PHILIPPE GIRARD

LEONARD COHEN

ON A WIRE

**Translated by Helge Dascher
and Karen Houle**

Drawn & Quarterly

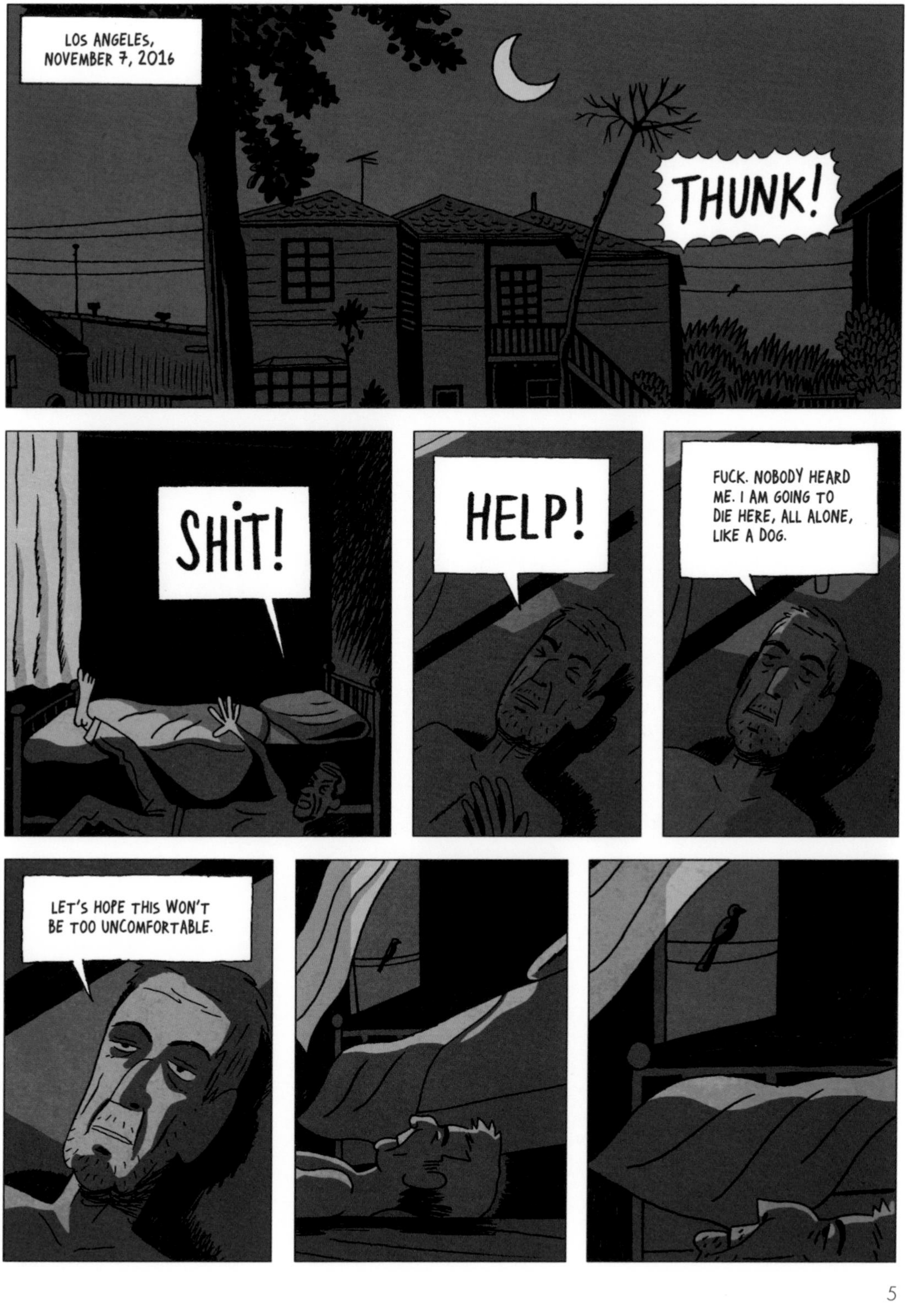
LOS ANGELES,
NOVEMBER 7, 2016
THUNK!
SHIT!
HELP!
FUCK. NOBODY HEARD ME. I AM GOING TO DIE HERE, ALL ALONE, LIKE A DOG.
LET'S HOPE THIS WON'T BE TOO UNCOMFORTABLE.

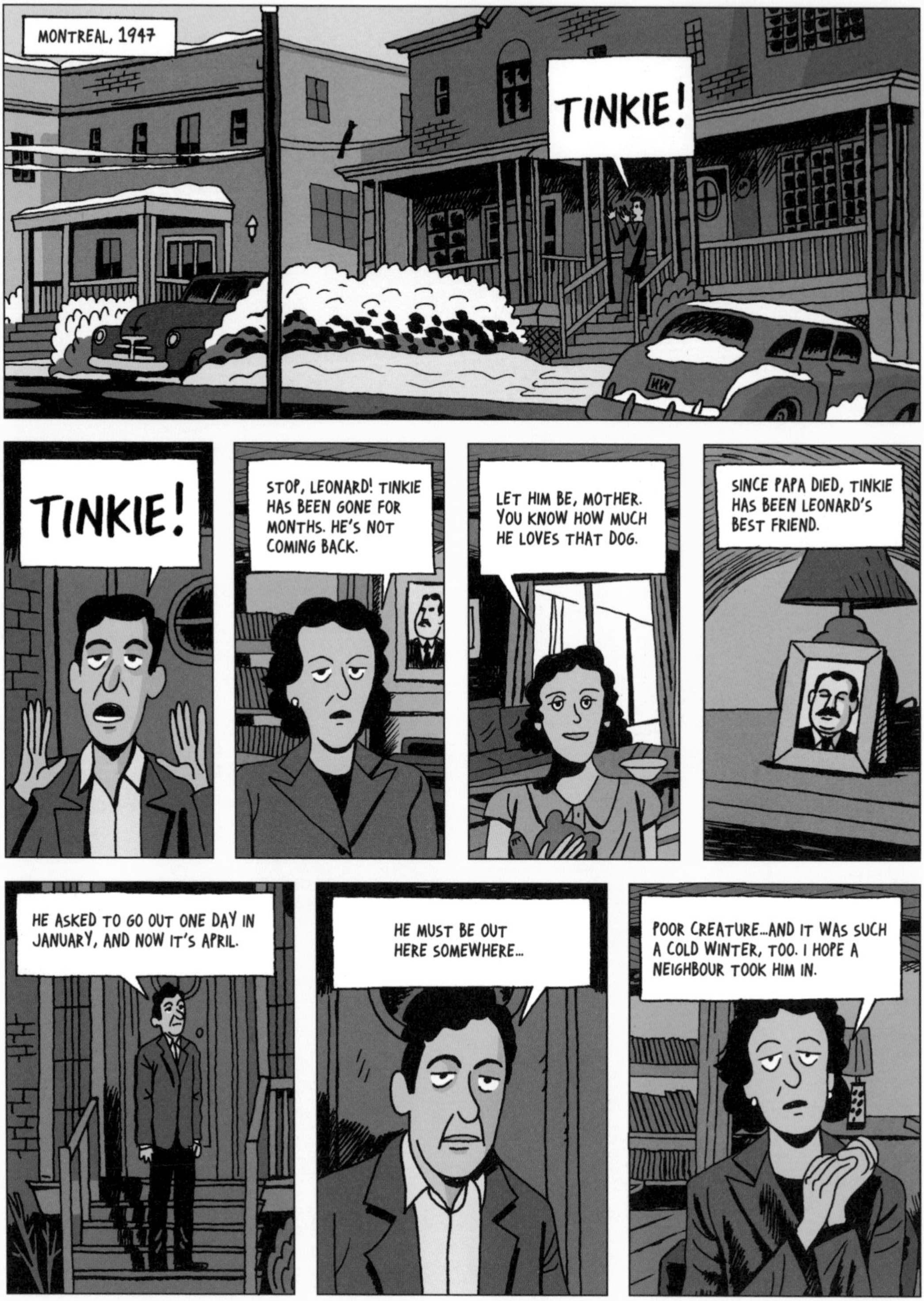

MONTREAL, 1947
TINKIE!
TINKIE!
STOP, LEONARD! TINKIE HAS BEEN GONE FOR MONTHS. HE'S NOT COMING BACK.
LET HIM BE, MOTHER. YOU KNOW HOW MUCH HE LOVES THAT DOG.
SINCE PAPA DIED, TINKIE HAS BEEN LEONARD'S BEST FRIEND.
HE ASKED TO GO OUT ONE DAY IN JANUARY, AND NOW IT'S APRIL.
HE MUST BE OUT HERE SOMEWHERE...
POOR CREATURE...AND IT WAS SUCH A COLD WINTER, TOO. I HOPE A NEIGHBOUR TOOK HIM IN.

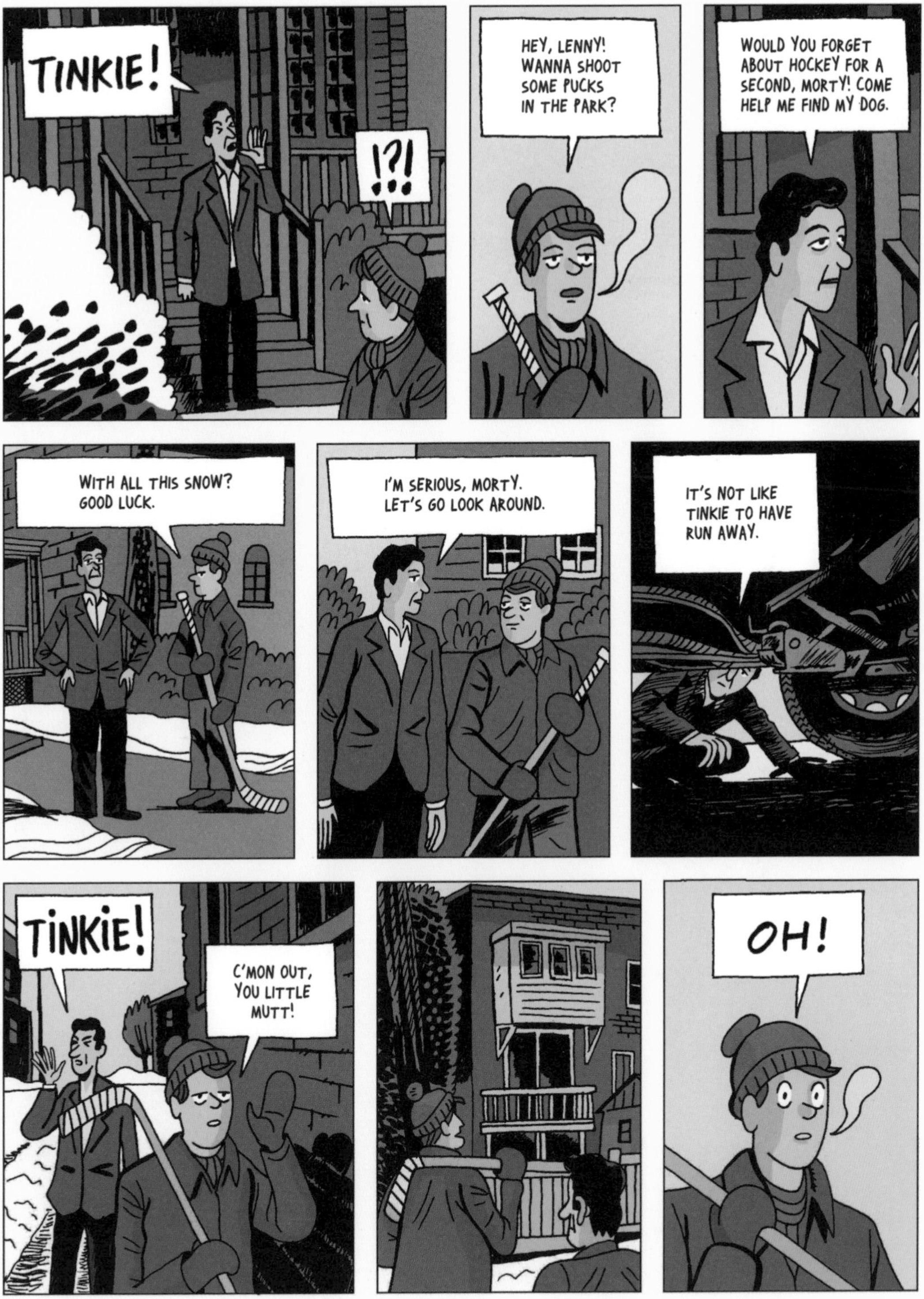
TINKIE!
!?!
HEY, LENNY! WANNA SHOOT SOME PUCKS IN THE PARK?
WOULD YOU FORGET ABOUT HOCKEY FOR A SECOND, MORTY! COME HELP ME FIND MY DOG.
WITH ALL THIS SNOW? GOOD LUCK.
I'M SERIOUS, MORTY. LET'S GO LOOK AROUND.
IT'S NOT LIKE TINKIE TO HAVE RUN AWAY.
TINKIE!
C'MON OUT, YOU LITTLE MUTT!
OH!

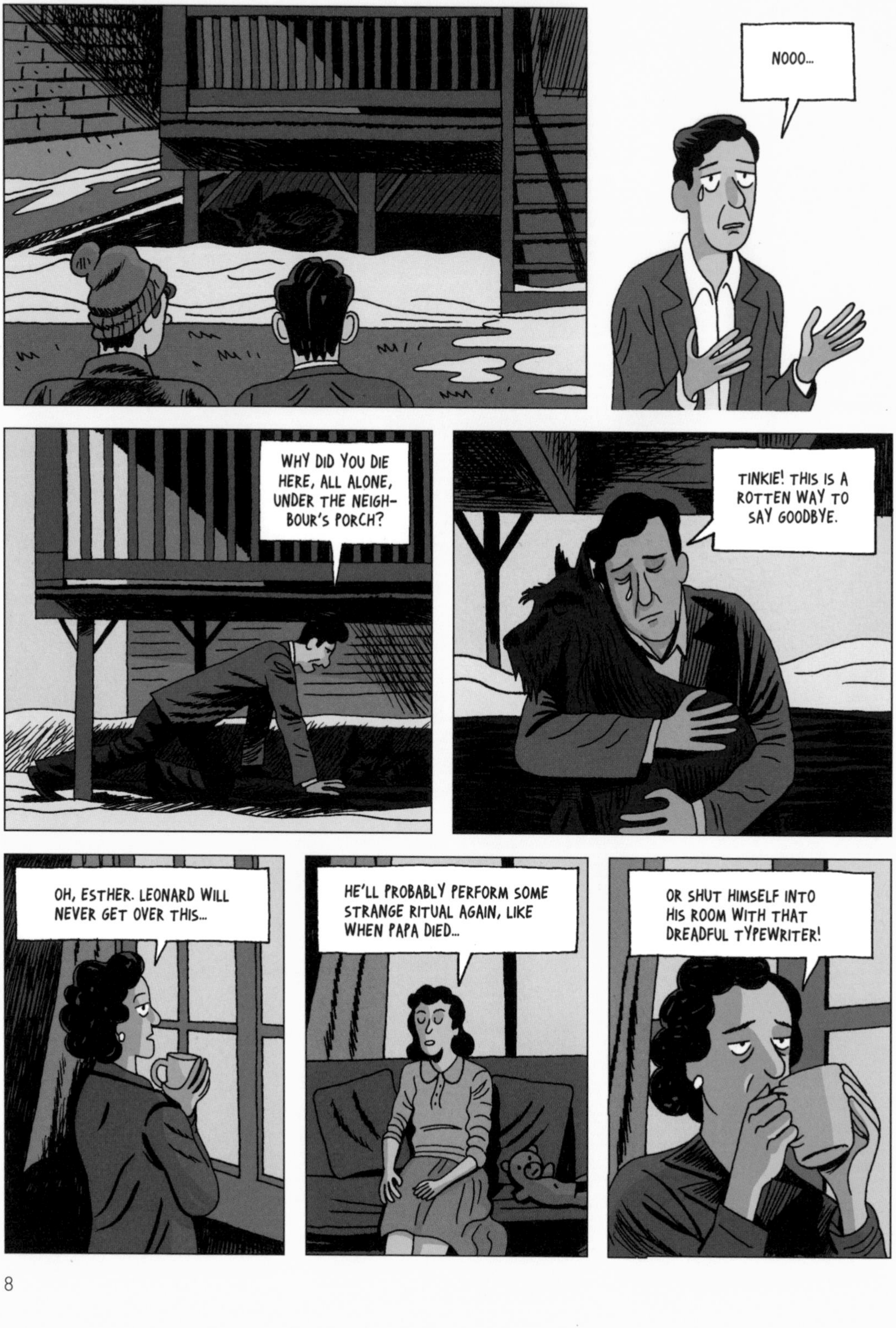
NOOO...
WHY DID YOU DIE HERE, ALL ALONE, UNDER THE NEIGHBOUR'S PORCH?
TINKIE! THIS IS A ROTTEN WAY TO SAY GOODBYE.
OH, ESTHER. LEONARD WILL NEVER GET OVER THIS...
HE'LL PROBABLY PERFORM SOME STRANGE RITUAL AGAIN, LIKE WHEN PAPA DIED...
OR SHUT HIMSELF INTO HIS ROOM WITH THAT DREADFUL TYPEWRITER!

A FEW MONTHS LATER...

TAPTAPTAPTAPTAP
TAPTAPTAP
TAPTAPTAPTAPTAP

TAPTAPTAPTAPTAP
TAP

ENOUGH ALREADY!

TAPTAPT

TAPT
PTAPT
APTA
TA

EVER SINCE ZAIDA SOLOMON MOVED IN, YOU'VE BEEN TRYING TO COPY HIM.

AND WHAT'S WRONG WITH THAT? HE'S A DISTINGUISHED RABBI. HE WROTE A TALMUDIC THESAURUS. IT'S NOBLE TO BE AS LEARNED AS HE IS.

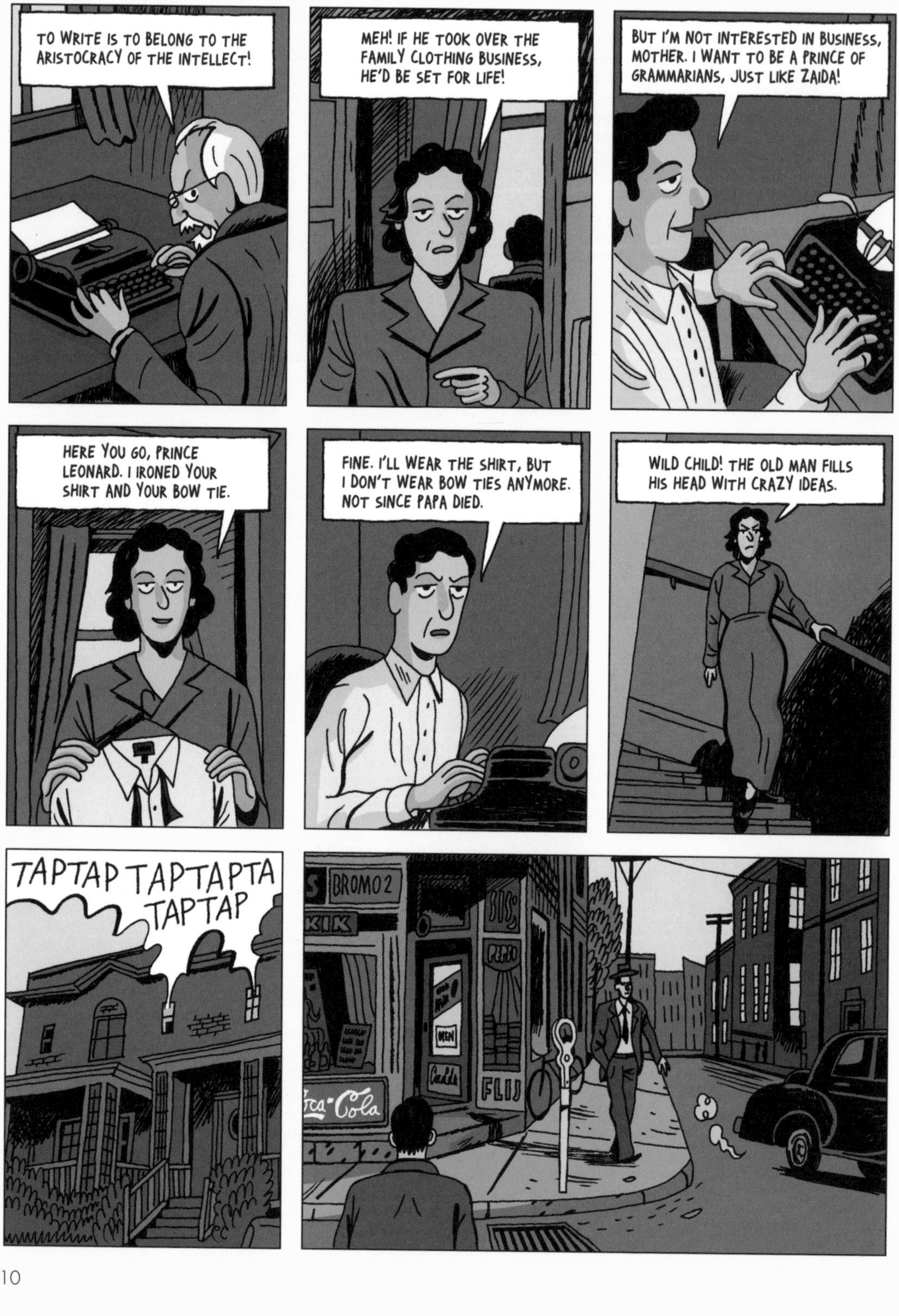
TO WRITE IS TO BELONG TO THE ARISTOCRACY OF THE INTELLECT!
MEH! IF HE TOOK OVER THE FAMILY CLOTHING BUSINESS, HE'D BE SET FOR LIFE!
BUT I'M NOT INTERESTED IN BUSINESS, MOTHER. I WANT TO BE A PRINCE OF GRAMMARIANS, JUST LIKE ZAIDA!
HERE YOU GO, PRINCE LEONARD. I IRONED YOUR SHIRT AND YOUR BOW TIE.
FINE. I'LL WEAR THE SHIRT, BUT I DON'T WEAR BOW TIES ANYMORE. NOT SINCE PAPA DIED.
WILD CHILD! THE OLD MAN FILLS HIS HEAD WITH CRAZY IDEAS.
TAPTAP TAPTAPTA TAPTAP
BROMO 2

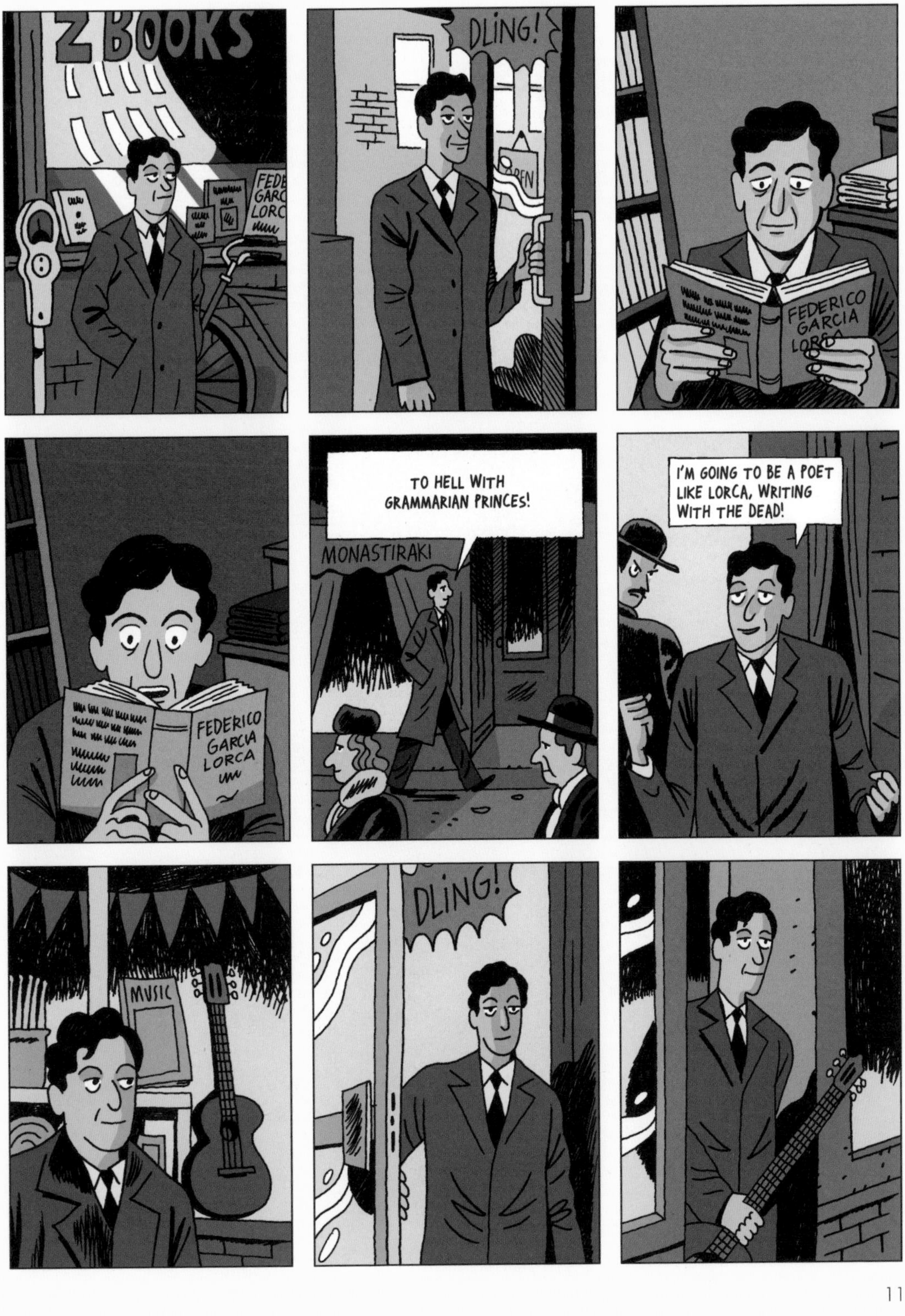
Z BOOKS
FEDE
GARC
LORC
DLING!
OPEN
FEDERICO
GARCIA
LORCA
FEDERICO
GARCIA
LORCA
TO HELL WITH GRAMMARIAN PRINCES!
MONASTIRAKI
I'M GOING TO BE A POET LIKE LORCA, WRITING WITH THE DEAD!
MUSIC
DLING!

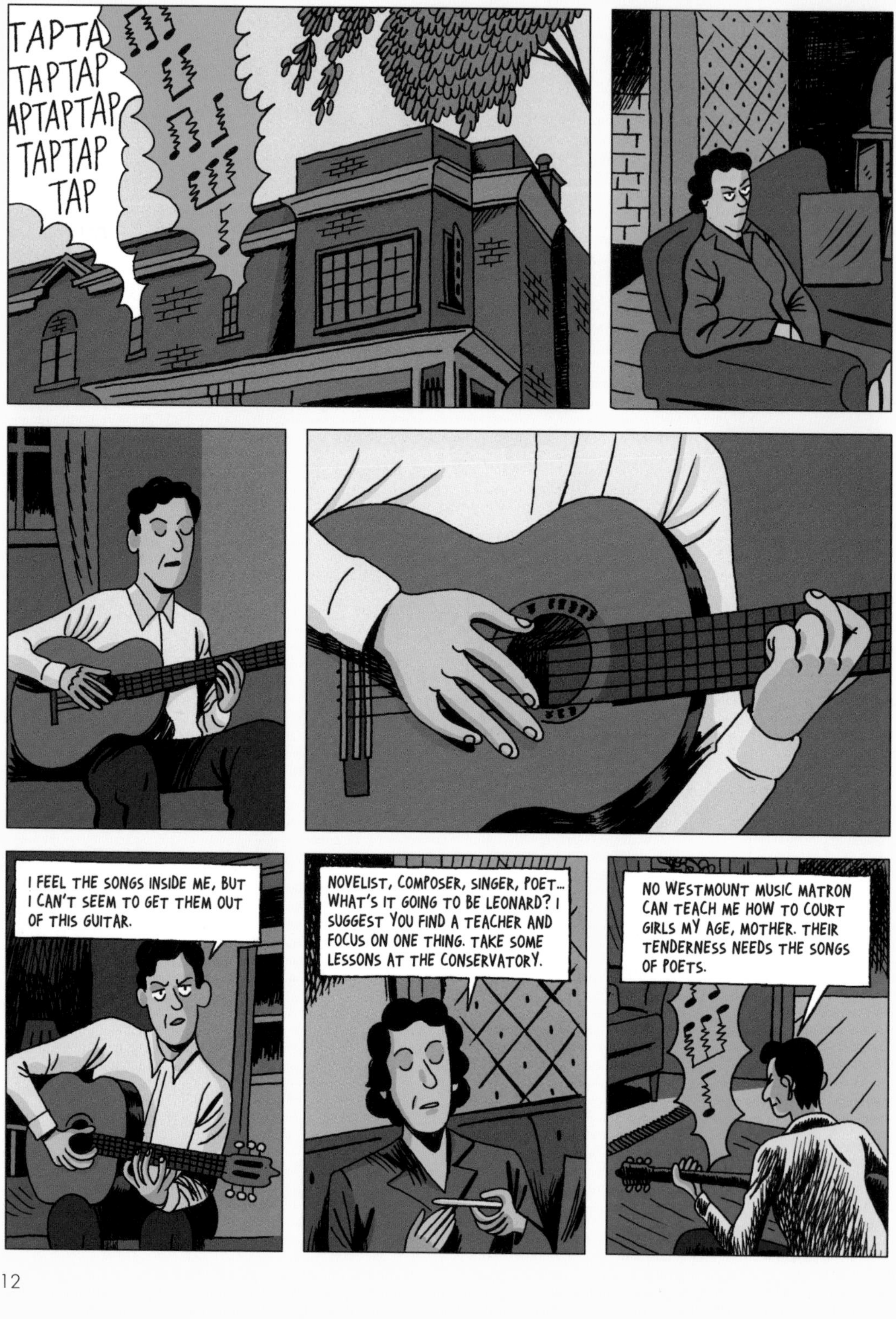
TAPTA
TAPTAP
APTAPTAP
TAPTAP
TAP
I FEEL THE SONGS INSIDE ME, BUT I CAN'T SEEM TO GET THEM OUT OF THIS GUITAR.
NOVELIST, COMPOSER, SINGER, POET... WHAT'S IT GOING TO BE LEONARD? I SUGGEST YOU FIND A TEACHER AND FOCUS ON ONE THING. TAKE SOME LESSONS AT THE CONSERVATORY.
NO WESTMOUNT MUSIC MATRON CAN TEACH ME HOW TO COURT GIRLS MY AGE, MOTHER. THEIR TENDERNESS NEEDS THE SONGS OF POETS.

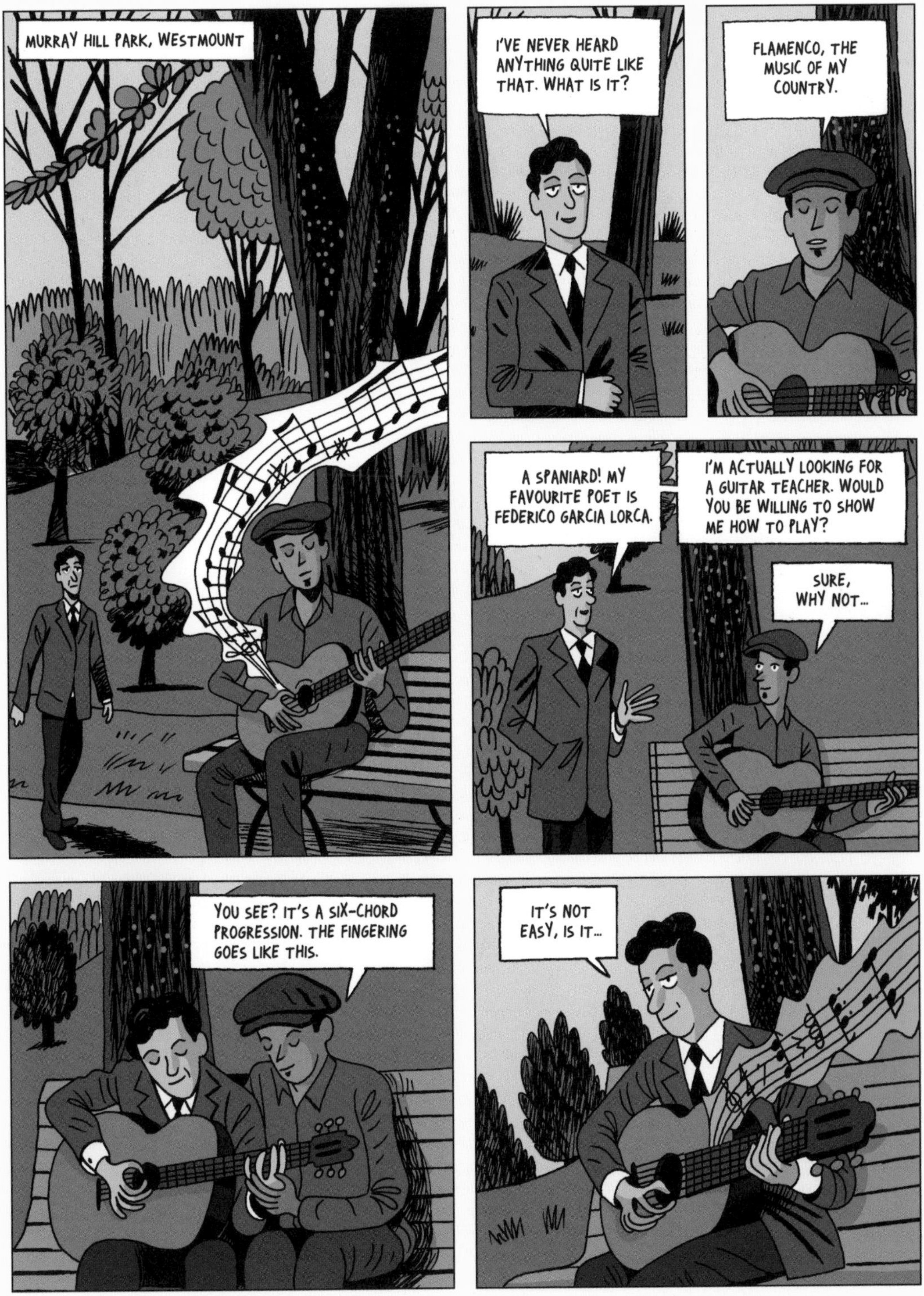
MURRAY HILL PARK, WESTMOUNT
I'VE NEVER HEARD ANYTHING QUITE LIKE THAT. WHAT IS IT?
FLAMENCO, THE MUSIC OF MY COUNTRY.
A SPANIARD! MY FAVOURITE POET IS FEDERICO GARCIA LORCA.
I'M ACTUALLY LOOKING FOR A GUITAR TEACHER. WOULD YOU BE WILLING TO SHOW ME HOW TO PLAY?
SURE, WHY NOT...
YOU SEE? IT'S A SIX-CHORD PROGRESSION. THE FINGERING GOES LIKE THIS.
IT'S NOT EASY, IS IT...

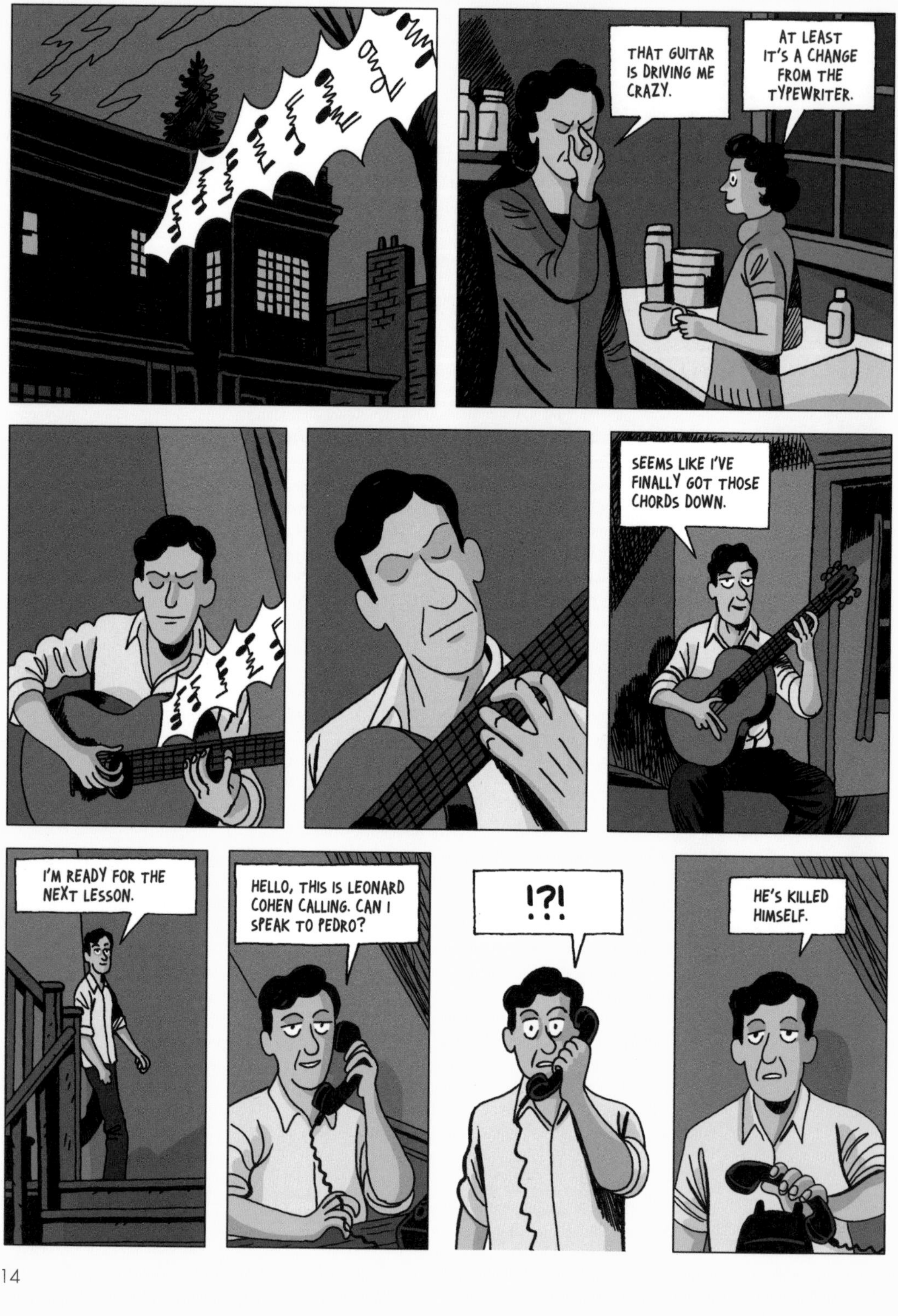
THAT GUITAR IS DRIVING ME CRAZY.
AT LEAST IT'S A CHANGE FROM THE TYPEWRITER.
SEEMS LIKE I'VE FINALLY GOT THOSE CHORDS DOWN.
I'M READY FOR THE NEXT LESSON.
HELLO, THIS IS LEONARD COHEN CALLING. CAN I SPEAK TO PEDRO?
!?!
HE'S KILLED HIMSELF.

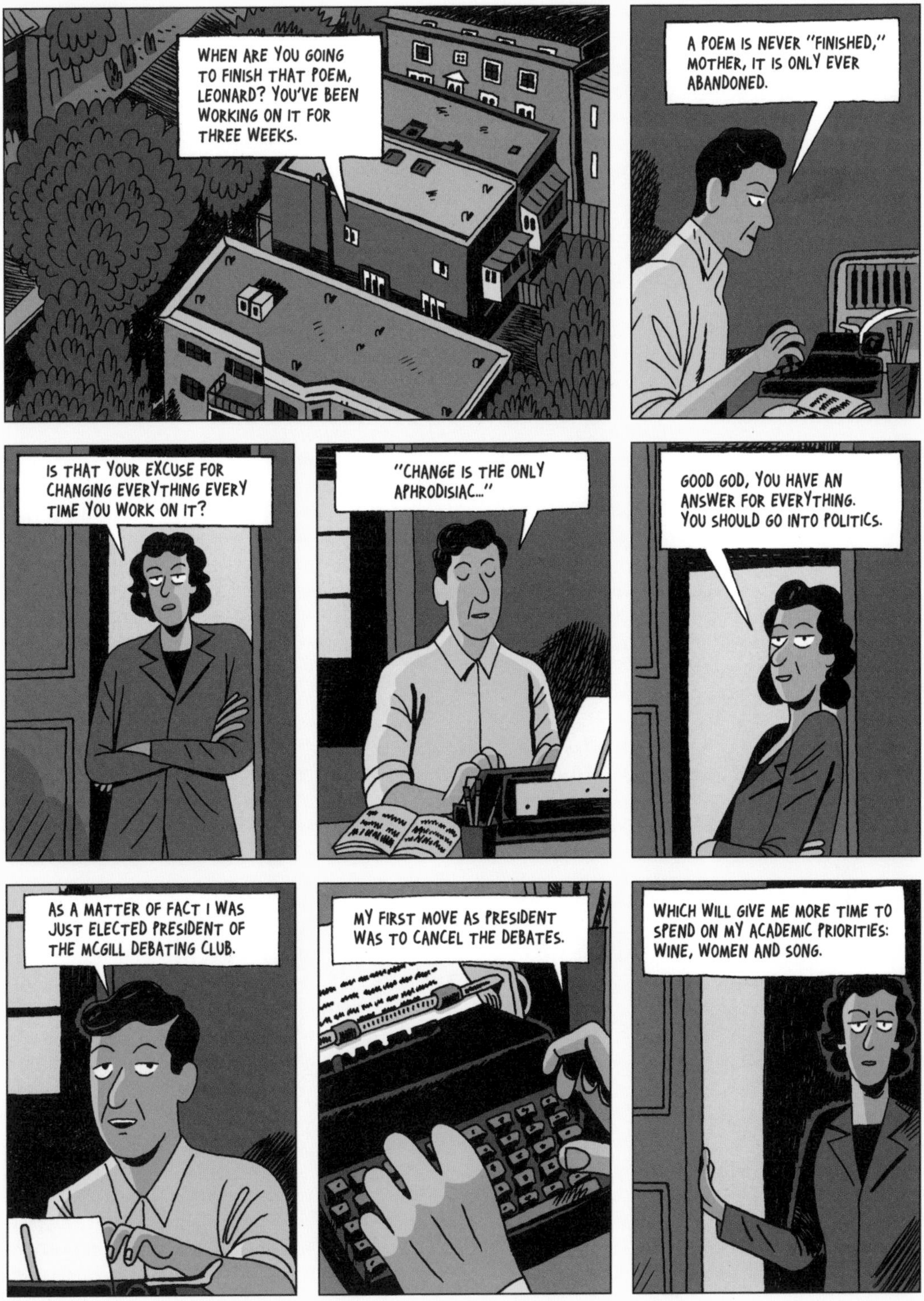
WHEN ARE YOU GOING TO FINISH THAT POEM, LEONARD? YOU'VE BEEN WORKING ON IT FOR THREE WEEKS.
A POEM IS NEVER "FINISHED," MOTHER, IT IS ONLY EVER ABANDONED.
IS THAT YOUR EXCUSE FOR CHANGING EVERYTHING EVERY TIME YOU WORK ON IT?
"CHANGE IS THE ONLY APHRODISIAC..."
GOOD GOD, YOU HAVE AN ANSWER FOR EVERYTHING. YOU SHOULD GO INTO POLITICS.
AS A MATTER OF FACT I WAS JUST ELECTED PRESIDENT OF THE MCGILL DEBATING CLUB.
MY FIRST MOVE AS PRESIDENT WAS TO CANCEL THE DEBATES.
WHICH WILL GIVE ME MORE TIME TO SPEND ON MY ACADEMIC PRIORITIES: WINE, WOMEN AND SONG.

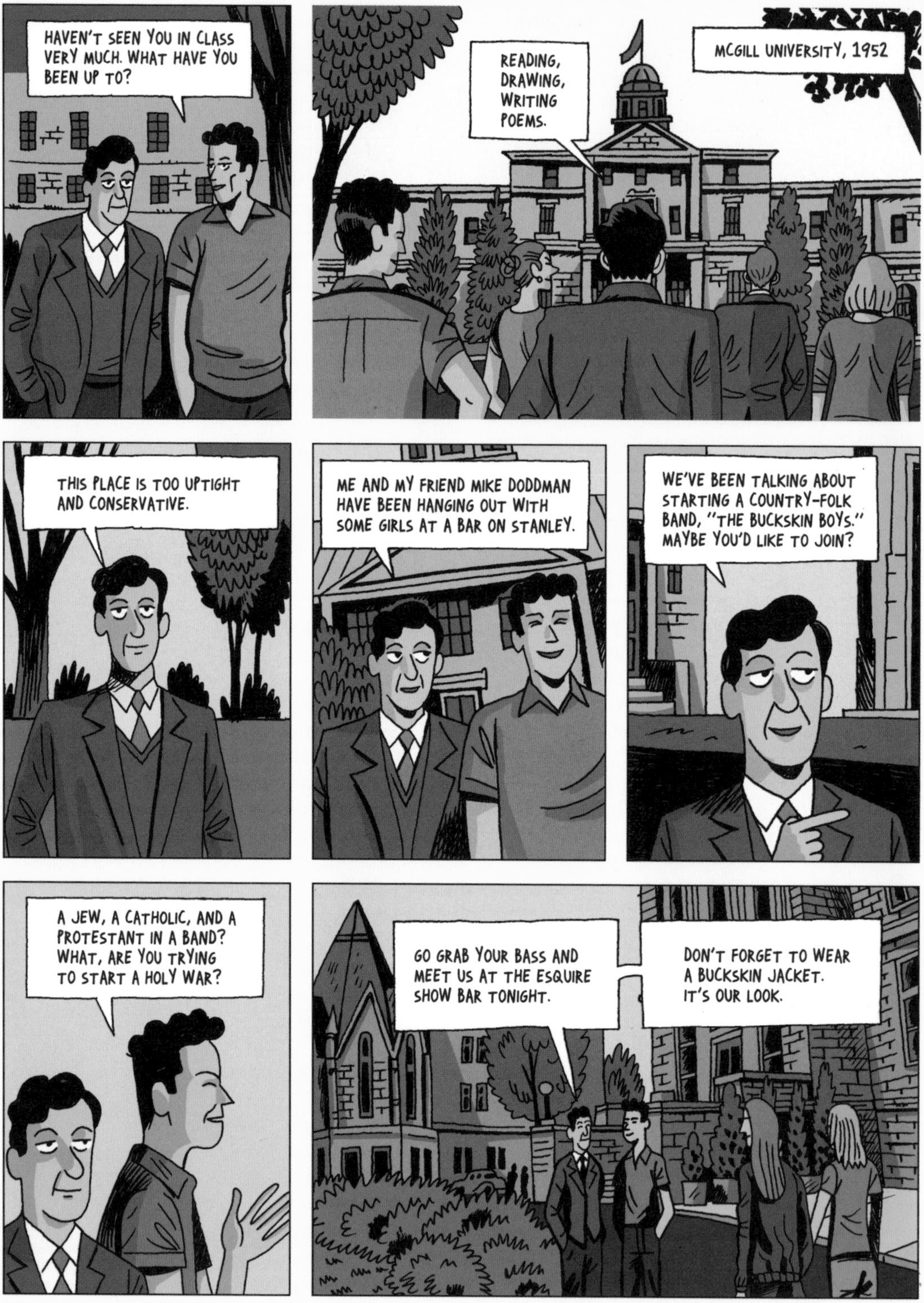
HAVEN'T SEEN YOU IN CLASS VERY MUCH. WHAT HAVE YOU BEEN UP TO?
MCGILL UNIVERSITY, 1952
READING, DRAWING, WRITING POEMS.
THIS PLACE IS TOO UPTIGHT AND CONSERVATIVE.
ME AND MY FRIEND MIKE DODDMAN HAVE BEEN HANGING OUT WITH SOME GIRLS AT A BAR ON STANLEY.
WE'VE BEEN TALKING ABOUT STARTING A COUNTRY-FOLK BAND, "THE BUCKSKIN BOYS." MAYBE YOU'D LIKE TO JOIN?
A JEW, A CATHOLIC, AND A PROTESTANT IN A BAND? WHAT, ARE YOU TRYING TO START A HOLY WAR?
GO GRAB YOUR BASS AND MEET US AT THE ESQUIRE SHOW BAR TONIGHT.
DON'T FORGET TO WEAR A BUCKSKIN JACKET. IT'S OUR LOOK.

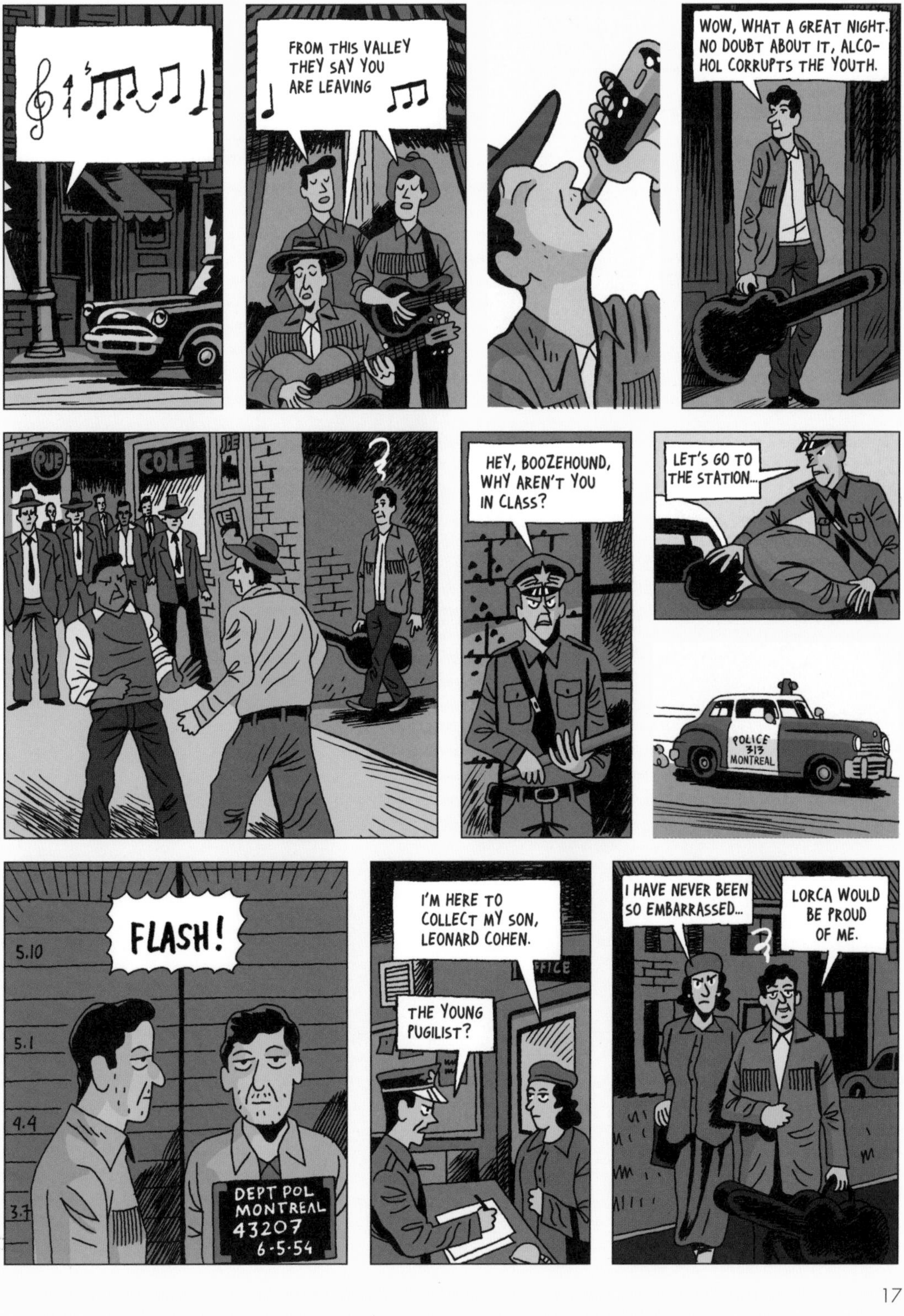
FROM THIS VALLEY THEY SAY YOU ARE LEAVING
WOW, WHAT A GREAT NIGHT. NO DOUBT ABOUT IT, ALCOHOL CORRUPTS THE YOUTH.
PUB
COLE
HEY, BOOZEHOUND, WHY AREN'T YOU IN CLASS?
LET'S GO TO THE STATION...
POLICE 313 MONTREAL
FLASH!
5.10
5.1
4.4
3.7
DEPT POL MONTREAL 43207 6-5-54
I'M HERE TO COLLECT MY SON, LEONARD COHEN.
THE YOUNG PUGILIST?
I HAVE NEVER BEEN SO EMBARRASSED...
LORCA WOULD BE PROUD OF ME.

MONTREAL, 1957

MISTER COHEN!

I SAW YOUR POEM "THE SPARROW" IN THE MCGILL DAILY. GREAT PIECE!

THANK YOU, PROFESSOR DUDEK.

I GOT A GRANT TO GO TO LONDON ONCE I GRADUATE. I'M LOOKING FORWARD TO DOING MORE WRITING THERE.

EXCELLENT. WE'RE JUST THRILLED TO BE LAUNCHING THE MCGILL POETRY SERIES WITH A VOLUME OF YOUR VERSE.

THANKS TO YOU, WE'VE PRE-SOLD 500 SUBSCRIPTIONS. AT A BUCK A PIECE, THAT'LL GET THIS SERIES ROLLING.

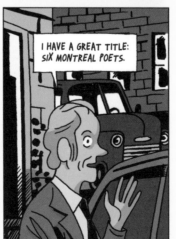

I'M HOPING YOU WOULD AGREE TO BE ON A RECORD I'M MAKING THIS WINTER.

I HAVE A GREAT TITLE: SIX MONTREAL POETS.

POET? WHY NOT? I FEEL LIKE AN IMPOSTER, BUT MAYBE THAT'S FOR OTHERS TO DECIDE...

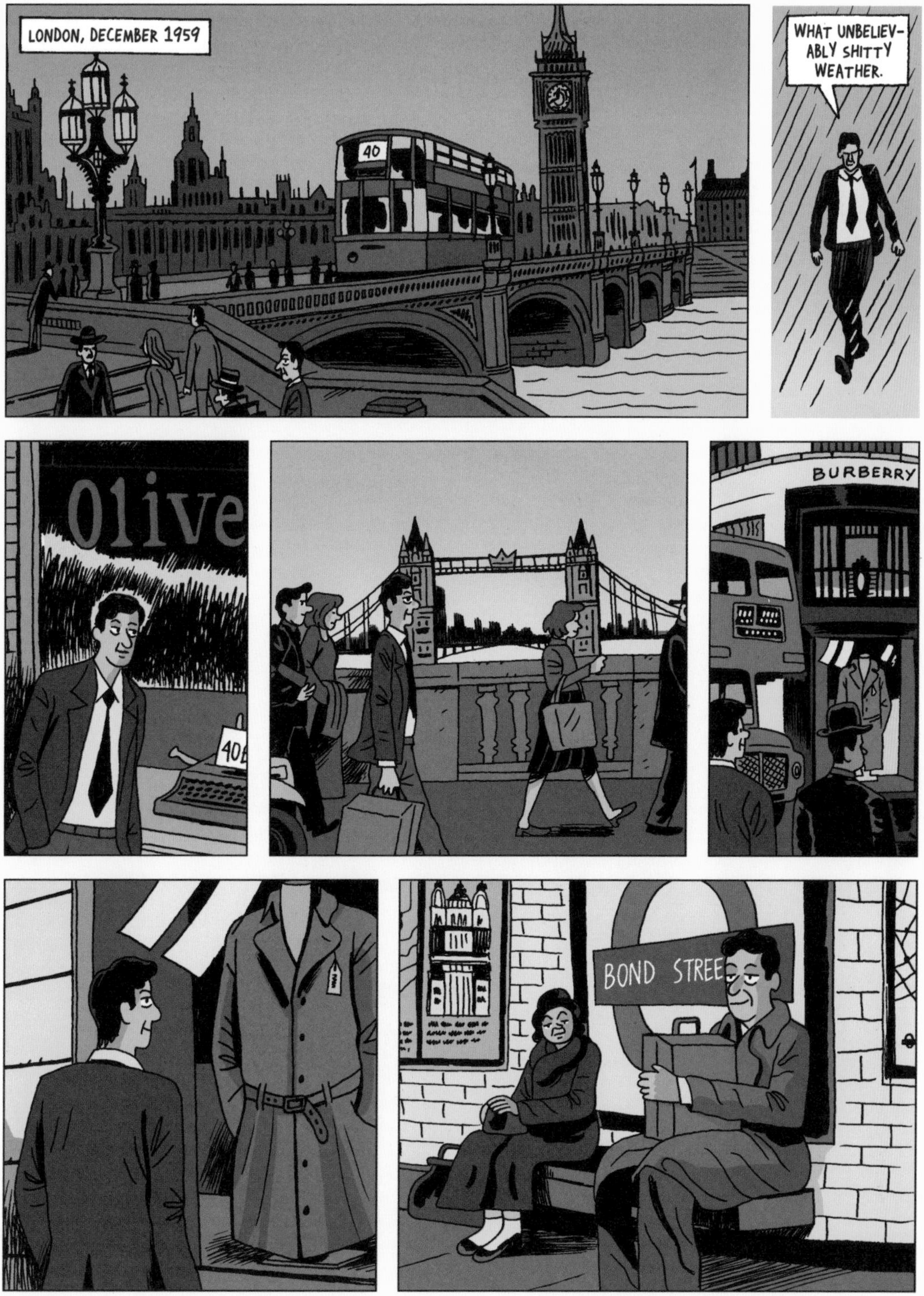
LONDON, DECEMBER 1959
40
WHAT UNBELIEV-ABLY SHITTY WEATHER.
Olive
BURBERRY
BOND STREE

YOU HAVE TWO LOVELY BUSINESS CARDS THERE, MISTER COHEN.

SIX MONTREAL POETS
IRVING LAYTON
LEONARD COHEN

LET US COMPARE MYTHOLOGIES
Leonard Cohen

THE PARENTS OF YOUR FRIEND, MORT ROSENGARTEN, GAVE YOU GOOD REFERENCES. YOU CAN BOARD HERE DURING YOUR STAY IN LONDON.

IN EXCHANGE FOR MY HOSPITALITY, YOUR DUTIES ARE TO FILL THE FURNACE EVERY MORNING WITH COAL, LIGHT THE FIRE, AND WRITE THREE PAGES OF YOUR NOVEL EACH DAY.

JANUARY

FEBRUARY

MARCH

MY BOOK IS PROGRESSING LIKE A CHARM...

EXCEPT THAT I DON'T WANT TO BE A MAGICIAN. I WANT TO BE THE MAGIC.

WHAT'S THE WEATHER LIKE IN GREECE RIGHT NOW?

IT'S SPRING-TIME EVERY DAY, MY FRIEND.

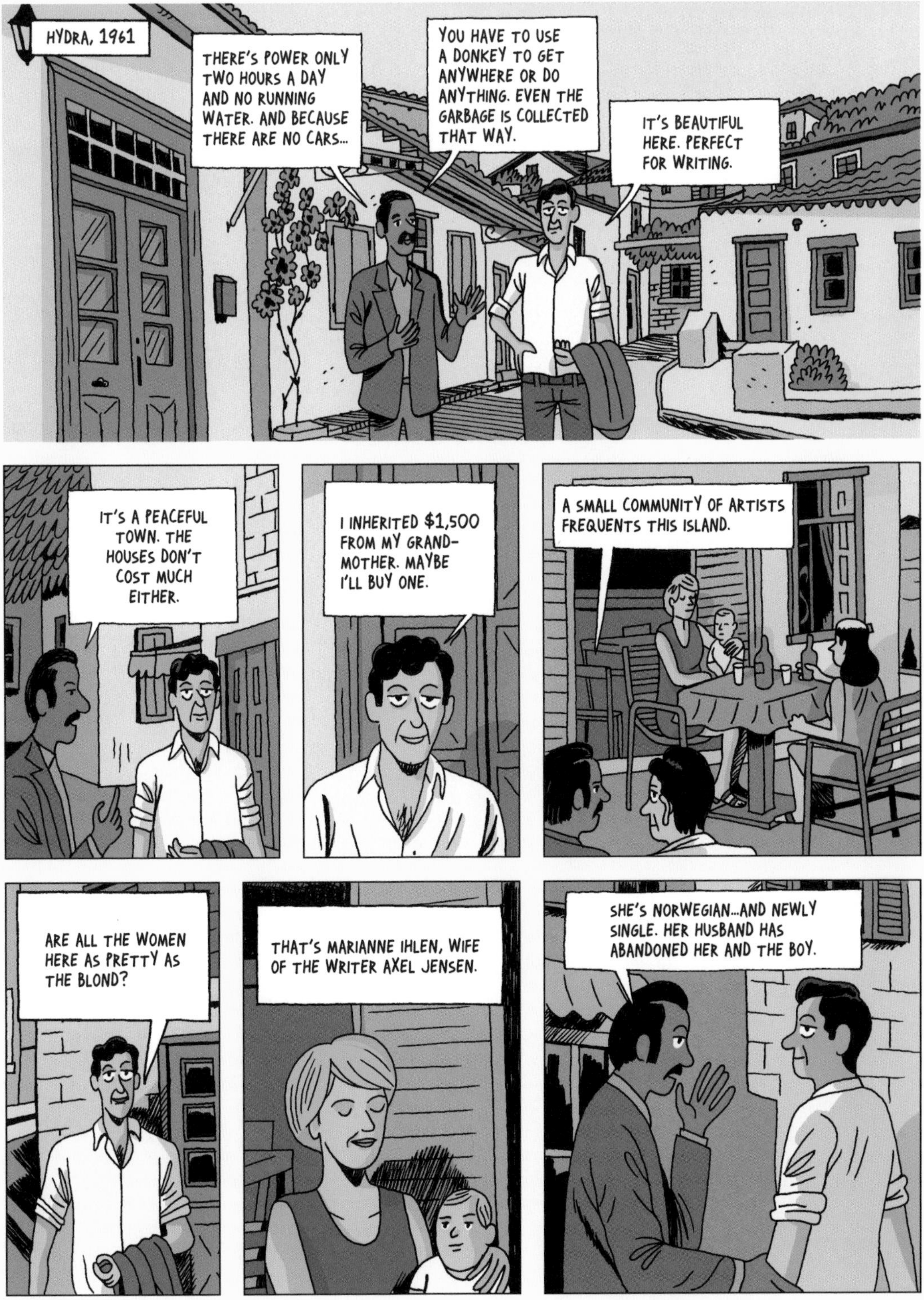
HYDRA, 1961
THERE'S POWER ONLY TWO HOURS A DAY AND NO RUNNING WATER. AND BECAUSE THERE ARE NO CARS...
YOU HAVE TO USE A DONKEY TO GET ANYWHERE OR DO ANYTHING. EVEN THE GARBAGE IS COLLECTED THAT WAY.
IT'S BEAUTIFUL HERE. PERFECT FOR WRITING.
IT'S A PEACEFUL TOWN. THE HOUSES DON'T COST MUCH EITHER.
I INHERITED $1,500 FROM MY GRAND-MOTHER. MAYBE I'LL BUY ONE.
A SMALL COMMUNITY OF ARTISTS FREQUENTS THIS ISLAND.
ARE ALL THE WOMEN HERE AS PRETTY AS THE BLOND?
THAT'S MARIANNE IHLEN, WIFE OF THE WRITER AXEL JENSEN.
SHE'S NORWEGIAN...AND NEWLY SINGLE. HER HUSBAND HAS ABANDONED HER AND THE BOY.

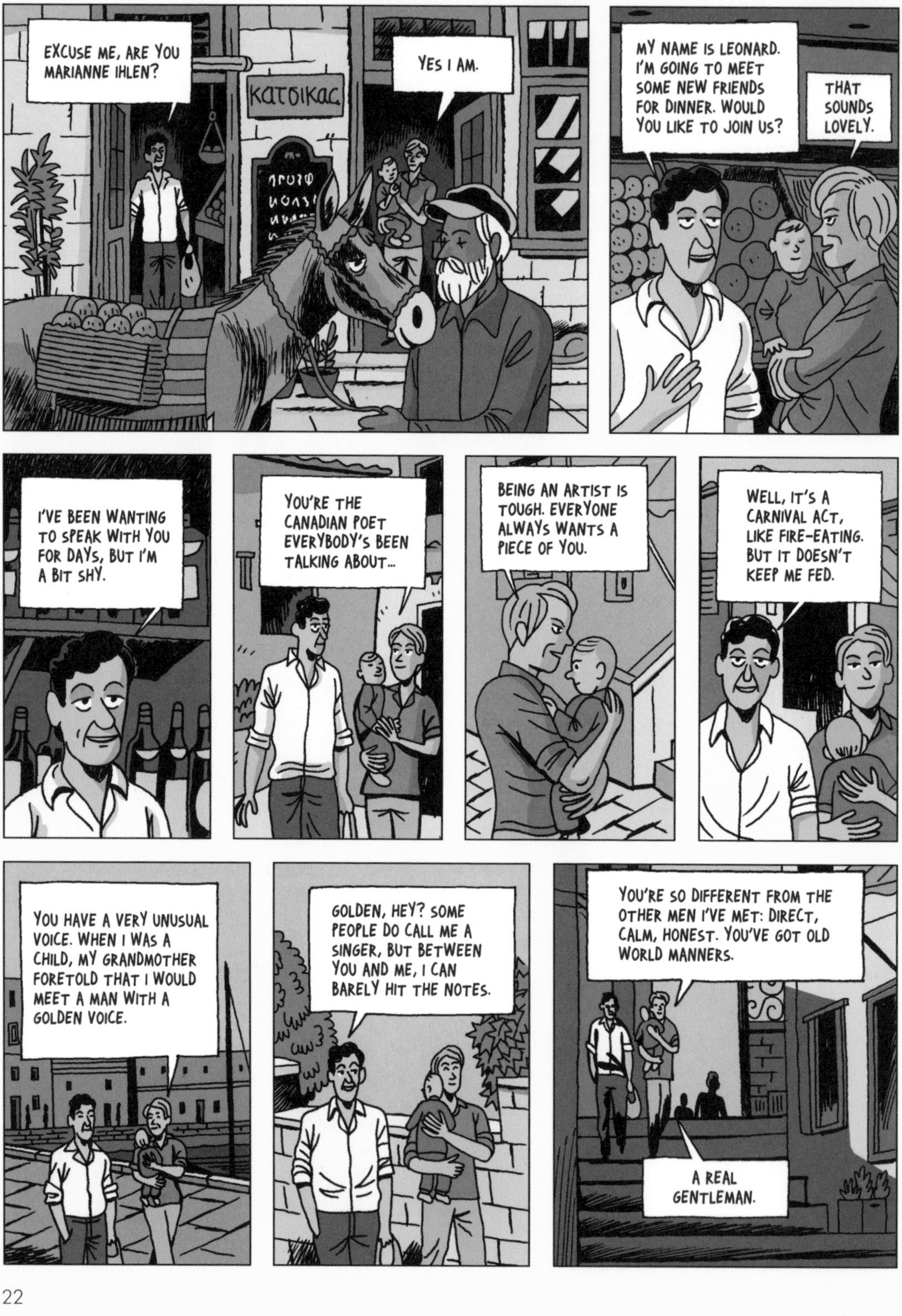
EXCUSE ME, ARE YOU MARIANNE IHLEN?
YES I AM.
KATOIKAC
MY NAME IS LEONARD. I'M GOING TO MEET SOME NEW FRIENDS FOR DINNER. WOULD YOU LIKE TO JOIN US?
THAT SOUNDS LOVELY.
I'VE BEEN WANTING TO SPEAK WITH YOU FOR DAYS, BUT I'M A BIT SHY.
YOU'RE THE CANADIAN POET EVERYBODY'S BEEN TALKING ABOUT...
BEING AN ARTIST IS TOUGH. EVERYONE ALWAYS WANTS A PIECE OF YOU.
WELL, IT'S A CARNIVAL ACT, LIKE FIRE-EATING. BUT IT DOESN'T KEEP ME FED.
YOU HAVE A VERY UNUSUAL VOICE. WHEN I WAS A CHILD, MY GRANDMOTHER FORETOLD THAT I WOULD MEET A MAN WITH A GOLDEN VOICE.
GOLDEN, HEY? SOME PEOPLE DO CALL ME A SINGER, BUT BETWEEN YOU AND ME, I CAN BARELY HIT THE NOTES.
YOU'RE SO DIFFERENT FROM THE OTHER MEN I'VE MET: DIRECT, CALM, HONEST. YOU'VE GOT OLD WORLD MANNERS.
A REAL GENTLEMAN.

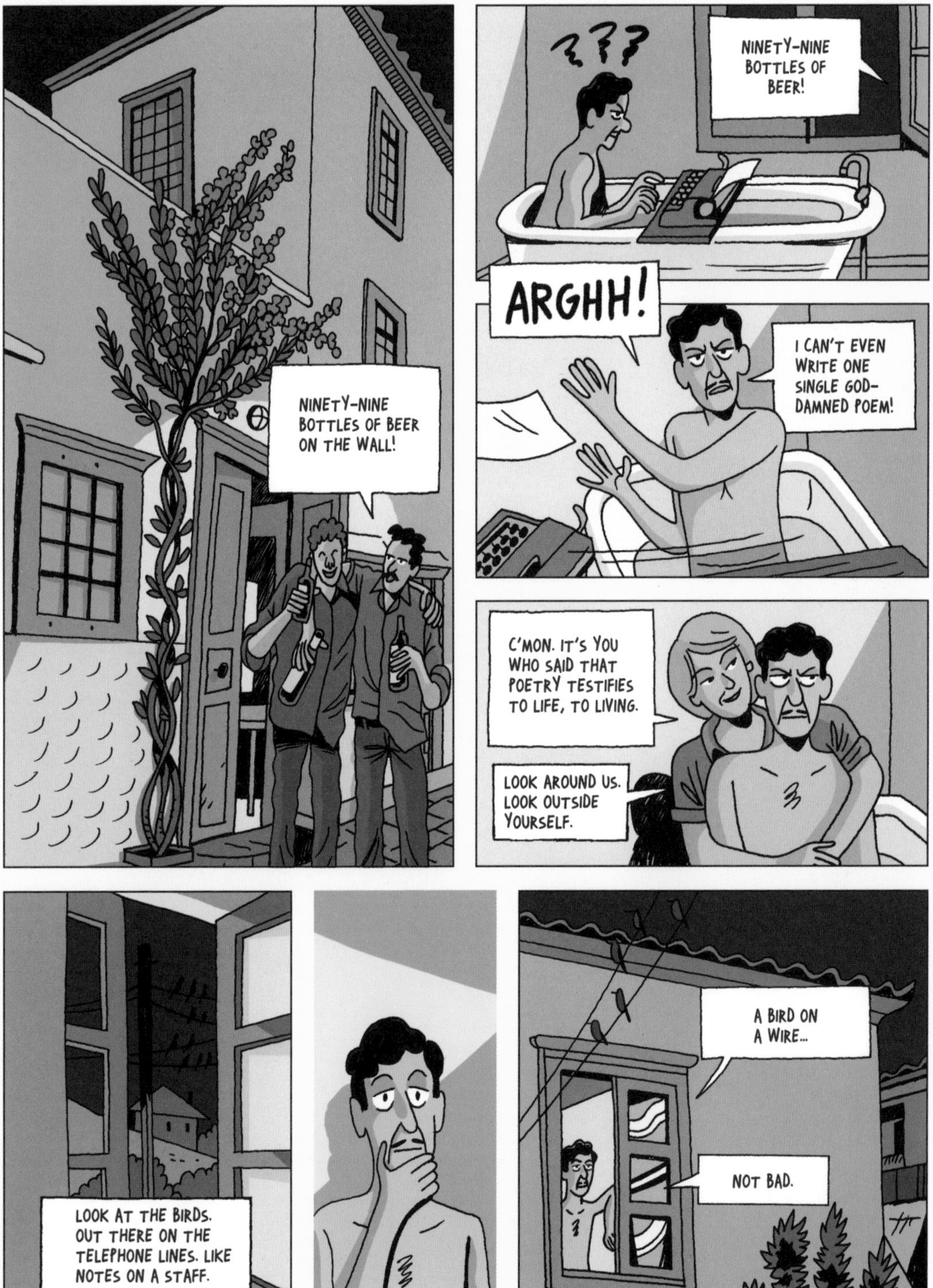

NINETY-NINE BOTTLES OF BEER ON THE WALL!
NINETY-NINE BOTTLES OF BEER!
ARGHH!
I CAN'T EVEN WRITE ONE SINGLE GOD-DAMNED POEM!
C'MON. IT'S YOU WHO SAID THAT POETRY TESTIFIES TO LIFE, TO LIVING.
LOOK AROUND US. LOOK OUTSIDE YOURSELF.
LOOK AT THE BIRDS. OUT THERE ON THE TELEPHONE LINES. LIKE NOTES ON A STAFF.
A BIRD ON A WIRE...
NOT BAD.

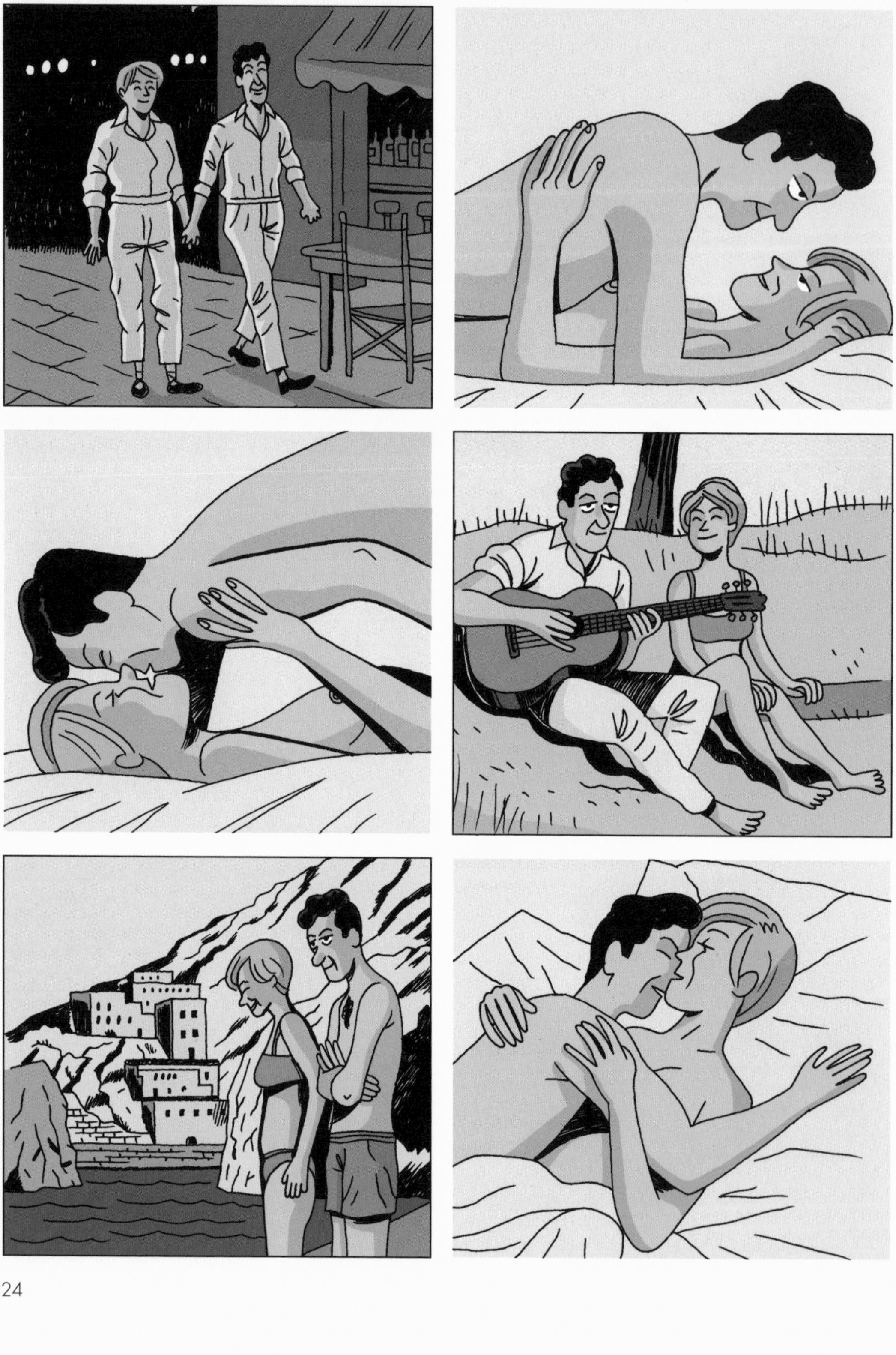

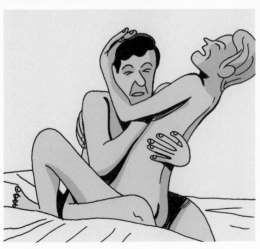

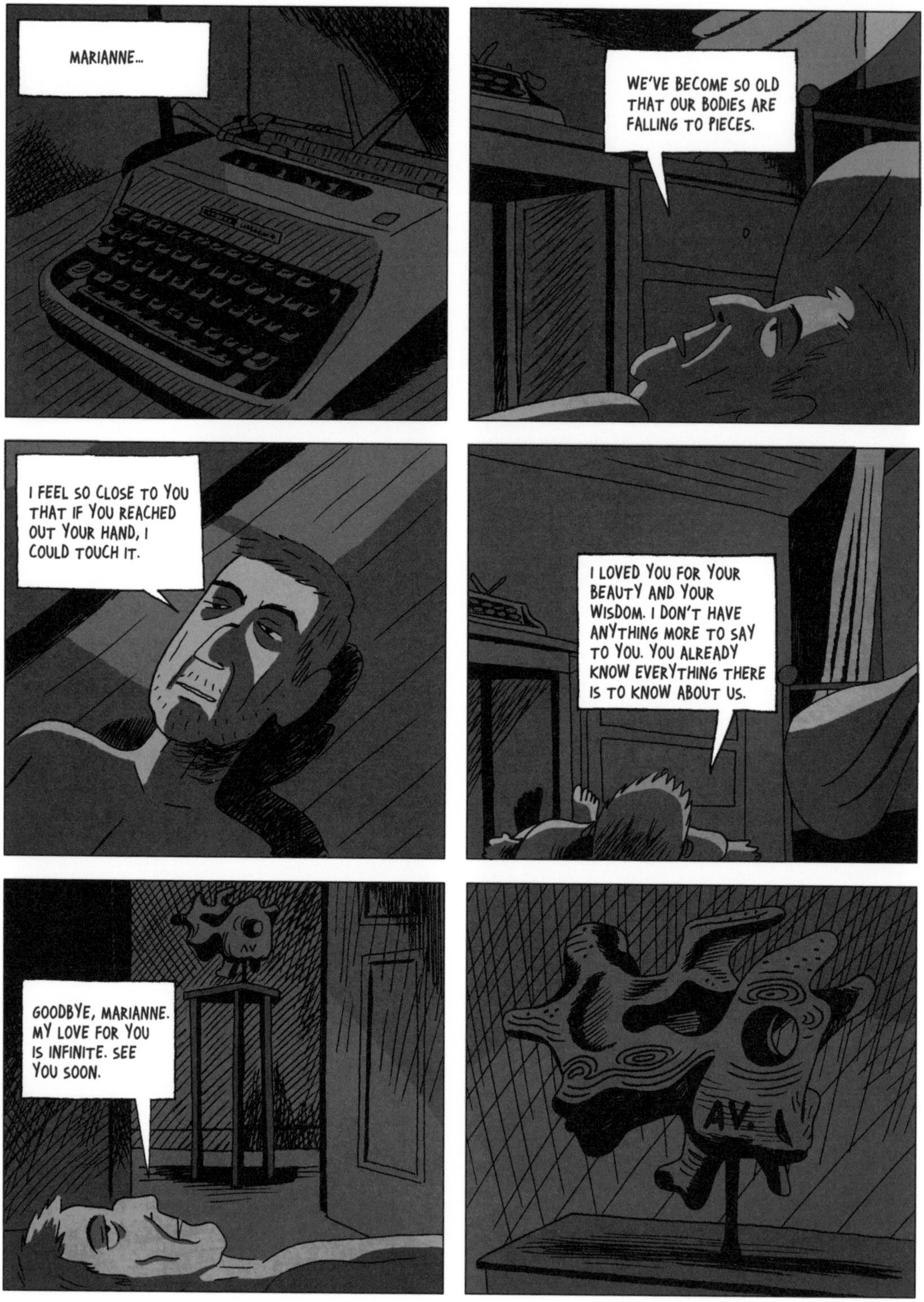
MARIANNE...
WE'VE BECOME SO OLD THAT OUR BODIES ARE FALLING TO PIECES.
I FEEL SO CLOSE TO YOU THAT IF YOU REACHED OUT YOUR HAND, I COULD TOUCH IT.
I LOVED YOU FOR YOUR BEAUTY AND YOUR WISDOM. I DON'T HAVE ANYTHING MORE TO SAY TO YOU. YOU ALREADY KNOW EVERYTHING THERE IS TO KNOW ABOUT US.
GOODBYE, MARIANNE. MY LOVE FOR YOU IS INFINITE. SEE YOU SOON.
AV.

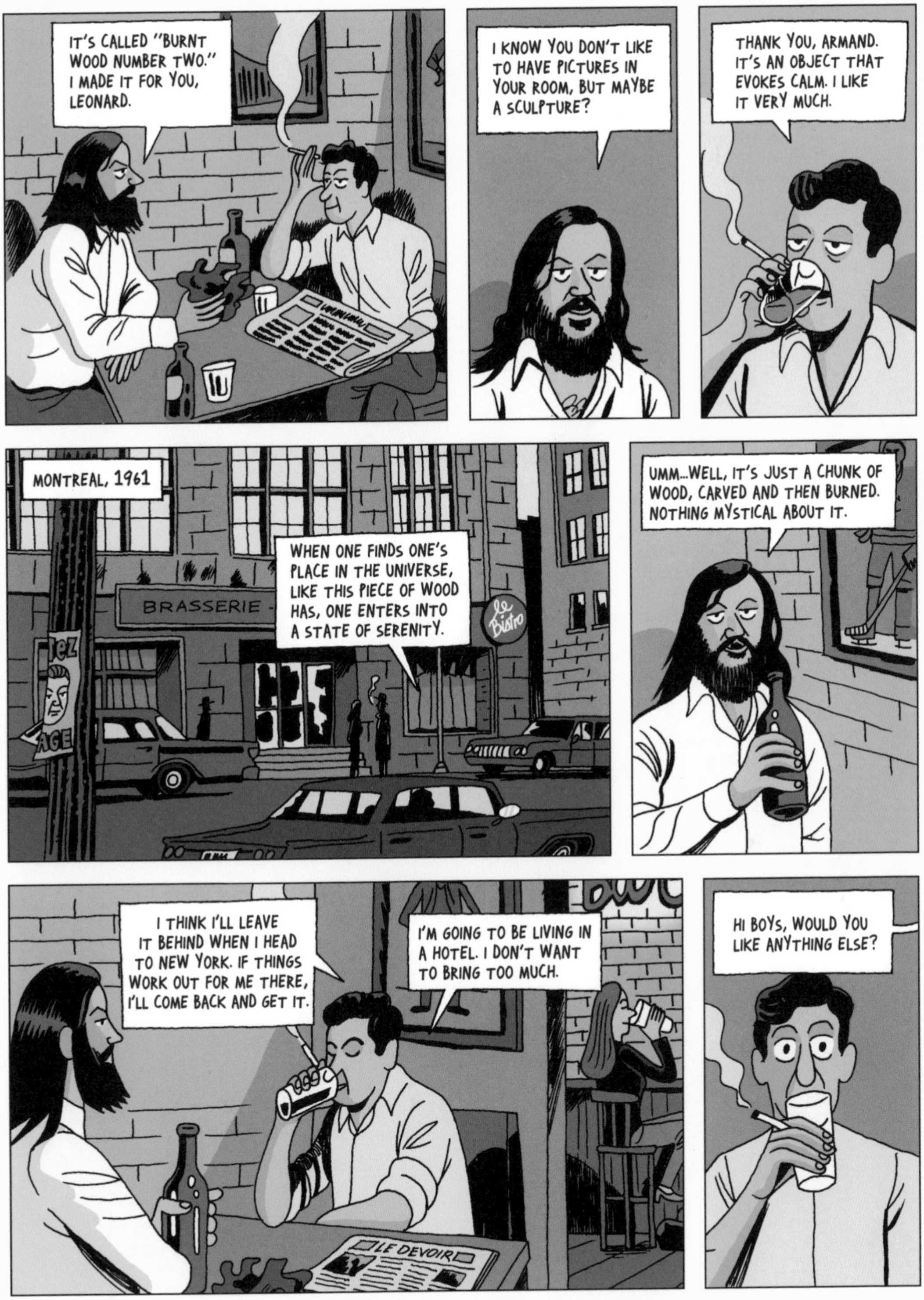
IT'S CALLED "BURNT WOOD NUMBER TWO." I MADE IT FOR YOU, LEONARD.
I KNOW YOU DON'T LIKE TO HAVE PICTURES IN YOUR ROOM, BUT MAYBE A SCULPTURE?
THANK YOU, ARMAND. IT'S AN OBJECT THAT EVOKES CALM. I LIKE IT VERY MUCH.
MONTREAL, 1961
BRASSERIE
Le Bistro
WHEN ONE FINDS ONE'S PLACE IN THE UNIVERSE, LIKE THIS PIECE OF WOOD HAS, ONE ENTERS INTO A STATE OF SERENITY.
UMM...WELL, IT'S JUST A CHUNK OF WOOD, CARVED AND THEN BURNED. NOTHING MYSTICAL ABOUT IT.
I THINK I'LL LEAVE IT BEHIND WHEN I HEAD TO NEW YORK. IF THINGS WORK OUT FOR ME THERE, I'LL COME BACK AND GET IT.
I'M GOING TO BE LIVING IN A HOTEL. I DON'T WANT TO BRING TOO MUCH.
LE DEVOIR
HI BOYS, WOULD YOU LIKE ANYTHING ELSE?

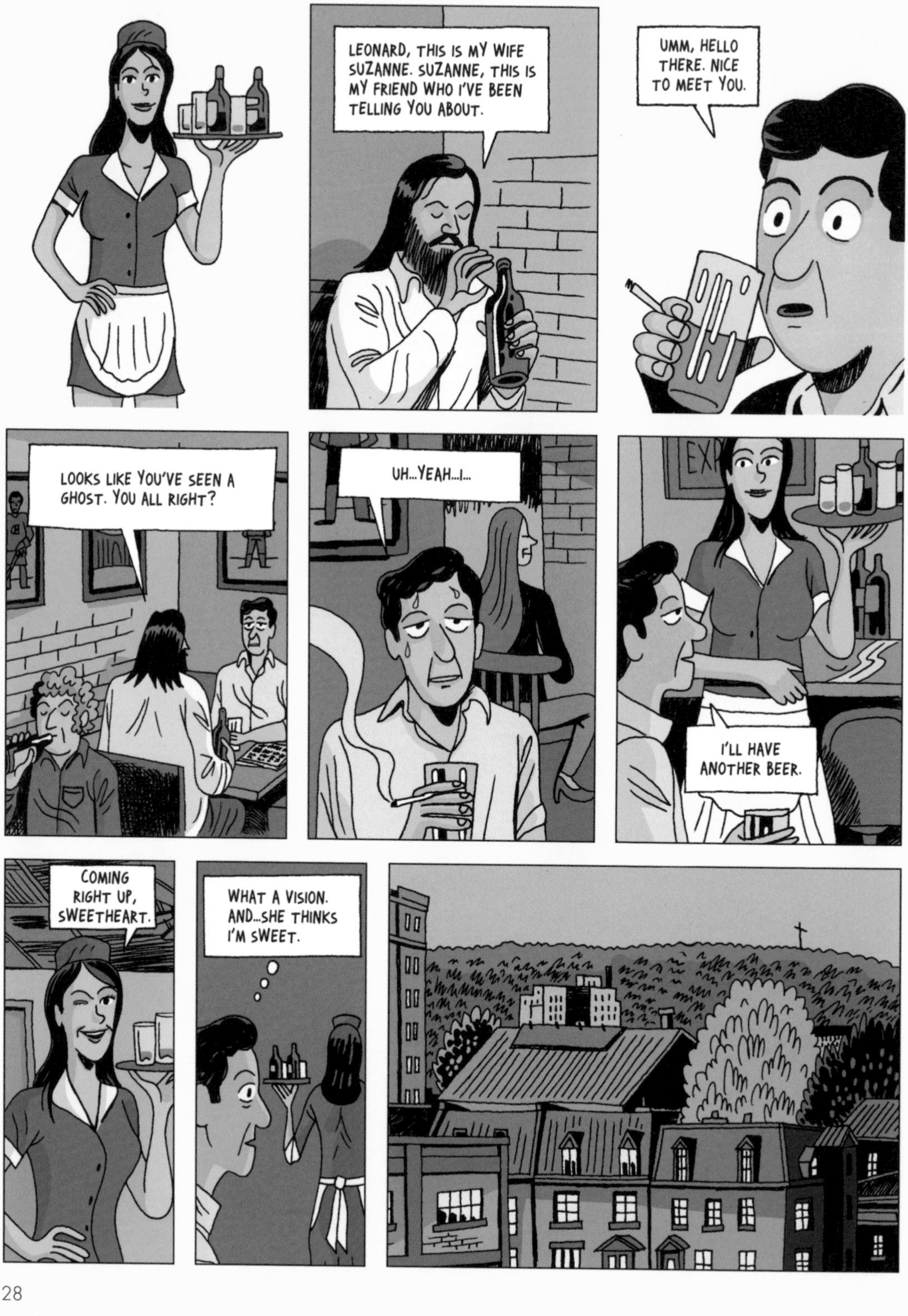
LEONARD, THIS IS MY WIFE SUZANNE. SUZANNE, THIS IS MY FRIEND WHO I'VE BEEN TELLING YOU ABOUT.
UMM, HELLO THERE. NICE TO MEET YOU.
LOOKS LIKE YOU'VE SEEN A GHOST. YOU ALL RIGHT?
UH...YEAH...I...
I'LL HAVE ANOTHER BEER.
COMING RIGHT UP, SWEETHEART.
WHAT A VISION. AND...SHE THINKS I'M SWEET.

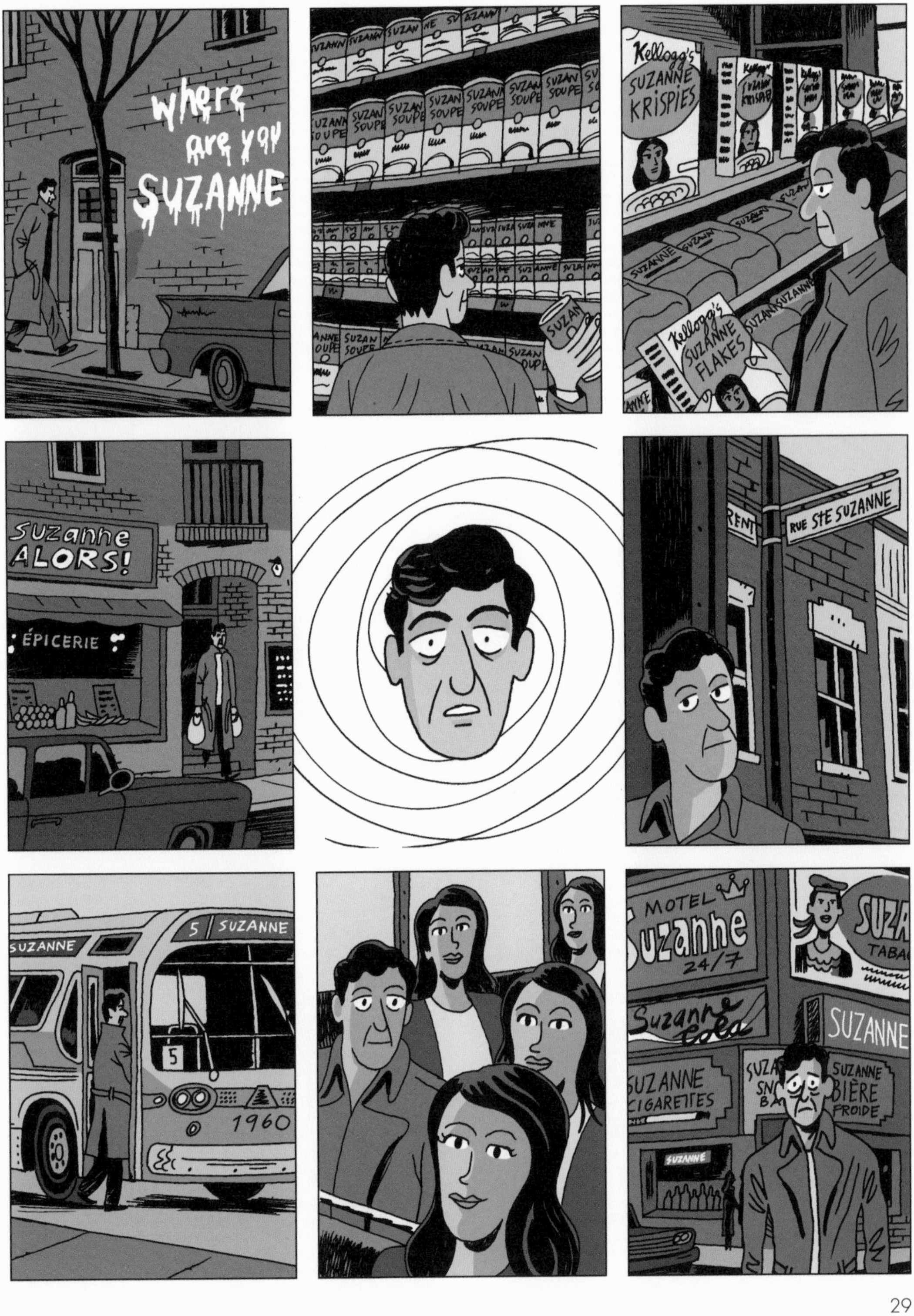
where are you SUZANNE
SUZAN SOUPE
Kellogg's SUZANNE KRISPIES
Kellogg's SUZANNE FLAKES
Suzanne ALORS!
ÉPICERIE
RUE STE SUZANNE
SUZANNE
5 SUZANNE
5
1960
MOTEL Suzanne 24/7
Suzanne cola
SUZANNE
SUZANNE CIGARETTES
SUZANNE BIÈRE FROIDE
SUZANNE

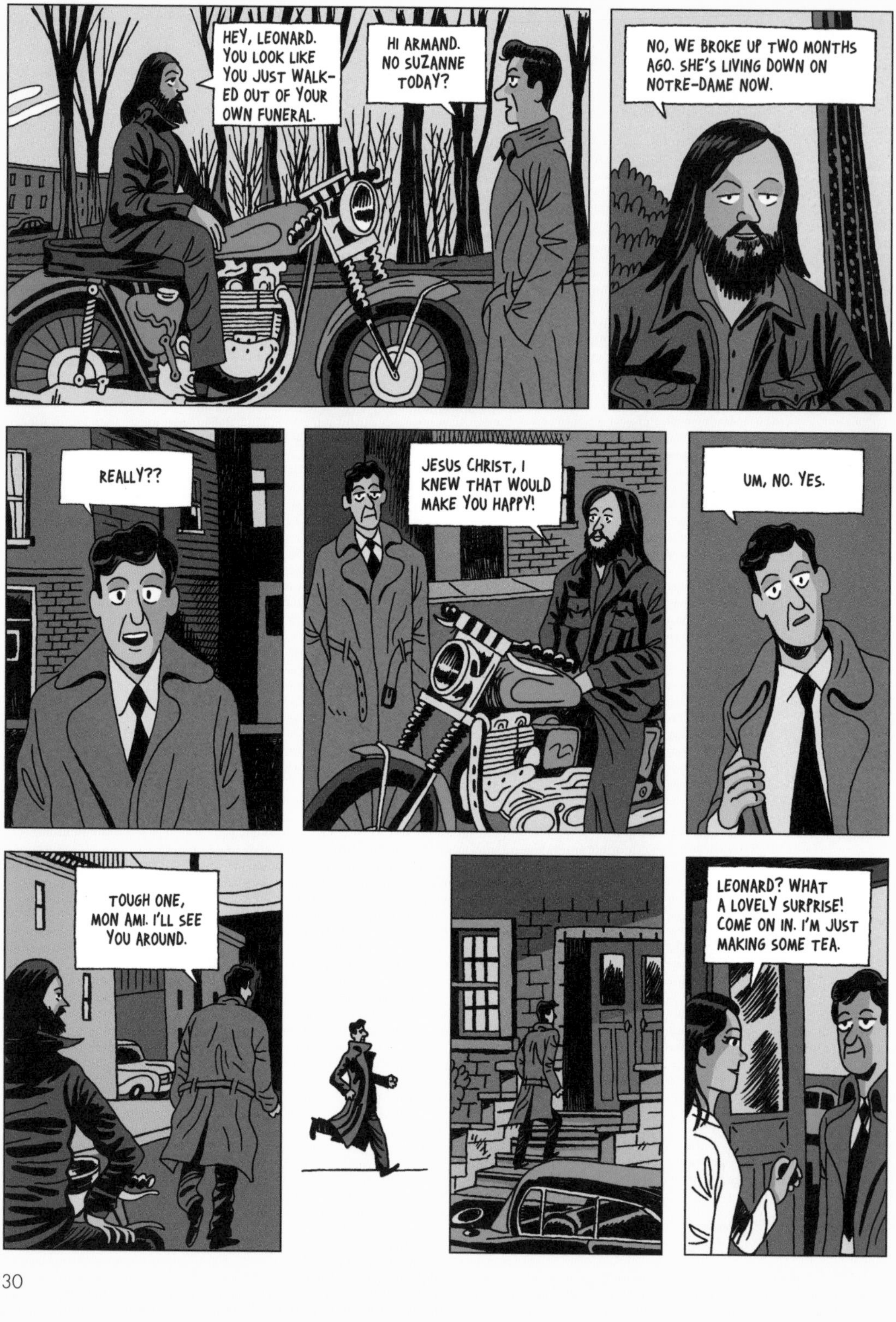
HEY, LEONARD. YOU LOOK LIKE YOU JUST WALK-ED OUT OF YOUR OWN FUNERAL.
HI ARMAND. NO SUZANNE TODAY?
NO, WE BROKE UP TWO MONTHS AGO. SHE'S LIVING DOWN ON NOTRE-DAME NOW.
REALLY??
JESUS CHRIST, I KNEW THAT WOULD MAKE YOU HAPPY!
UM, NO. YES.
TOUGH ONE, MON AMI. I'LL SEE YOU AROUND.
LEONARD? WHAT A LOVELY SURPRISE! COME ON IN. I'M JUST MAKING SOME TEA.

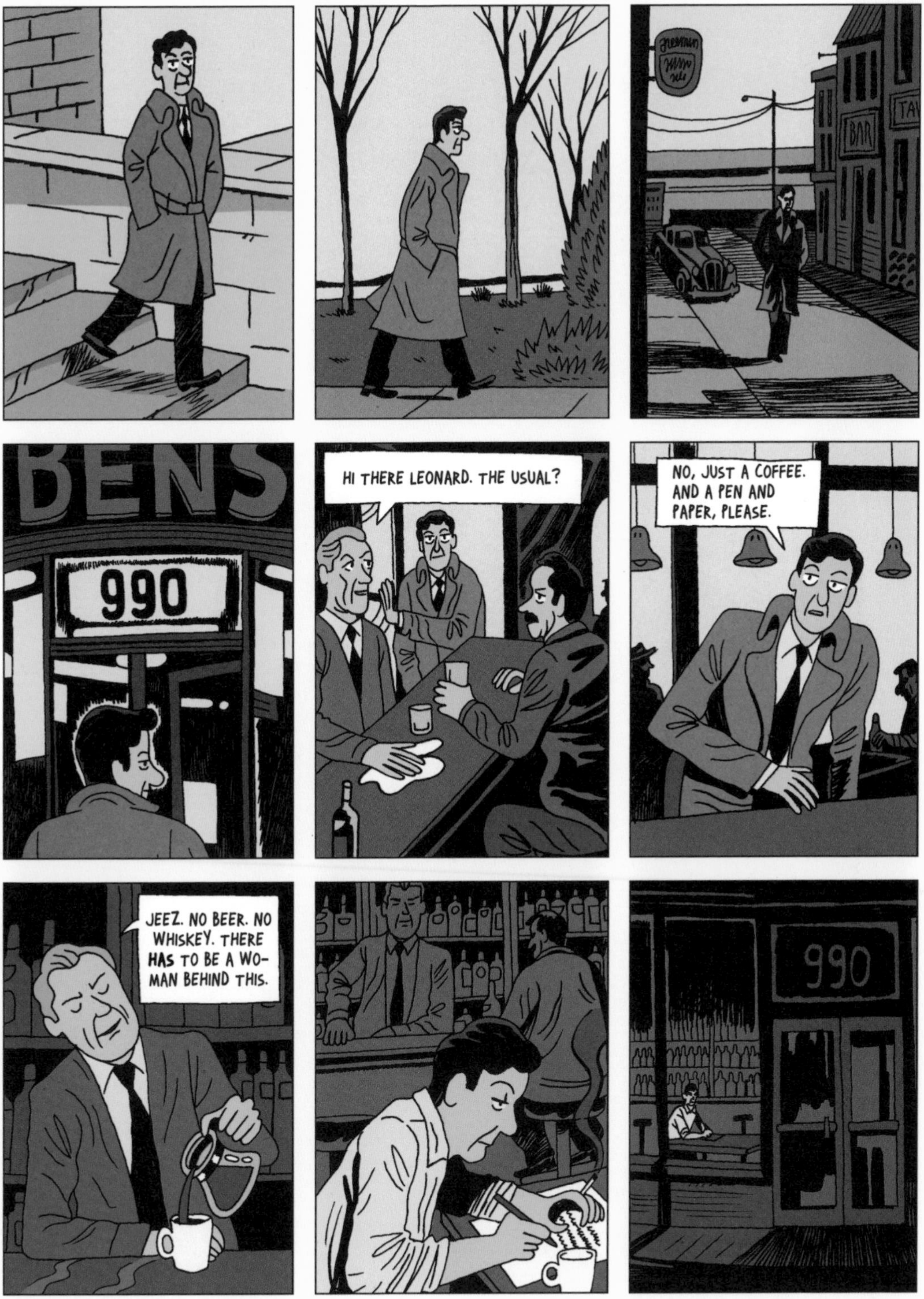
BAR
BENS
990
HI THERE LEONARD. THE USUAL?
NO, JUST A COFFEE. AND A PEN AND PAPER, PLEASE.
JEEZ. NO BEER. NO WHISKEY. THERE **HAS** TO BE A WO-MAN BEHIND THIS.
990

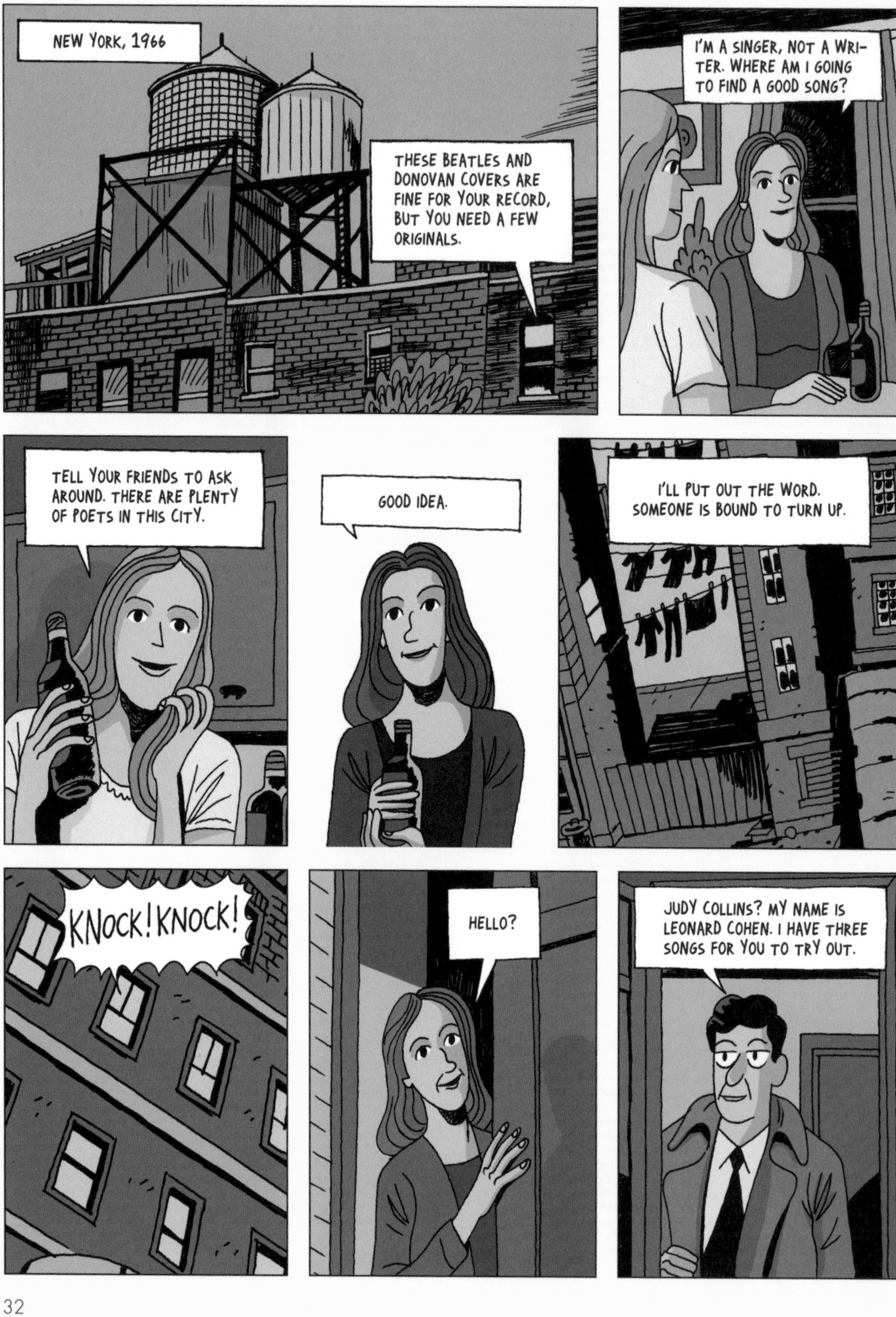
NEW YORK, 1966
THESE BEATLES AND DONOVAN COVERS ARE FINE FOR YOUR RECORD, BUT YOU NEED A FEW ORIGINALS.
I'M A SINGER, NOT A WRITER. WHERE AM I GOING TO FIND A GOOD SONG?
TELL YOUR FRIENDS TO ASK AROUND. THERE ARE PLENTY OF POETS IN THIS CITY.
GOOD IDEA.
I'LL PUT OUT THE WORD. SOMEONE IS BOUND TO TURN UP.
KNOCK! KNOCK!
HELLO?
JUDY COLLINS? MY NAME IS LEONARD COHEN. I HAVE THREE SONGS FOR YOU TO TRY OUT.

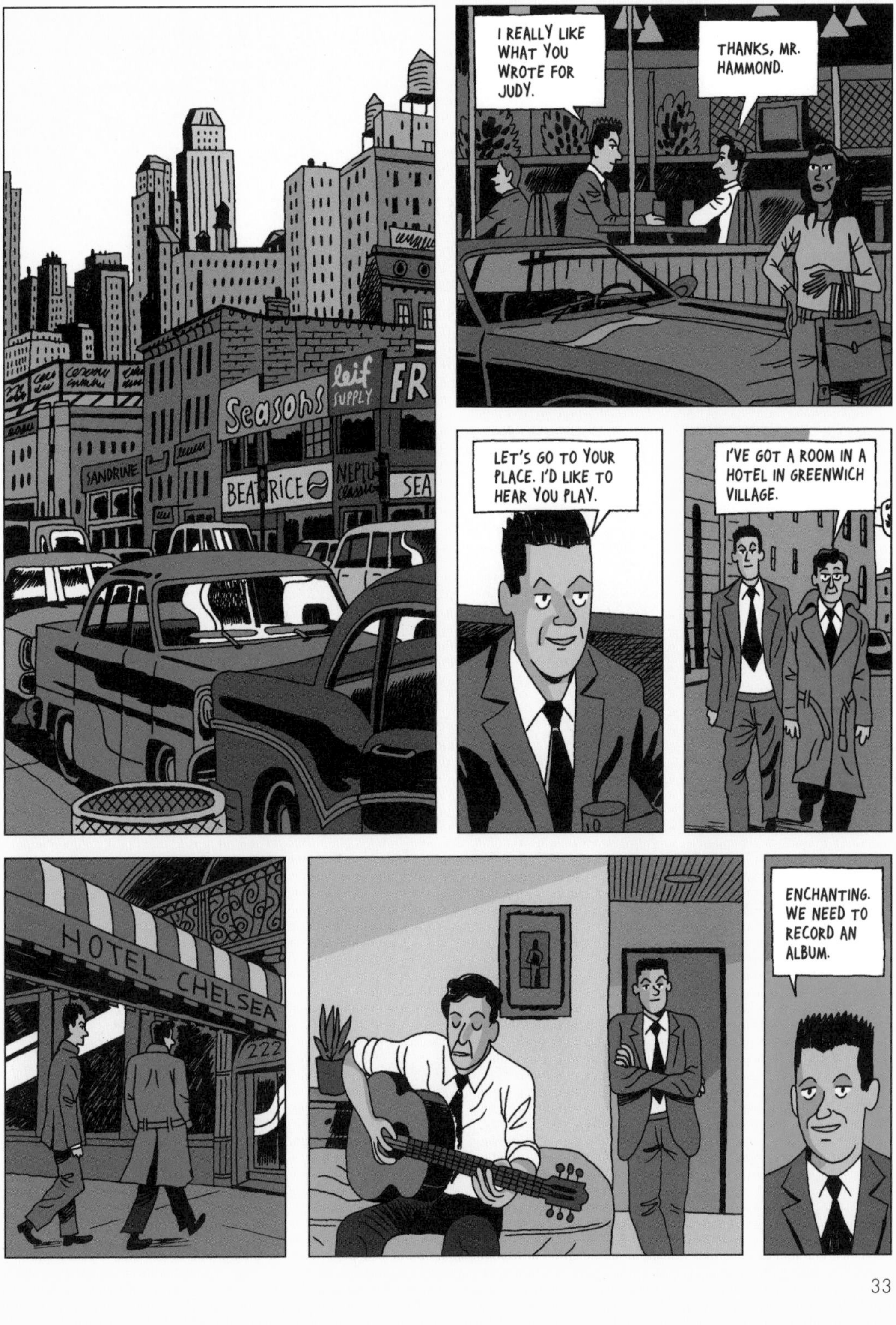
Seasons
leif SUPPLY
FR
SANDRINE
BEATRICE
NEPTU
SEA
I REALLY LIKE WHAT YOU WROTE FOR JUDY.
THANKS, MR. HAMMOND.
LET'S GO TO YOUR PLACE. I'D LIKE TO HEAR YOU PLAY.
I'VE GOT A ROOM IN A HOTEL IN GREENWICH VILLAGE.
HOTEL CHELSEA
222
ENCHANTING. WE NEED TO RECORD AN ALBUM.

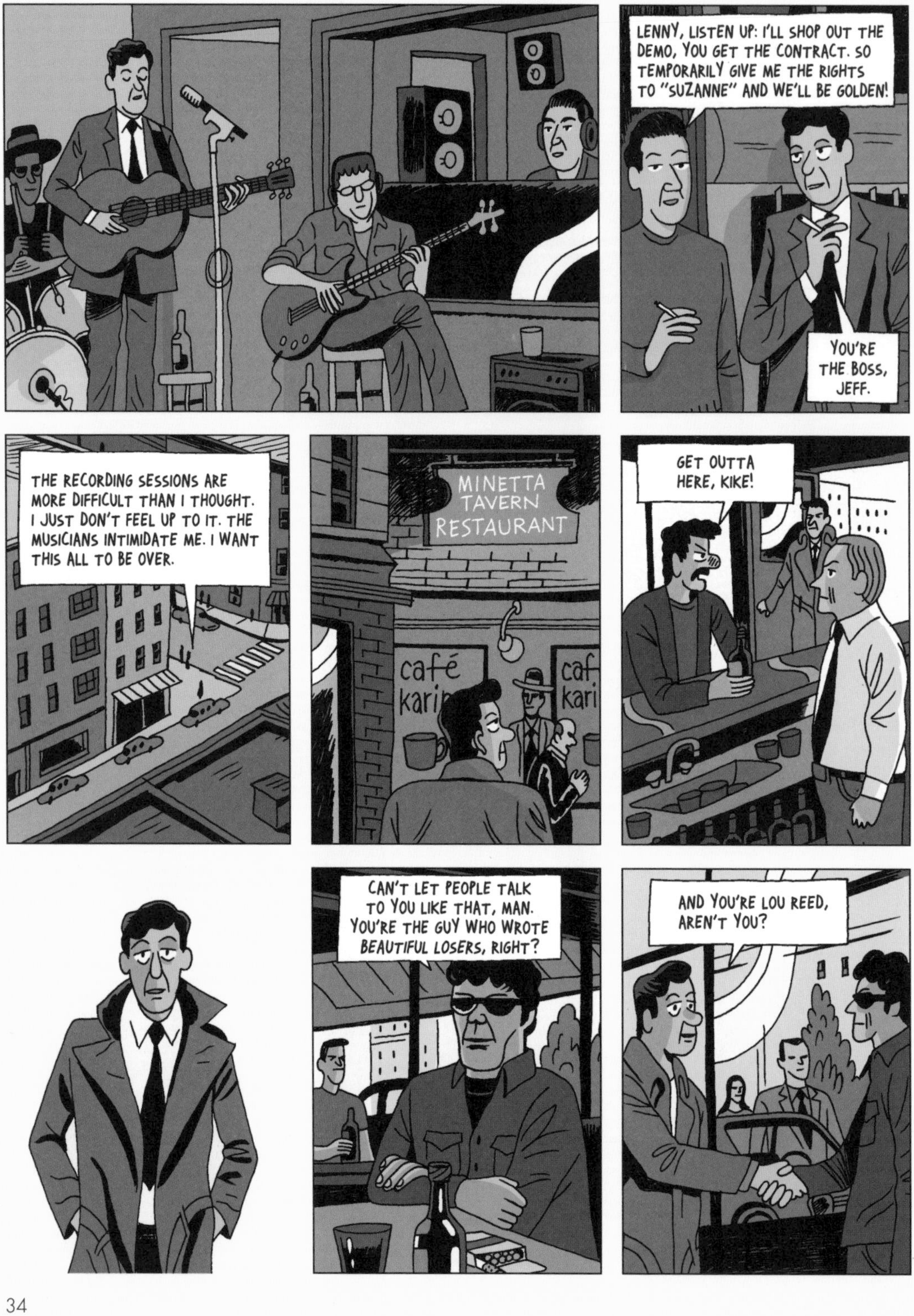

LENNY, LISTEN UP: I'LL SHOP OUT THE DEMO, YOU GET THE CONTRACT. SO TEMPORARILY GIVE ME THE RIGHTS TO "SUZANNE" AND WE'LL BE GOLDEN!
YOU'RE THE BOSS, JEFF.
THE RECORDING SESSIONS ARE MORE DIFFICULT THAN I THOUGHT. I JUST DON'T FEEL UP TO IT. THE MUSICIANS INTIMIDATE ME. I WANT THIS ALL TO BE OVER.
MINETTA TAVERN RESTAURANT
café kari
caf kari
GET OUTTA HERE, KIKE!
CAN'T LET PEOPLE TALK TO YOU LIKE THAT, MAN. YOU'RE THE GUY WHO WROTE *BEAUTIFUL LOSERS*, RIGHT?
AND YOU'RE LOU REED, AREN'T YOU?

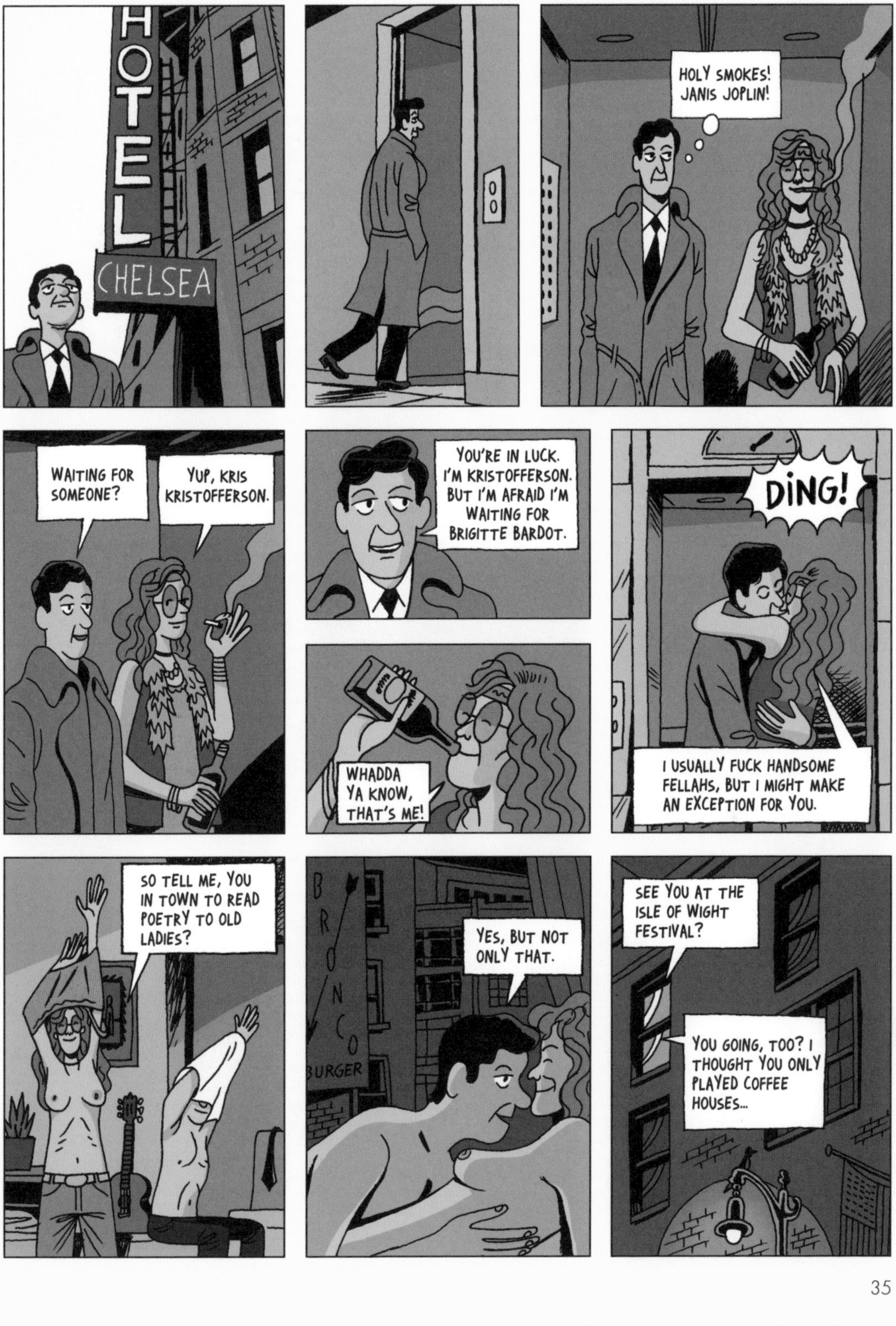

HOTEL
CHELSEA
HOLY SMOKES! JANIS JOPLIN!
WAITING FOR SOMEONE?
YUP, KRIS KRISTOFFERSON.
YOU'RE IN LUCK. I'M KRISTOFFERSON. BUT I'M AFRAID I'M WAITING FOR BRIGITTE BARDOT.
WHADDA YA KNOW, THAT'S ME!
DING!
I USUALLY FUCK HANDSOME FELLAHS, BUT I MIGHT MAKE AN EXCEPTION FOR YOU.
SO TELL ME, YOU IN TOWN TO READ POETRY TO OLD LADIES?
BRONCO
BURGER
YES, BUT NOT ONLY THAT.
SEE YOU AT THE ISLE OF WIGHT FESTIVAL?
YOU GOING, TOO? I THOUGHT YOU ONLY PLAYED COFFEE HOUSES...

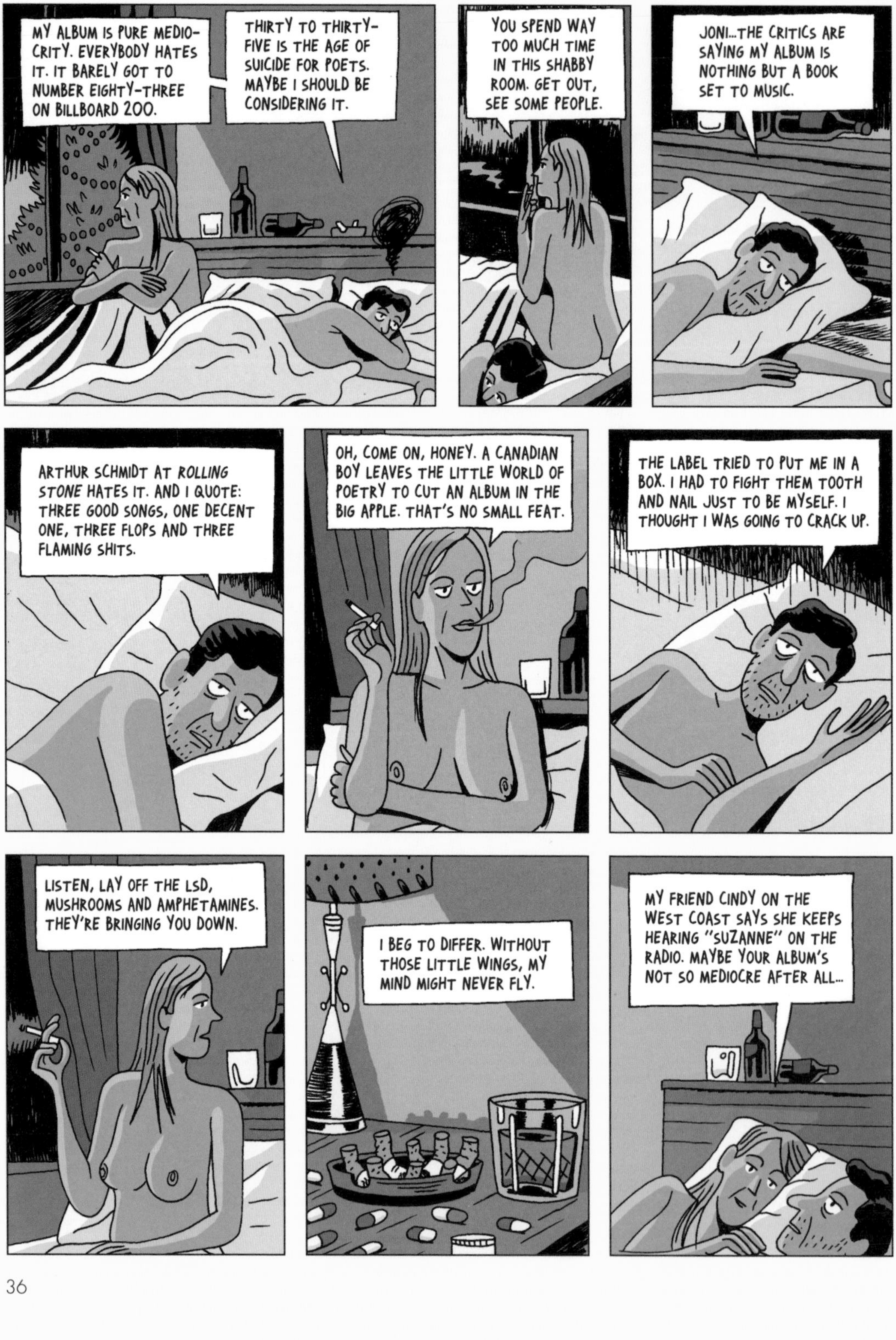

MY ALBUM IS PURE MEDIOCRITY. EVERYBODY HATES IT. IT BARELY GOT TO NUMBER EIGHTY-THREE ON BILLBOARD 200.
THIRTY TO THIRTY-FIVE IS THE AGE OF SUICIDE FOR POETS. MAYBE I SHOULD BE CONSIDERING IT.
YOU SPEND WAY TOO MUCH TIME IN THIS SHABBY ROOM. GET OUT, SEE SOME PEOPLE.
JONI...THE CRITICS ARE SAYING MY ALBUM IS NOTHING BUT A BOOK SET TO MUSIC.
ARTHUR SCHMIDT AT *ROLLING STONE* HATES IT. AND I QUOTE: THREE GOOD SONGS, ONE DECENT ONE, THREE FLOPS AND THREE FLAMING SHITS.
OH, COME ON, HONEY. A CANADIAN BOY LEAVES THE LITTLE WORLD OF POETRY TO CUT AN ALBUM IN THE BIG APPLE. THAT'S NO SMALL FEAT.
THE LABEL TRIED TO PUT ME IN A BOX. I HAD TO FIGHT THEM TOOTH AND NAIL JUST TO BE MYSELF. I THOUGHT I WAS GOING TO CRACK UP.
LISTEN, LAY OFF THE LSD, MUSHROOMS AND AMPHETAMINES. THEY'RE BRINGING YOU DOWN.
I BEG TO DIFFER. WITHOUT THOSE LITTLE WINGS, MY MIND MIGHT NEVER FLY.
MY FRIEND CINDY ON THE WEST COAST SAYS SHE KEEPS HEARING "SUZANNE" ON THE RADIO. MAYBE YOUR ALBUM'S NOT SO MEDIOCRE AFTER ALL...

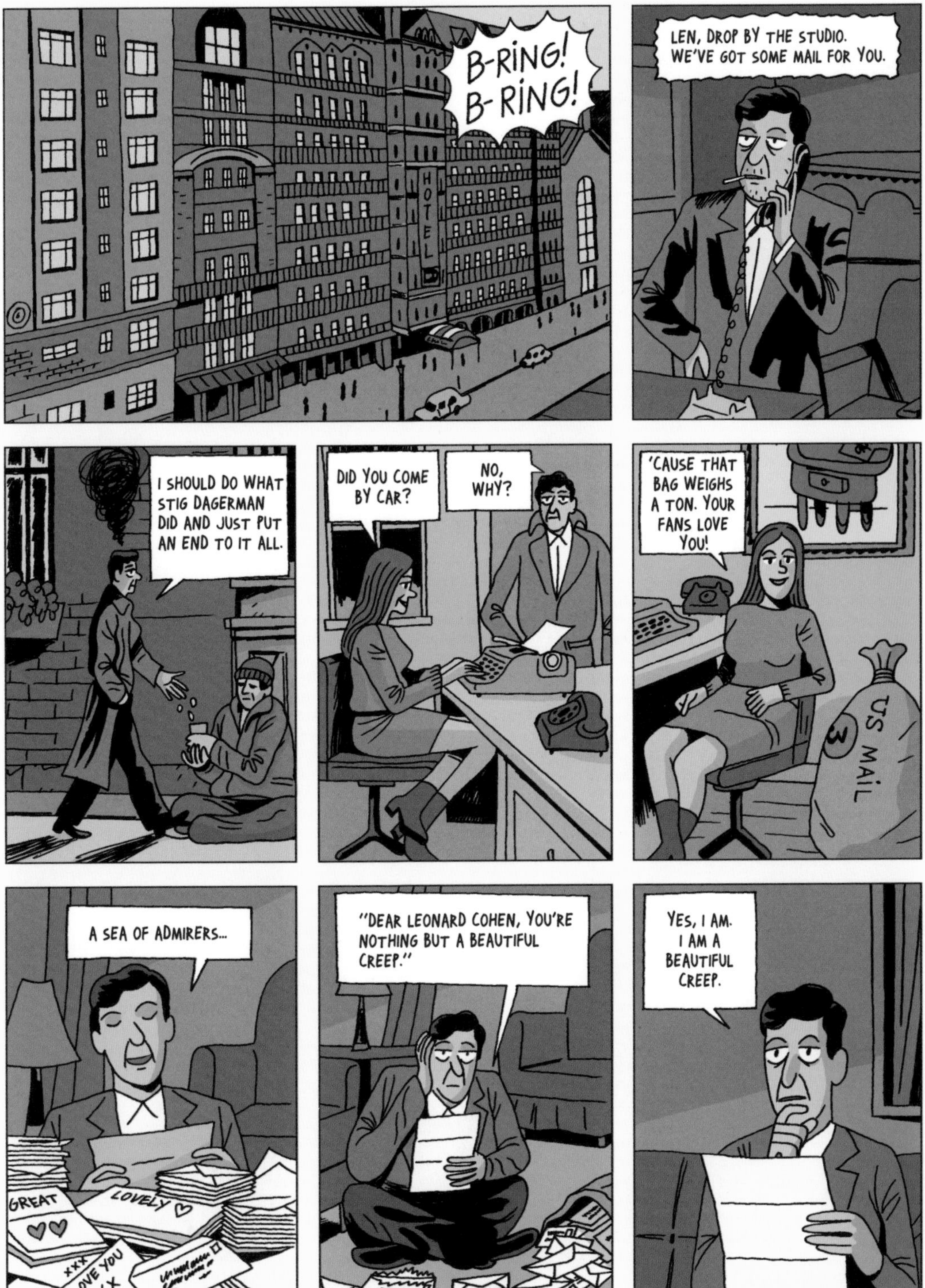
B-RING! B-RING!
LEN, DROP BY THE STUDIO. WE'VE GOT SOME MAIL FOR YOU.
I SHOULD DO WHAT STIG DAGERMAN DID AND JUST PUT AN END TO IT ALL.
DID YOU COME BY CAR?
NO, WHY?
'CAUSE THAT BAG WEIGHS A TON. YOUR FANS LOVE YOU!
US MAIL
A SEA OF ADMIRERS...
GREAT
LOVELY
LOVE YOU
XX
XXX
"DEAR LEONARD COHEN, YOU'RE NOTHING BUT A BEAUTIFUL CREEP."
YES, I AM. I AM A BEAUTIFUL CREEP.

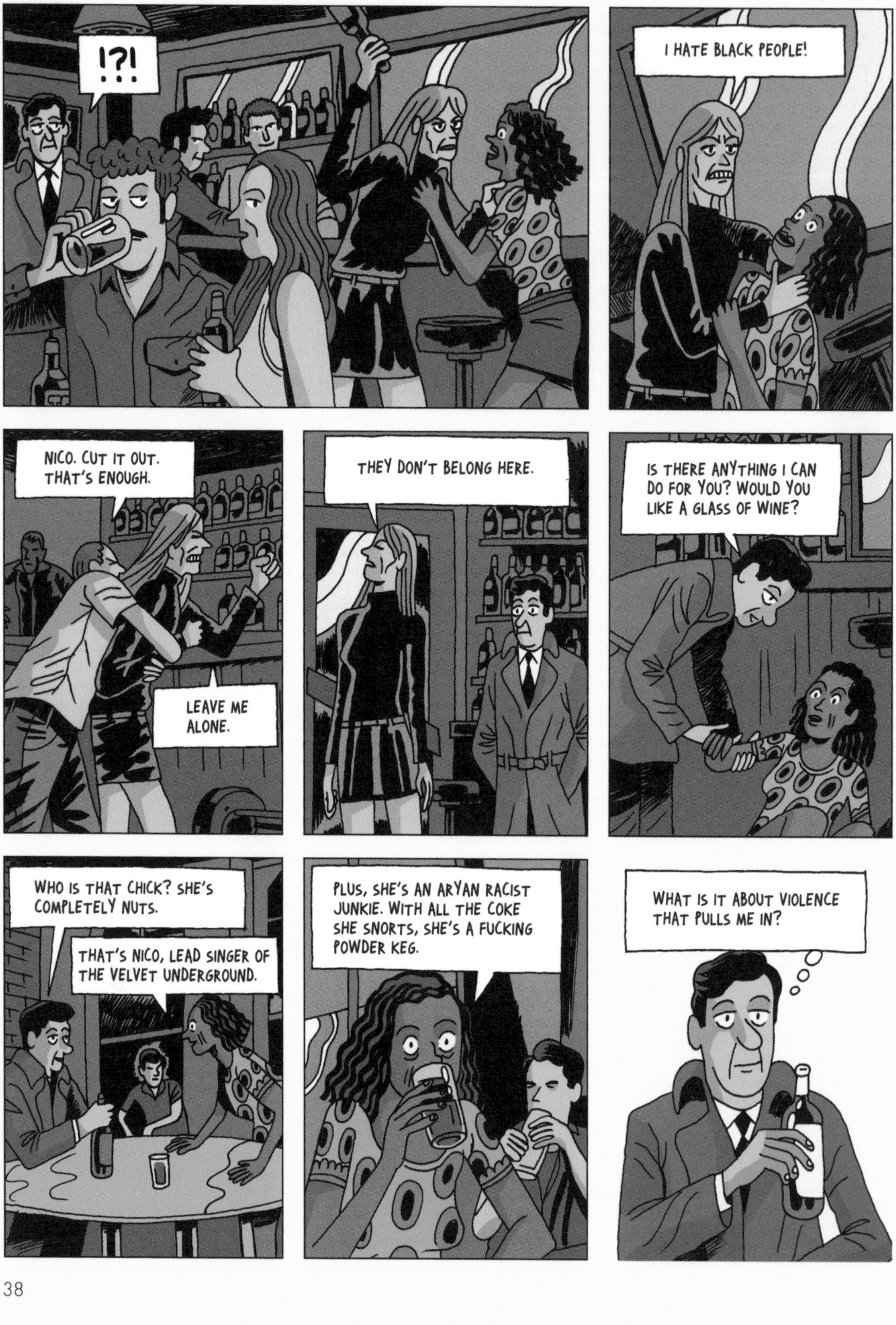
!?!
I HATE BLACK PEOPLE!
NICO. CUT IT OUT. THAT'S ENOUGH.
LEAVE ME ALONE.
THEY DON'T BELONG HERE.
IS THERE ANYTHING I CAN DO FOR YOU? WOULD YOU LIKE A GLASS OF WINE?
WHO IS THAT CHICK? SHE'S COMPLETELY NUTS.
THAT'S NICO, LEAD SINGER OF THE VELVET UNDERGROUND.
PLUS, SHE'S AN ARYAN RACIST JUNKIE. WITH ALL THE COKE SHE SNORTS, SHE'S A FUCKING POWDER KEG.
WHAT IS IT ABOUT VIOLENCE THAT PULLS ME IN?

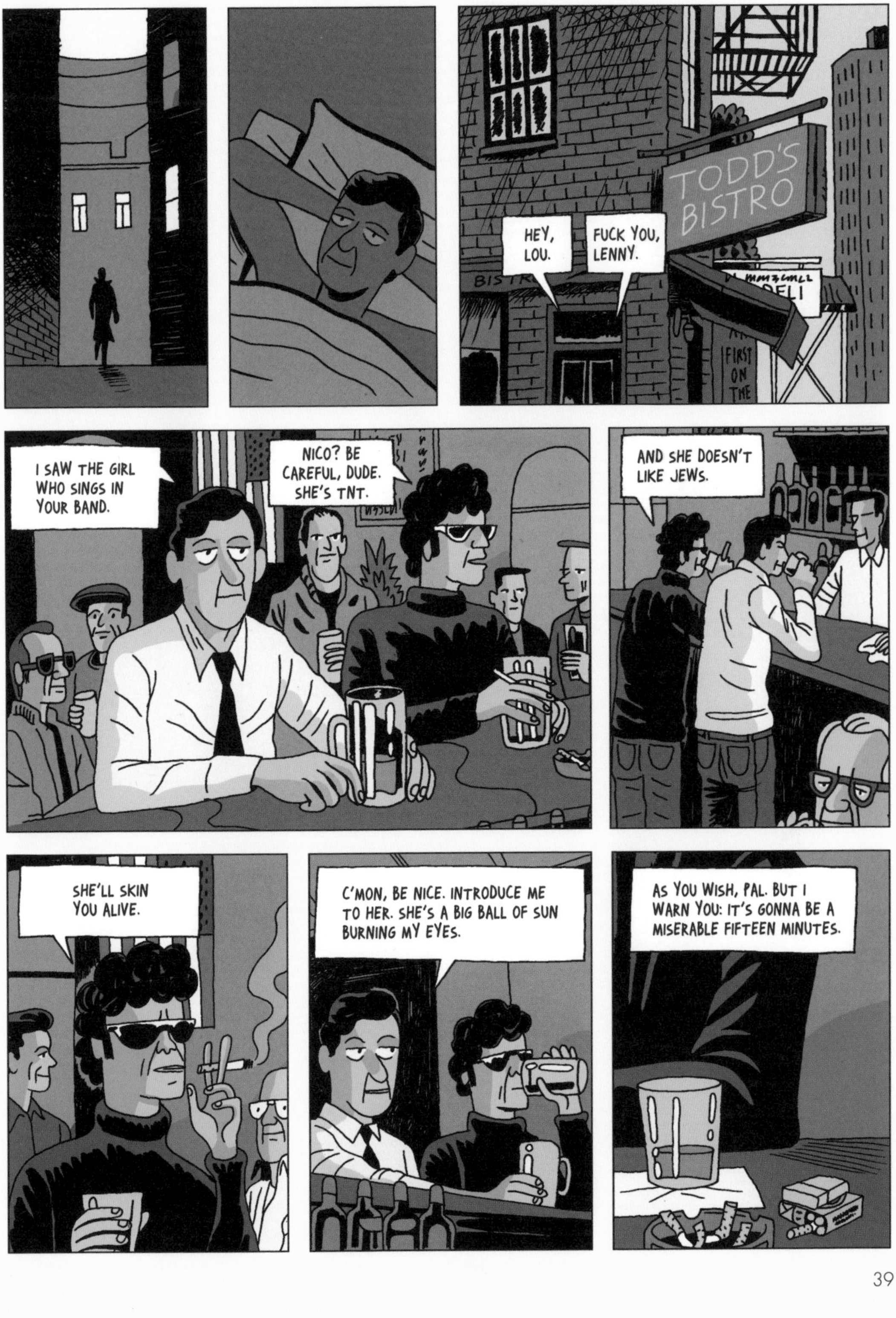
TODD'S BISTRO
HEY, LOU.
FUCK YOU, LENNY.
I SAW THE GIRL WHO SINGS IN YOUR BAND.
NICO? BE CAREFUL, DUDE. SHE'S TNT.
AND SHE DOESN'T LIKE JEWS.
SHE'LL SKIN YOU ALIVE.
C'MON, BE NICE. INTRODUCE ME TO HER. SHE'S A BIG BALL OF SUN BURNING MY EYES.
AS YOU WISH, PAL. BUT I WARN YOU: IT'S GONNA BE A MISERABLE FIFTEEN MINUTES.

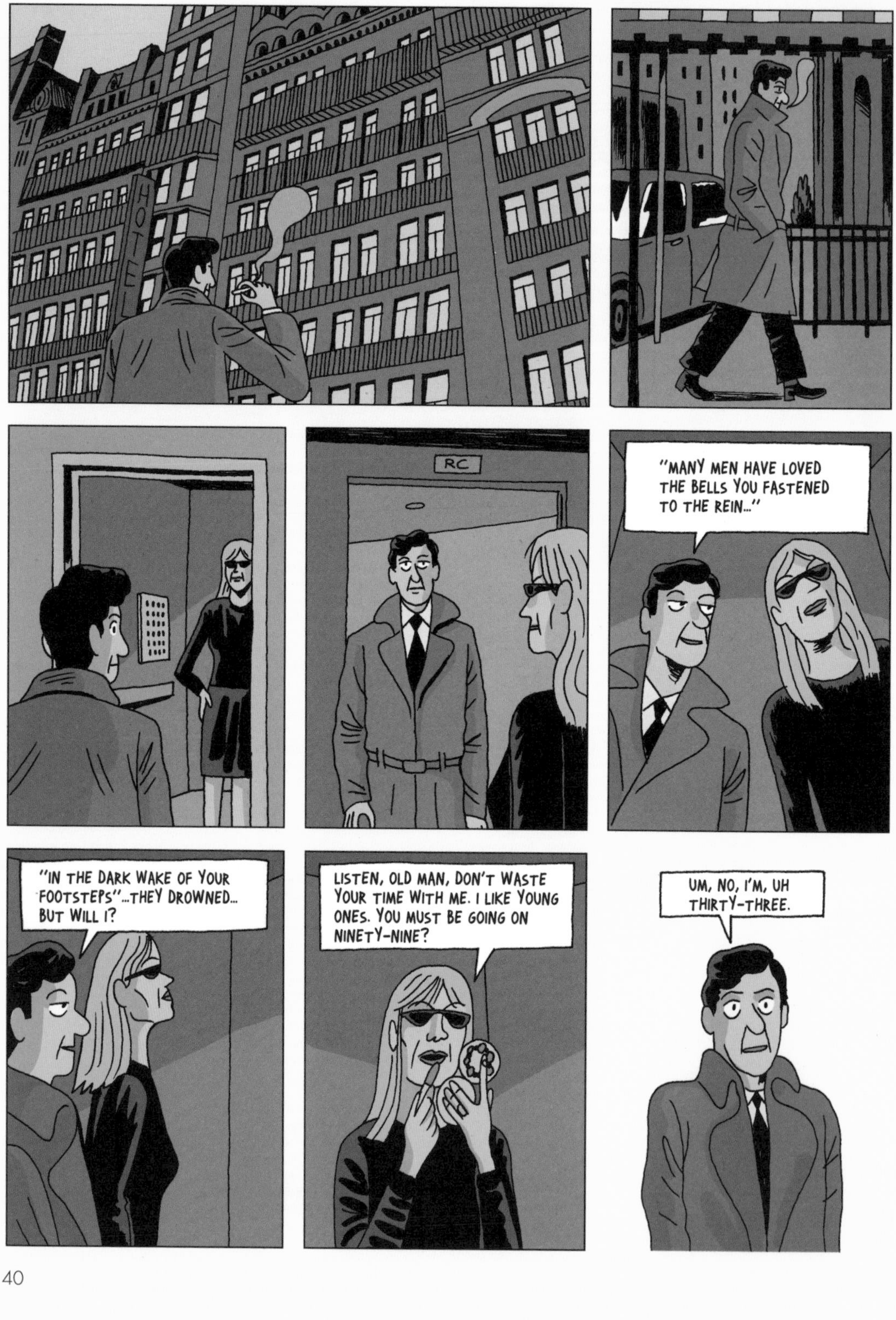
HOTEL
RC
"MANY MEN HAVE LOVED THE BELLS YOU FASTENED TO THE REIN..."
"IN THE DARK WAKE OF YOUR FOOTSTEPS"...THEY DROWNED... BUT WILL I?
LISTEN, OLD MAN, DON'T WASTE YOUR TIME WITH ME. I LIKE YOUNG ONES. YOU MUST BE GOING ON NINETY-NINE?
UM, NO, I'M, UH THIRTY-THREE.

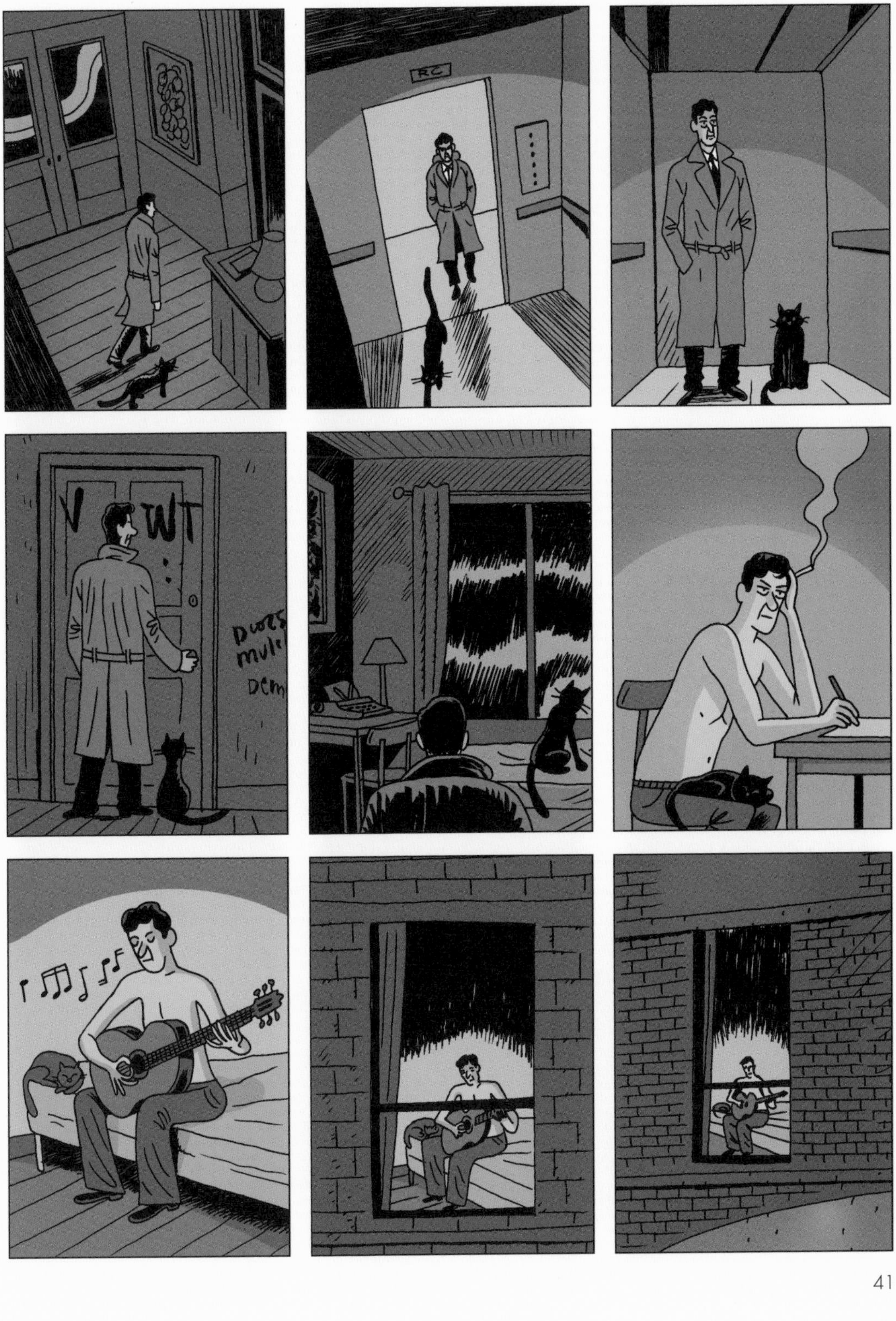
RC
V WT

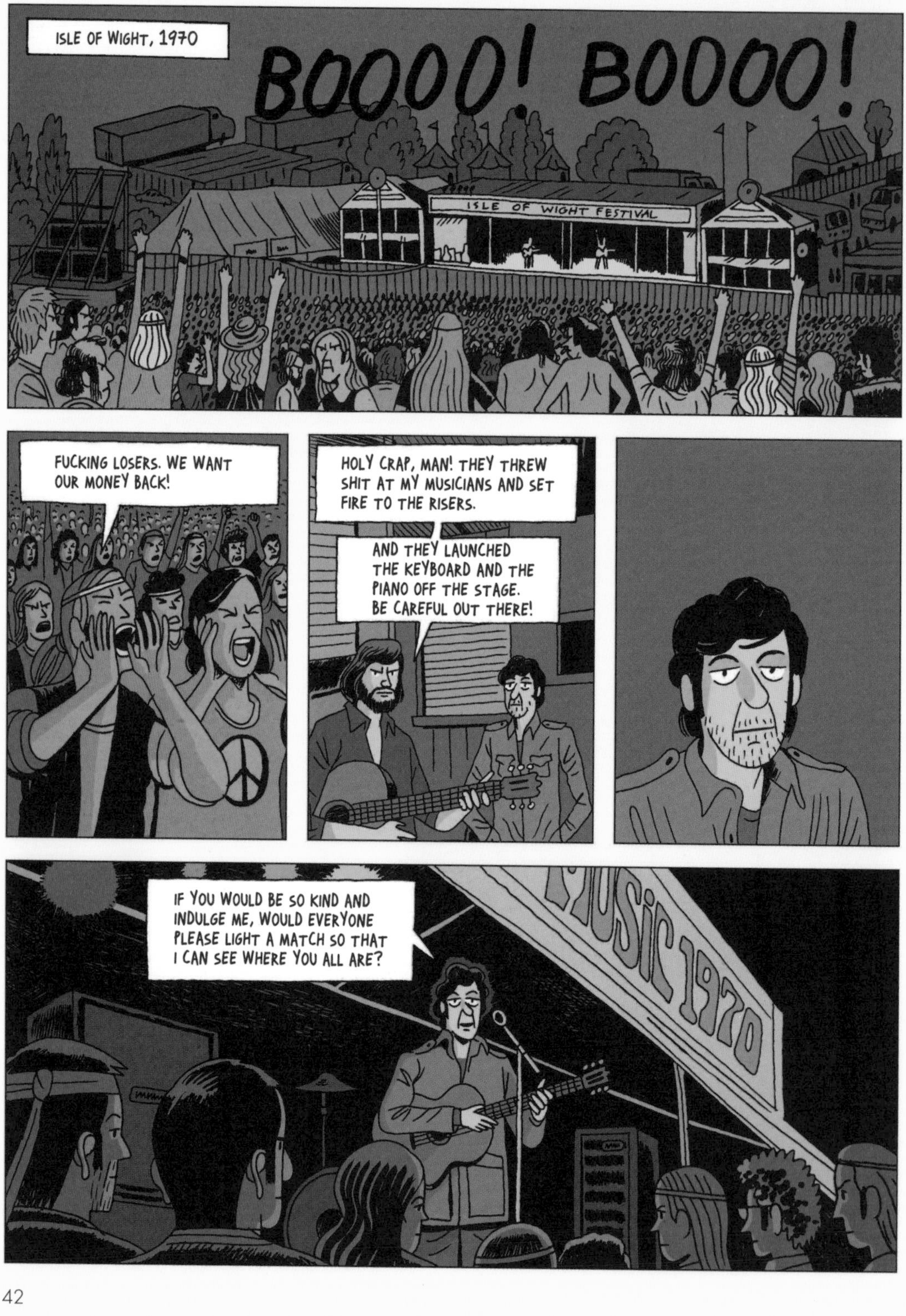

ISLE OF WIGHT, 1970
BOOOO! BOOOO!
ISLE OF WIGHT FESTIVAL
FUCKING LOSERS. WE WANT OUR MONEY BACK!
HOLY CRAP, MAN! THEY THREW SHIT AT MY MUSICIANS AND SET FIRE TO THE RISERS.
AND THEY LAUNCHED THE KEYBOARD AND THE PIANO OFF THE STAGE. BE CAREFUL OUT THERE!
IF YOU WOULD BE SO KIND AND INDULGE ME, WOULD EVERYONE PLEASE LIGHT A MATCH SO THAT I CAN SEE WHERE YOU ALL ARE?
MUSIC 1970

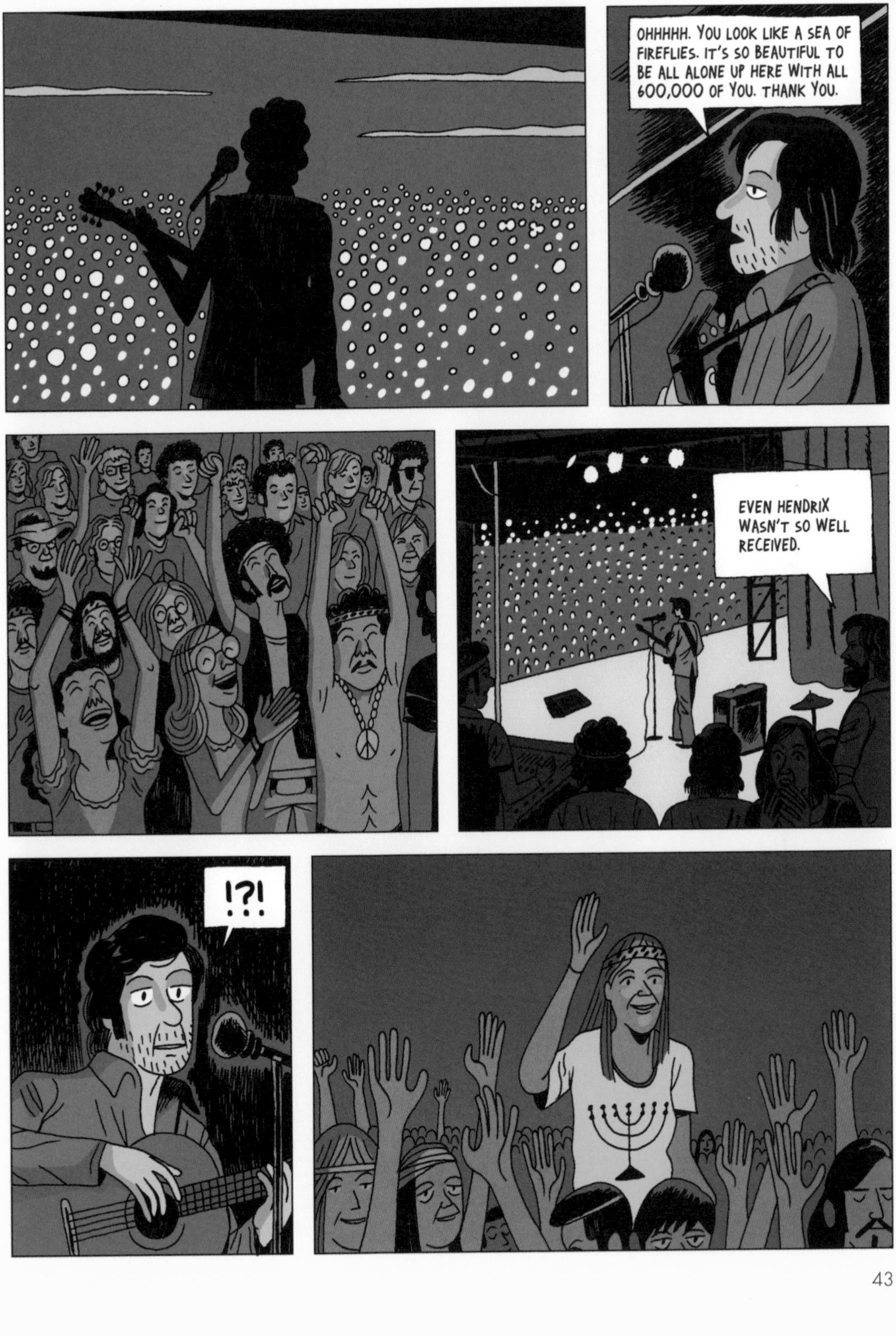
OHHHHH. YOU LOOK LIKE A SEA OF FIREFLIES. IT'S SO BEAUTIFUL TO BE ALL ALONE UP HERE WITH ALL 600,000 OF YOU. THANK YOU.
EVEN HENDRIX WASN'T SO WELL RECEIVED.
!?!

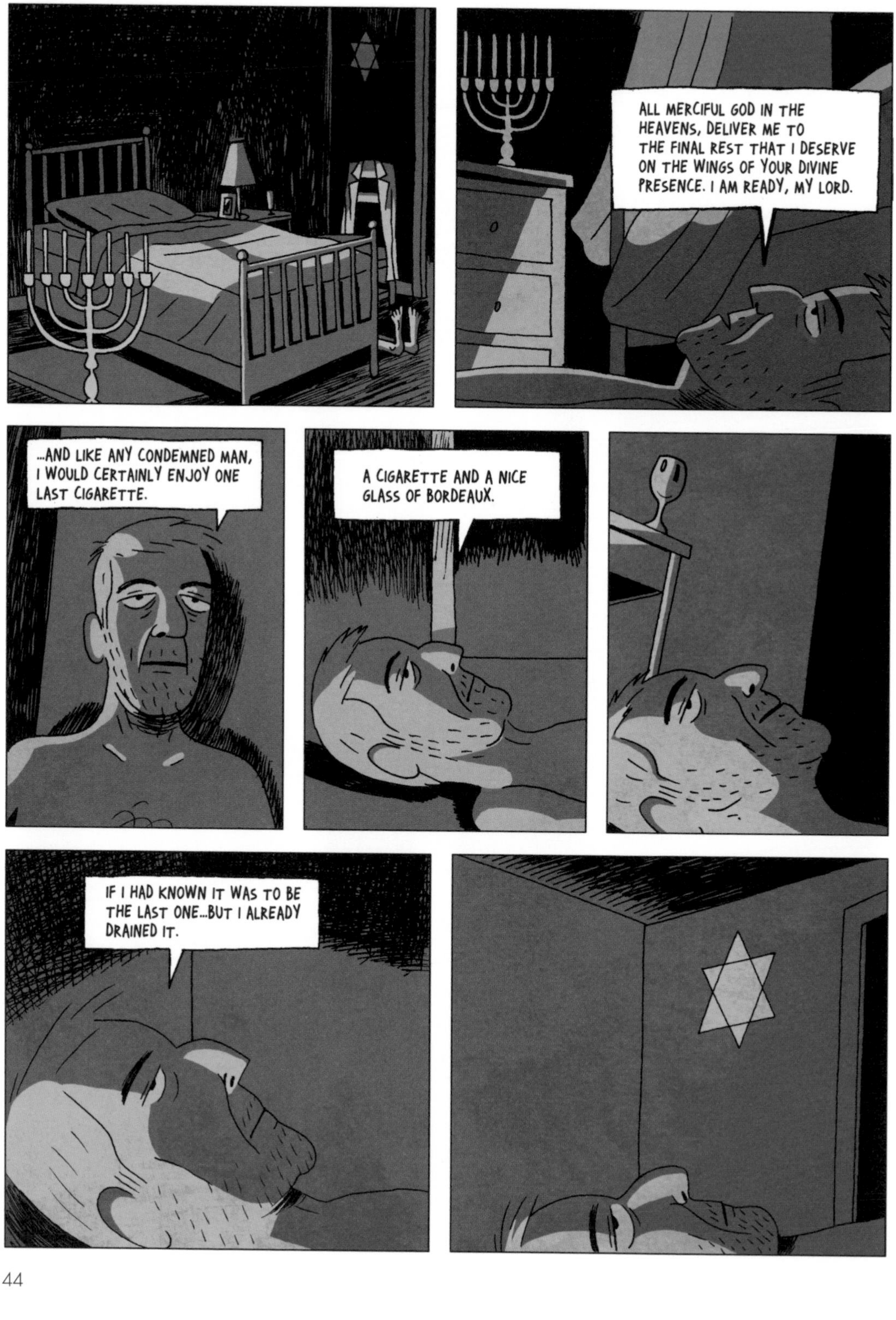
ALL MERCIFUL GOD IN THE HEAVENS, DELIVER ME TO THE FINAL REST THAT I DESERVE ON THE WINGS OF YOUR DIVINE PRESENCE. I AM READY, MY LORD.
...AND LIKE ANY CONDEMNED MAN, I WOULD CERTAINLY ENJOY ONE LAST CIGARETTE.
A CIGARETTE AND A NICE GLASS OF BORDEAUX.
IF I HAD KNOWN IT WAS TO BE THE LAST ONE...BUT I ALREADY DRAINED IT.

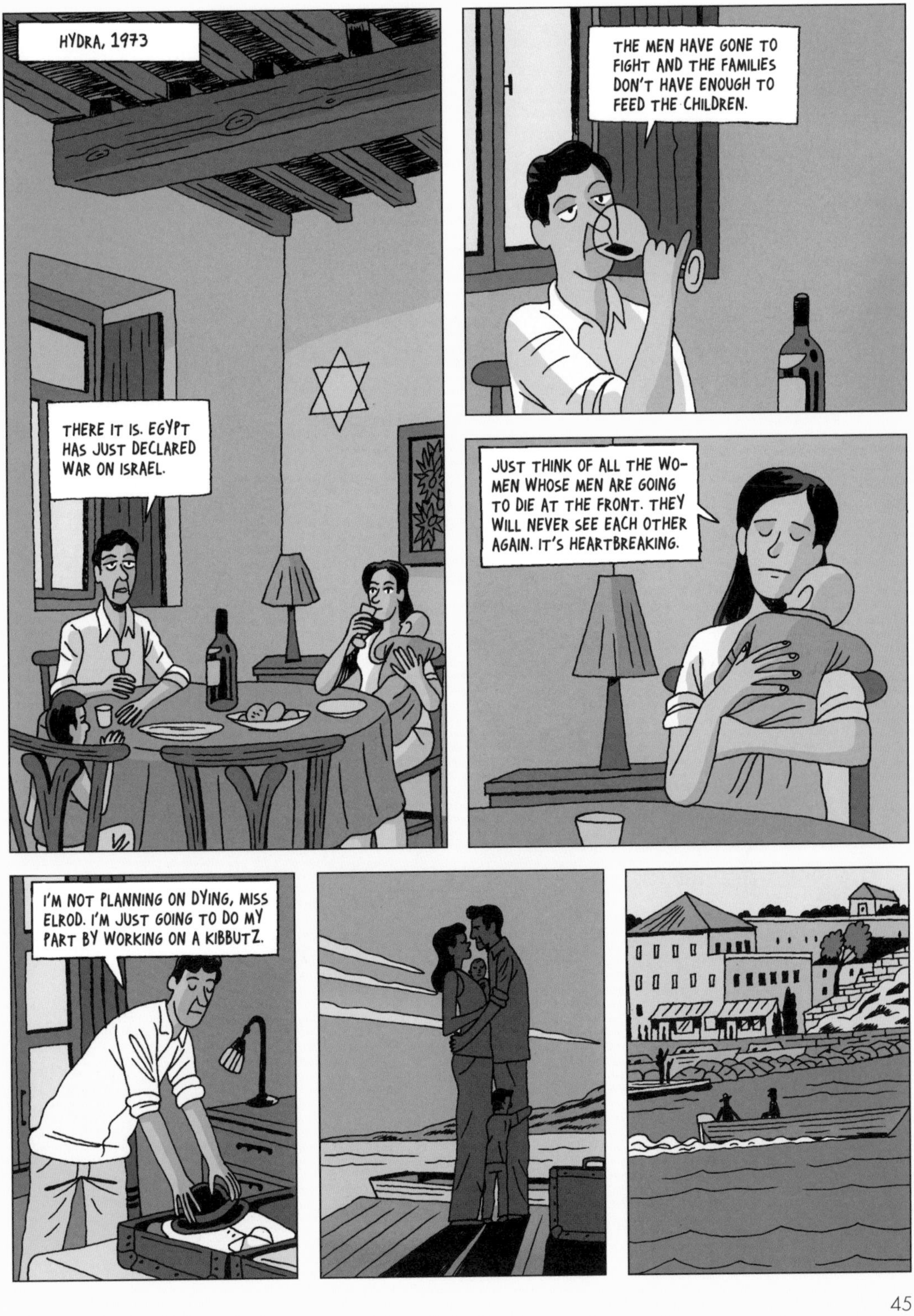
HYDRA, 1973
THERE IT IS. EGYPT HAS JUST DECLARED WAR ON ISRAEL.
THE MEN HAVE GONE TO FIGHT AND THE FAMILIES DON'T HAVE ENOUGH TO FEED THE CHILDREN.
JUST THINK OF ALL THE WO-MEN WHOSE MEN ARE GOING TO DIE AT THE FRONT. THEY WILL NEVER SEE EACH OTHER AGAIN. IT'S HEARTBREAKING.
I'M NOT PLANNING ON DYING, MISS ELROD. I'M JUST GOING TO DO MY PART BY WORKING ON A KIBBUTZ.

I JUST SAW LEONARD COHEN AT THE AIRPORT. I OVERHEARD HIM TELLING THE CAB DRIVER TO DROP HIM AT THE CAFE PINATI.

PARDON ME BUT AREN'T YOU LEONARD COHEN? WHAT ARE YOU DOING HERE IN ISRAEL?

I'VE COME TO WORK ON A KIBBUTZ.

IF YOU REALLY WANT TO HELP ISRAEL, COME WITH ME AND SING FOR THE TROOPS.

I'M NOT SO SURE THAT MY DREARY SONGS ARE GOING TO DO MUCH FOR MORALE.

I THINK YOU'RE WRONG ABOUT THAT. COME WITH ME AND SEE.

46

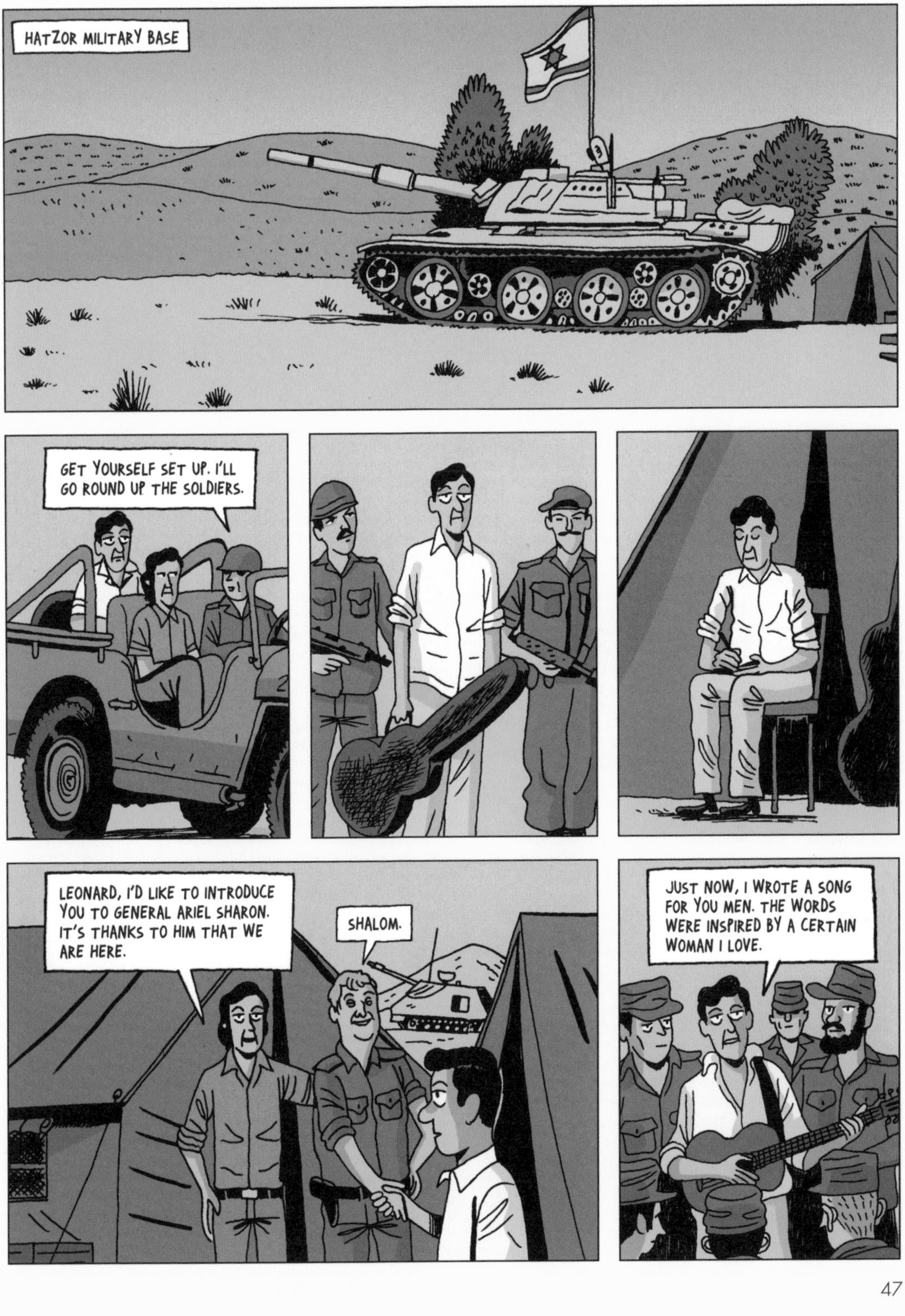
HATZOR MILITARY BASE
GET YOURSELF SET UP. I'LL GO ROUND UP THE SOLDIERS.
LEONARD, I'D LIKE TO INTRODUCE YOU TO GENERAL ARIEL SHARON. IT'S THANKS TO HIM THAT WE ARE HERE.
SHALOM.
JUST NOW, I WROTE A SONG FOR YOU MEN. THE WORDS WERE INSPIRED BY A CERTAIN WOMAN I LOVE.

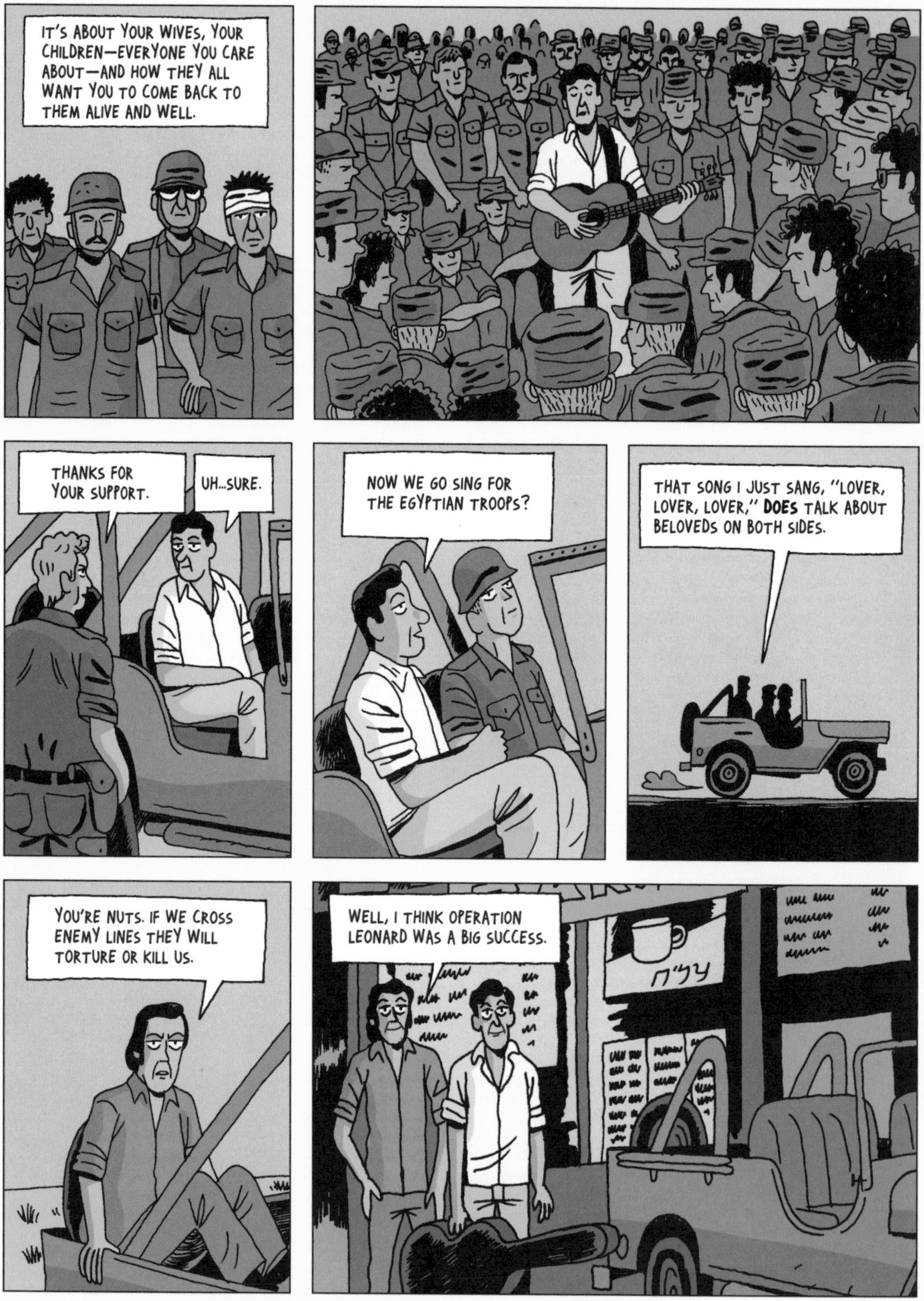
IT'S ABOUT YOUR WIVES, YOUR CHILDREN—EVERYONE YOU CARE ABOUT—AND HOW THEY ALL WANT YOU TO COME BACK TO THEM ALIVE AND WELL.
THANKS FOR YOUR SUPPORT.
UH...SURE.
NOW WE GO SING FOR THE EGYPTIAN TROOPS?
THAT SONG I JUST SANG, "LOVER, LOVER, LOVER," DOES TALK ABOUT BELOVEDS ON BOTH SIDES.
YOU'RE NUTS. IF WE CROSS ENEMY LINES THEY WILL TORTURE OR KILL US.
WELL, I THINK OPERATION LEONARD WAS A BIG SUCCESS.

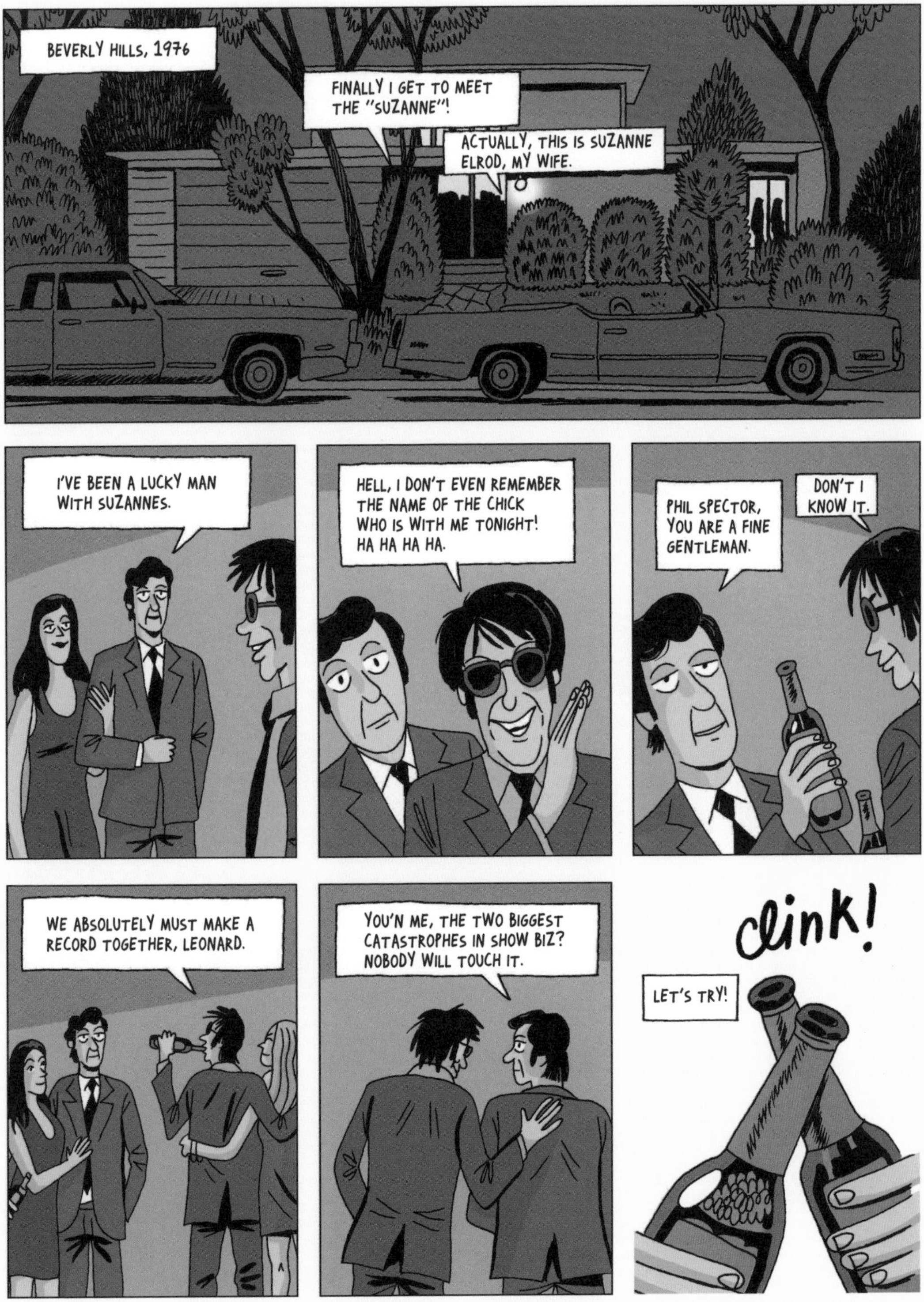
BEVERLY HILLS, 1976
FINALLY I GET TO MEET THE "SUZANNE"!
ACTUALLY, THIS IS SUZANNE ELROD, MY WIFE.
I'VE BEEN A LUCKY MAN WITH SUZANNES.
HELL, I DON'T EVEN REMEMBER THE NAME OF THE CHICK WHO IS WITH ME TONIGHT! HA HA HA HA.
PHIL SPECTOR, YOU ARE A FINE GENTLEMAN.
DON'T I KNOW IT.
WE ABSOLUTELY MUST MAKE A RECORD TOGETHER, LEONARD.
YOU'N ME, THE TWO BIGGEST CATASTROPHES IN SHOW BIZ? NOBODY WILL TOUCH IT.
LET'S TRY!
clink!

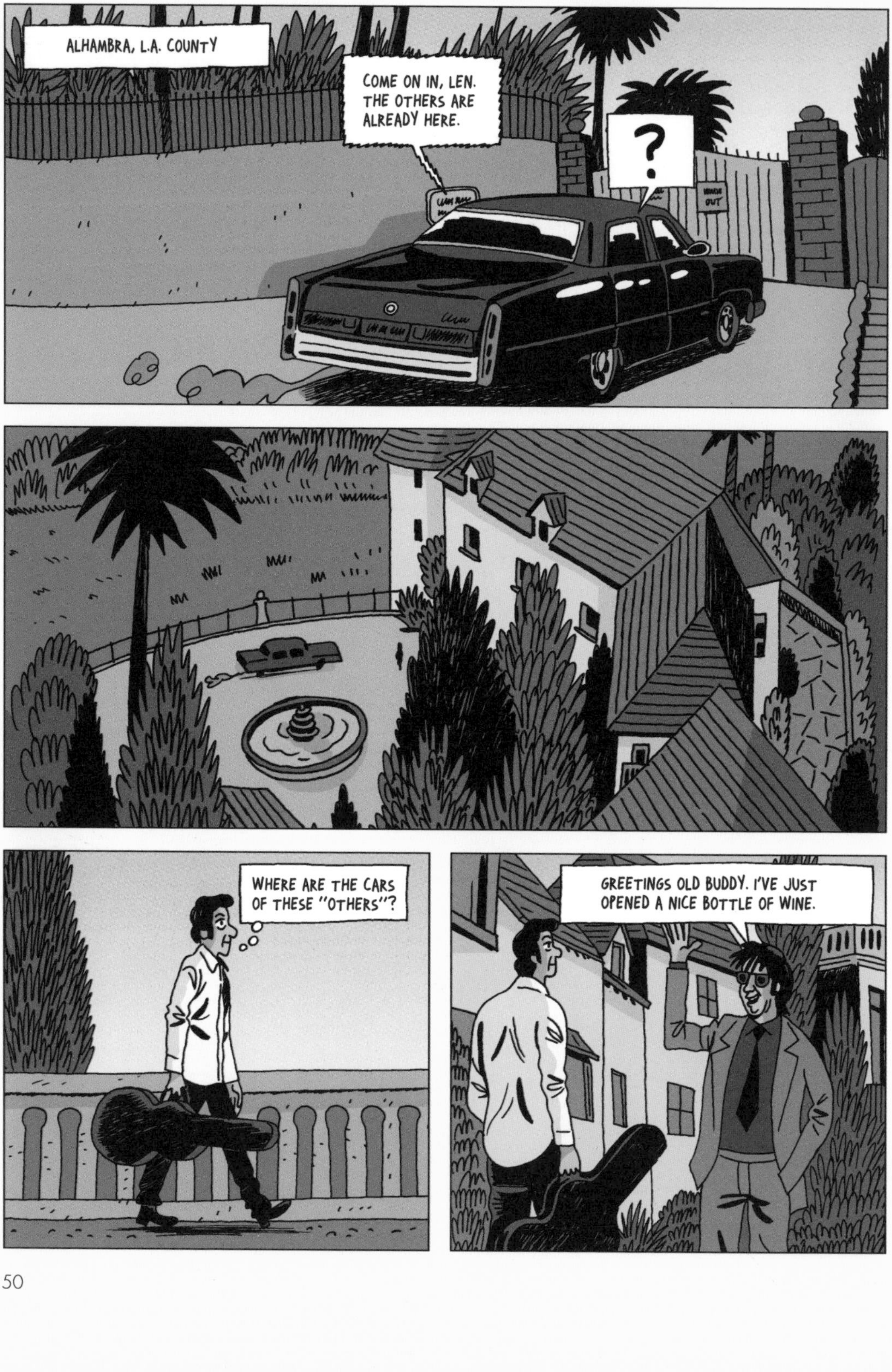
ALHAMBRA, L.A. COUNTY
COME ON IN, LEN. THE OTHERS ARE ALREADY HERE.
?
WHERE ARE THE CARS OF THESE "OTHERS"?
GREETINGS OLD BUDDY. I'VE JUST OPENED A NICE BOTTLE OF WINE.

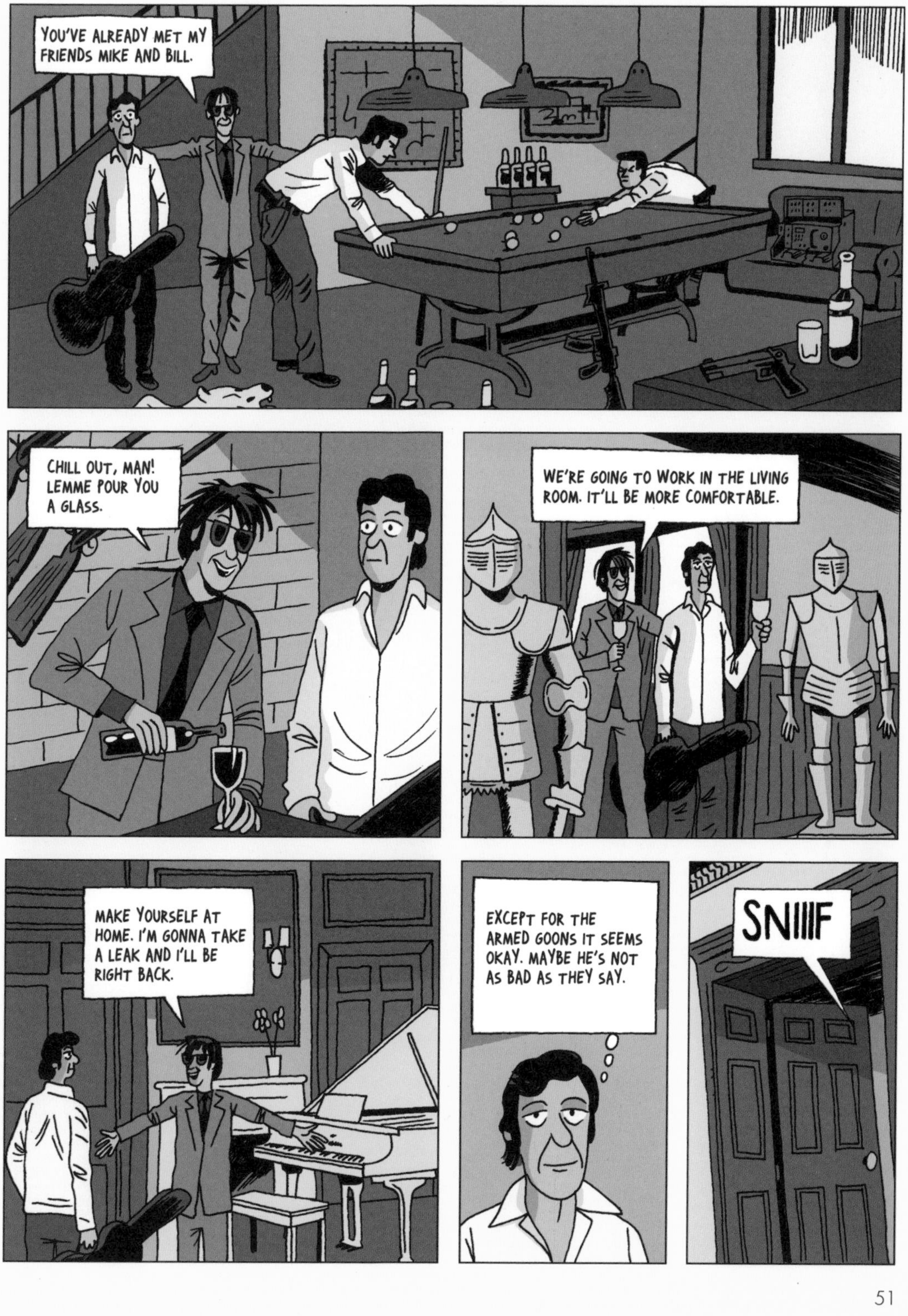
YOU'VE ALREADY MET MY FRIENDS MIKE AND BILL.
CHILL OUT, MAN! LEMME POUR YOU A GLASS.
WE'RE GOING TO WORK IN THE LIVING ROOM. IT'LL BE MORE COMFORTABLE.
MAKE YOURSELF AT HOME. I'M GONNA TAKE A LEAK AND I'LL BE RIGHT BACK.
EXCEPT FOR THE ARMED GOONS IT SEEMS OKAY. MAYBE HE'S NOT AS BAD AS THEY SAY.
SNIIIF

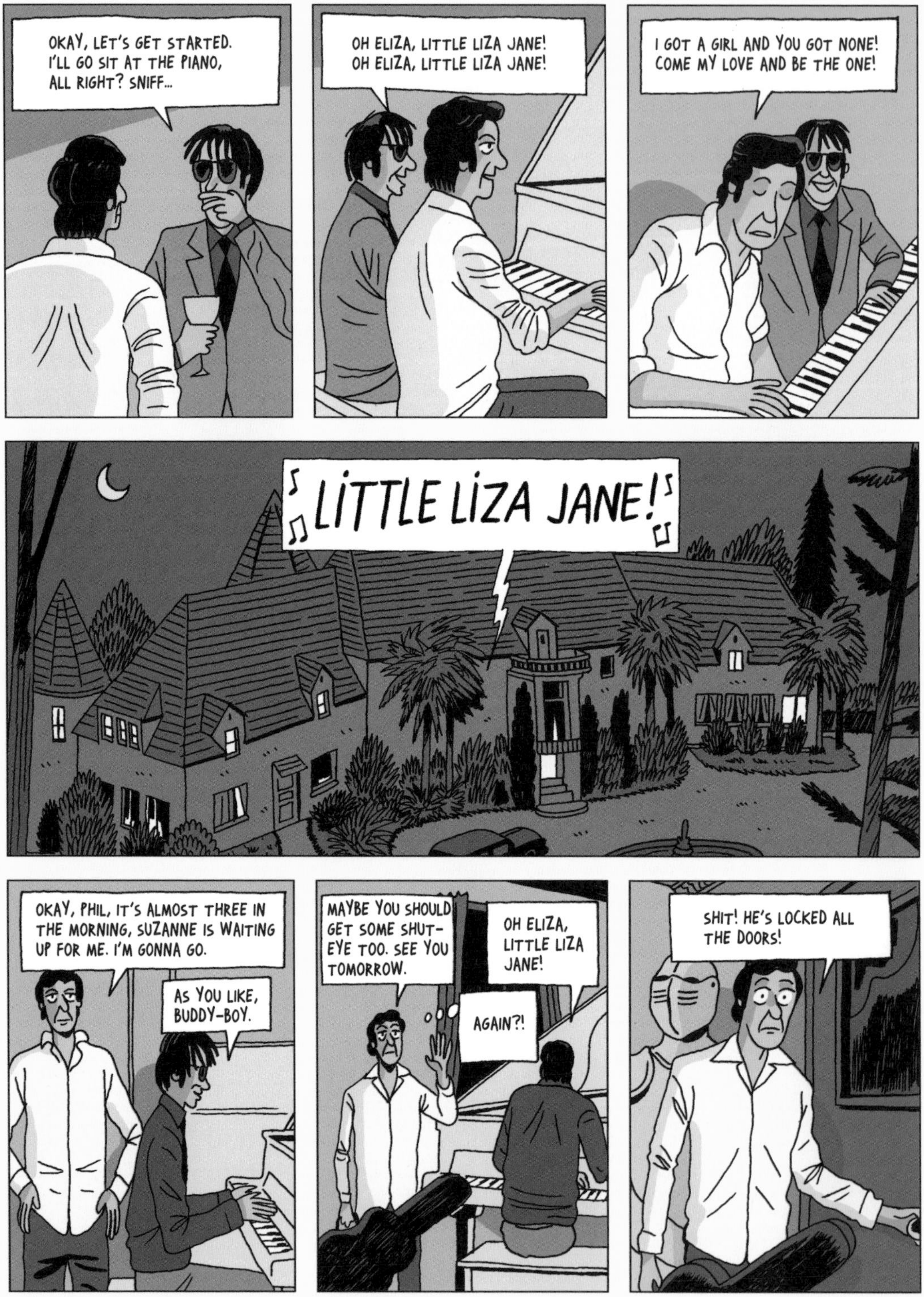
OKAY, LET'S GET STARTED. I'LL GO SIT AT THE PIANO, ALL RIGHT? SNIFF...
OH ELIZA, LITTLE LIZA JANE! OH ELIZA, LITTLE LIZA JANE!
I GOT A GIRL AND YOU GOT NONE! COME MY LOVE AND BE THE ONE!
LITTLE LIZA JANE!
OKAY, PHIL, IT'S ALMOST THREE IN THE MORNING, SUZANNE IS WAITING UP FOR ME. I'M GONNA GO.
AS YOU LIKE, BUDDY-BOY.
MAYBE YOU SHOULD GET SOME SHUT-EYE TOO. SEE YOU TOMORROW.
OH ELIZA, LITTLE LIZA JANE!
AGAIN?!
SHIT! HE'S LOCKED ALL THE DOORS!

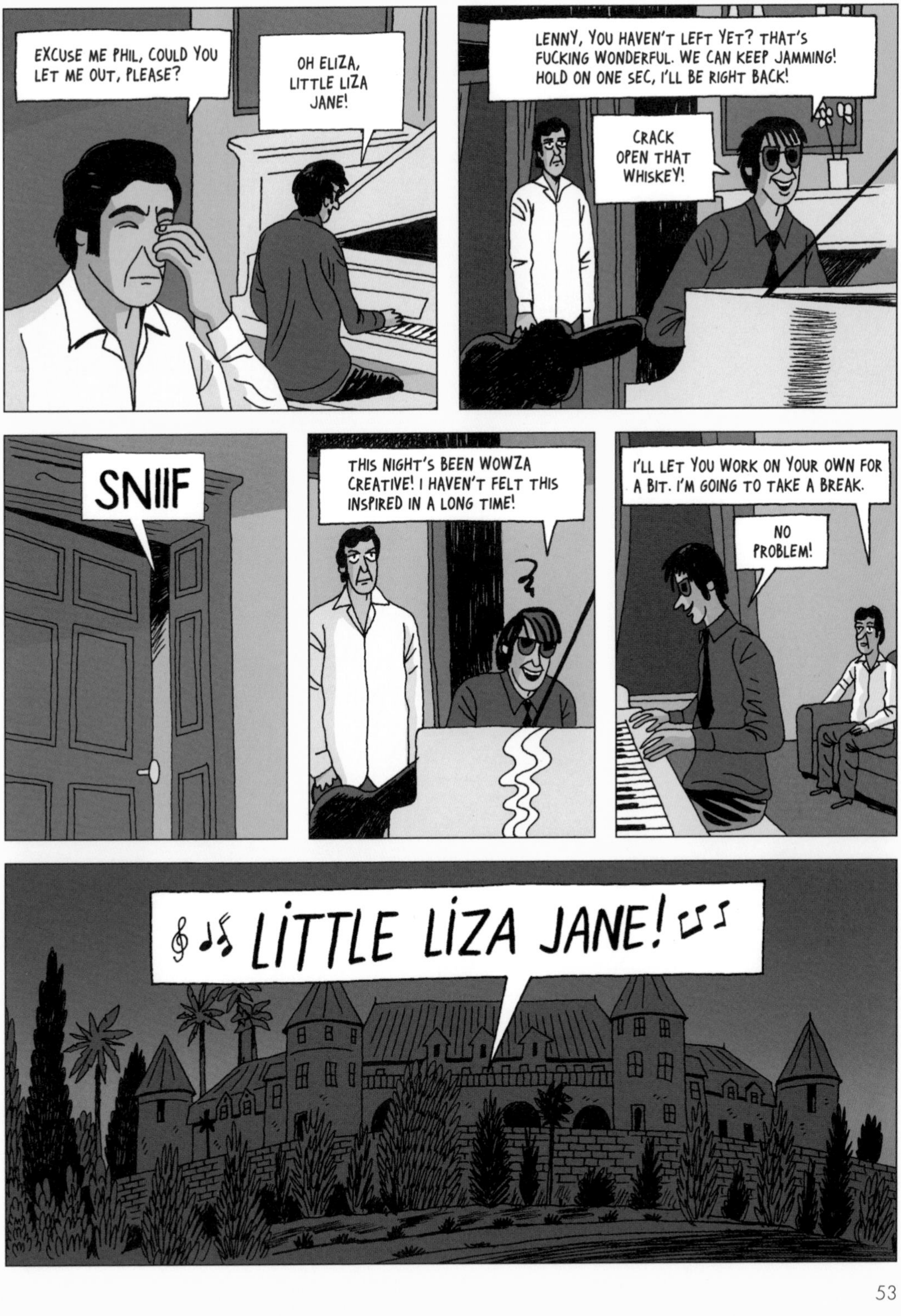
EXCUSE ME PHIL, COULD YOU LET ME OUT, PLEASE?
OH ELIZA, LITTLE LIZA JANE!
LENNY, YOU HAVEN'T LEFT YET? THAT'S FUCKING WONDERFUL. WE CAN KEEP JAMMING! HOLD ON ONE SEC, I'LL BE RIGHT BACK!
CRACK OPEN THAT WHISKEY!
SNIIF
THIS NIGHT'S BEEN WOWZA CREATIVE! I HAVEN'T FELT THIS INSPIRED IN A LONG TIME!
I'LL LET YOU WORK ON YOUR OWN FOR A BIT. I'M GOING TO TAKE A BREAK.
NO PROBLEM!
LITTLE LIZA JANE!

OKAY, THAT'S ENOUGH FOR ONE NIGHT. BEDTIME FOR SLEEPYHEADS! SEE YOU BACK HERE...LET'S SAY 5 P.M.?

LENNY! CAN'T WAIT TO DO THIS AGAIN!

FUCK! IT'S ALMOST EIGHT IN THE MORNING, SUZANNE IS GOING TO KILL ME.

HELLO, KIDS...

WHERE WERE YOU? I WAITED UP FOR YOU ALL NIGHT! YOU NEED TO CUT IT OUT, LEONARD. YOU POP MORE PILLS THAN ELVIS!

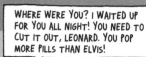

I WAS AT PHIL'S, WORKING.

LIKE HELL YOU WERE! YOU REEK OF BOOZE. YOU WERE OUT IN THE CLUBS AGAIN!

NO, I SWEAR...

YOU KNOW PHIL. HE'S A GENIUS. HE'S GOT UNCON-VENTIONAL METHODS.

I AM DONE WITH THIS, LEONARD. WHEN IT'S NOT A TOUR, IT'S DEPRESSION. OR ANOTHER WOMAN OR BUDDHISM! EVER NOTICE I'M ALWAYS LEFT ALONE!

THE ONLY THING WE EVER DO TOGETHER IS GO VISIT YOUR MOTHER, AND SHE CALLS ME MARIANNE! ISN'T THAT LOVELY?

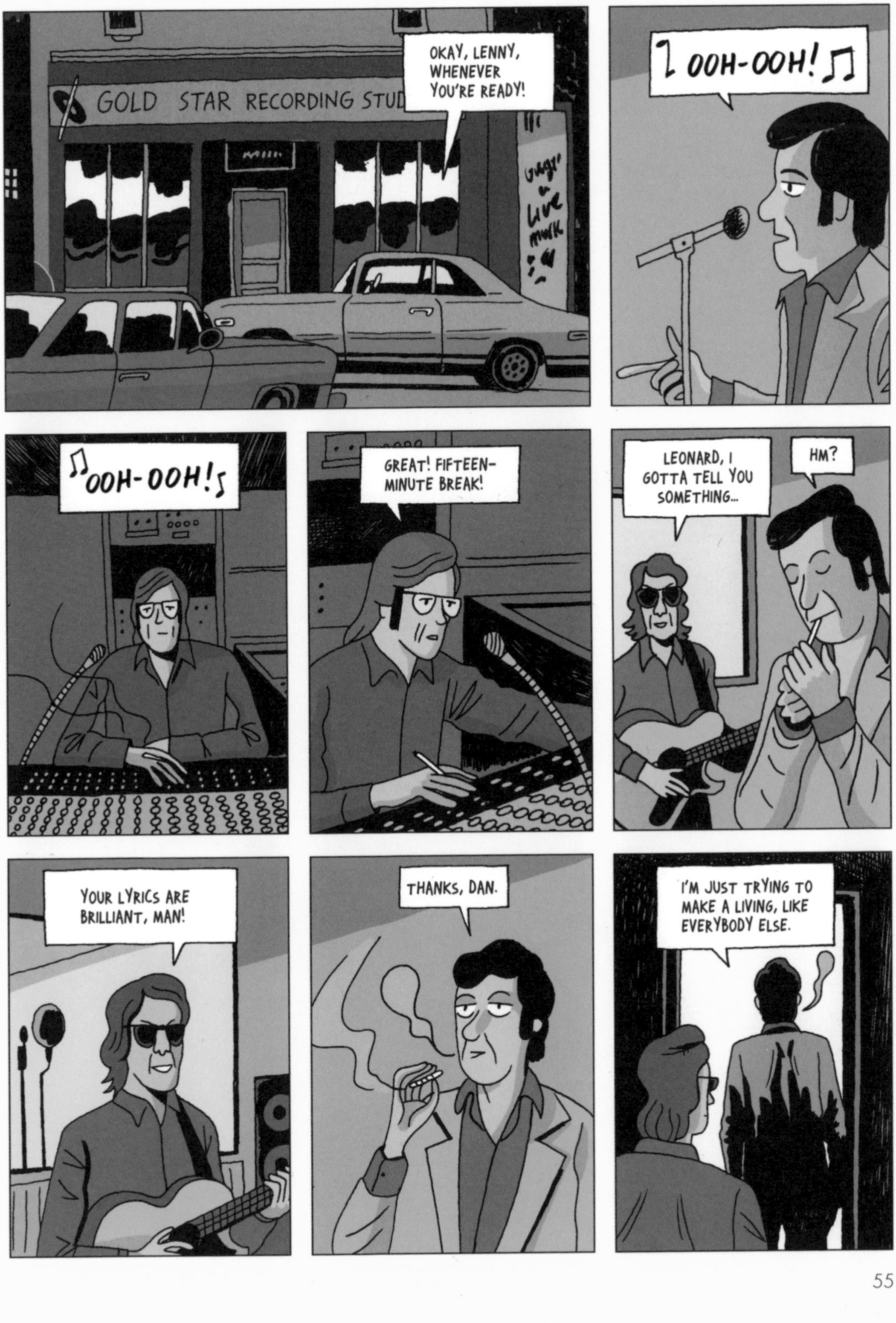
GOLD STAR RECORDING STUD
OKAY, LENNY, WHENEVER YOU'RE READY!
OOH-OOH!
OOH-OOH!
GREAT! FIFTEEN-MINUTE BREAK!
LEONARD, I GOTTA TELL YOU SOMETHING...
HM?
YOUR LYRICS ARE BRILLIANT, MAN!
THANKS, DAN.
I'M JUST TRYING TO MAKE A LIVING, LIKE EVERYBODY ELSE.

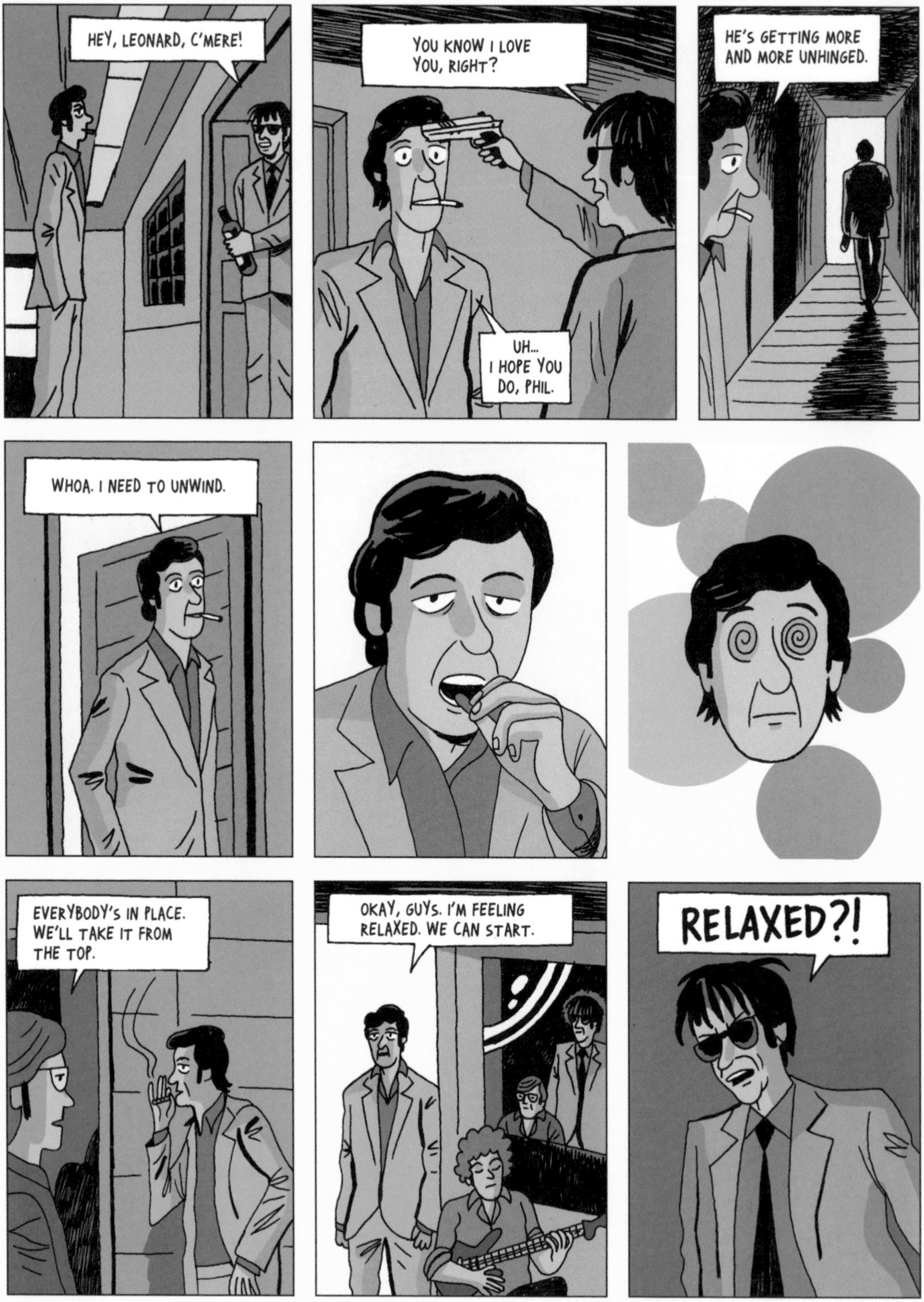
HEY, LEONARD, C'MERE!
YOU KNOW I LOVE YOU, RIGHT?
UH... I HOPE YOU DO, PHIL.
HE'S GETTING MORE AND MORE UNHINGED.
WHOA. I NEED TO UNWIND.
EVERYBODY'S IN PLACE. WE'LL TAKE IT FROM THE TOP.
OKAY, GUYS. I'M FEELING RELAXED. WE CAN START.
RELAXED?!

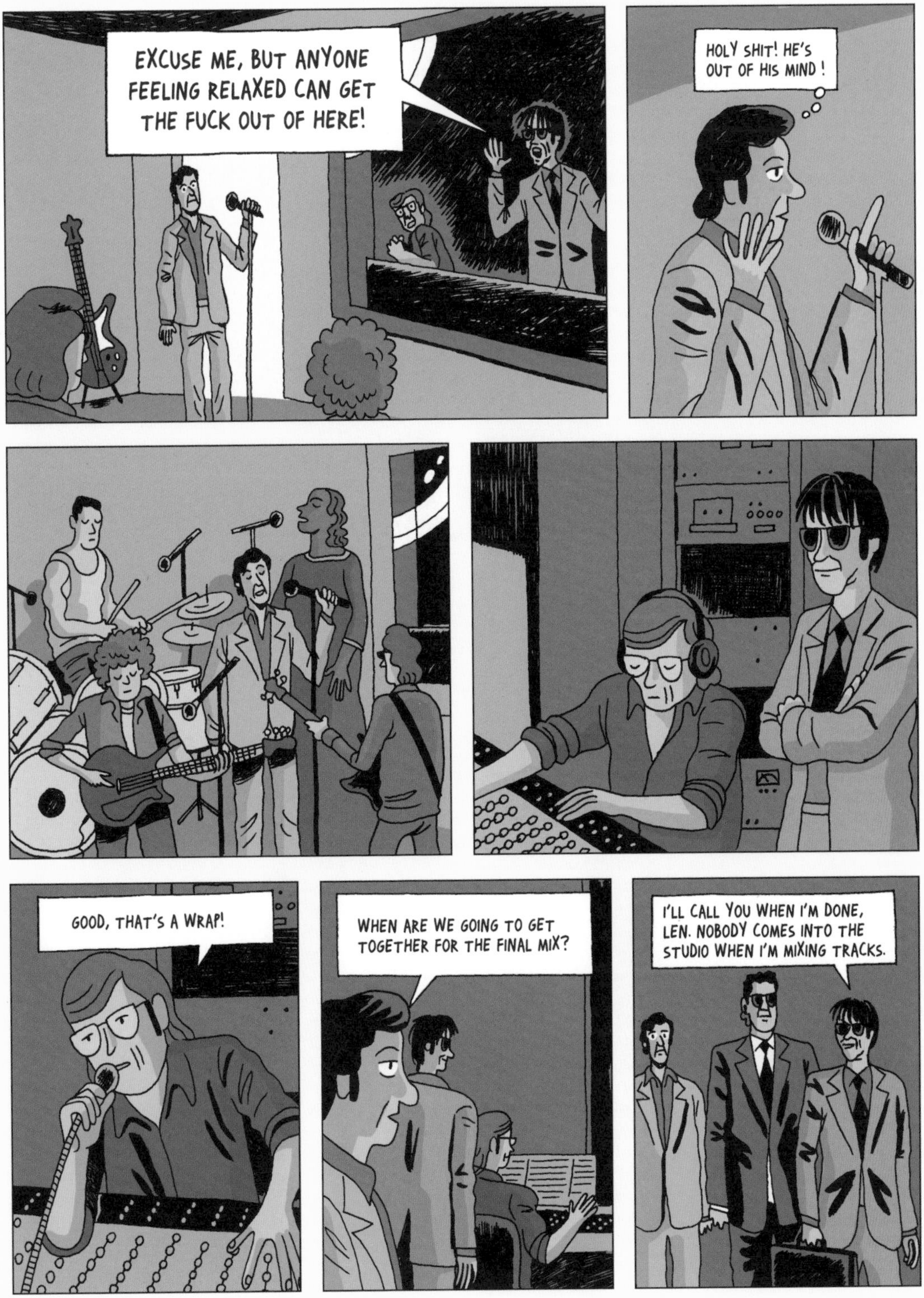
EXCUSE ME, BUT ANYONE FEELING RELAXED CAN GET THE FUCK OUT OF HERE!
HOLY SHIT! HE'S OUT OF HIS MIND!
GOOD, THAT'S A WRAP!
WHEN ARE WE GOING TO GET TOGETHER FOR THE FINAL MIX?
I'LL CALL YOU WHEN I'M DONE, LEN. NOBODY COMES INTO THE STUDIO WHEN I'M MIXING TRACKS.

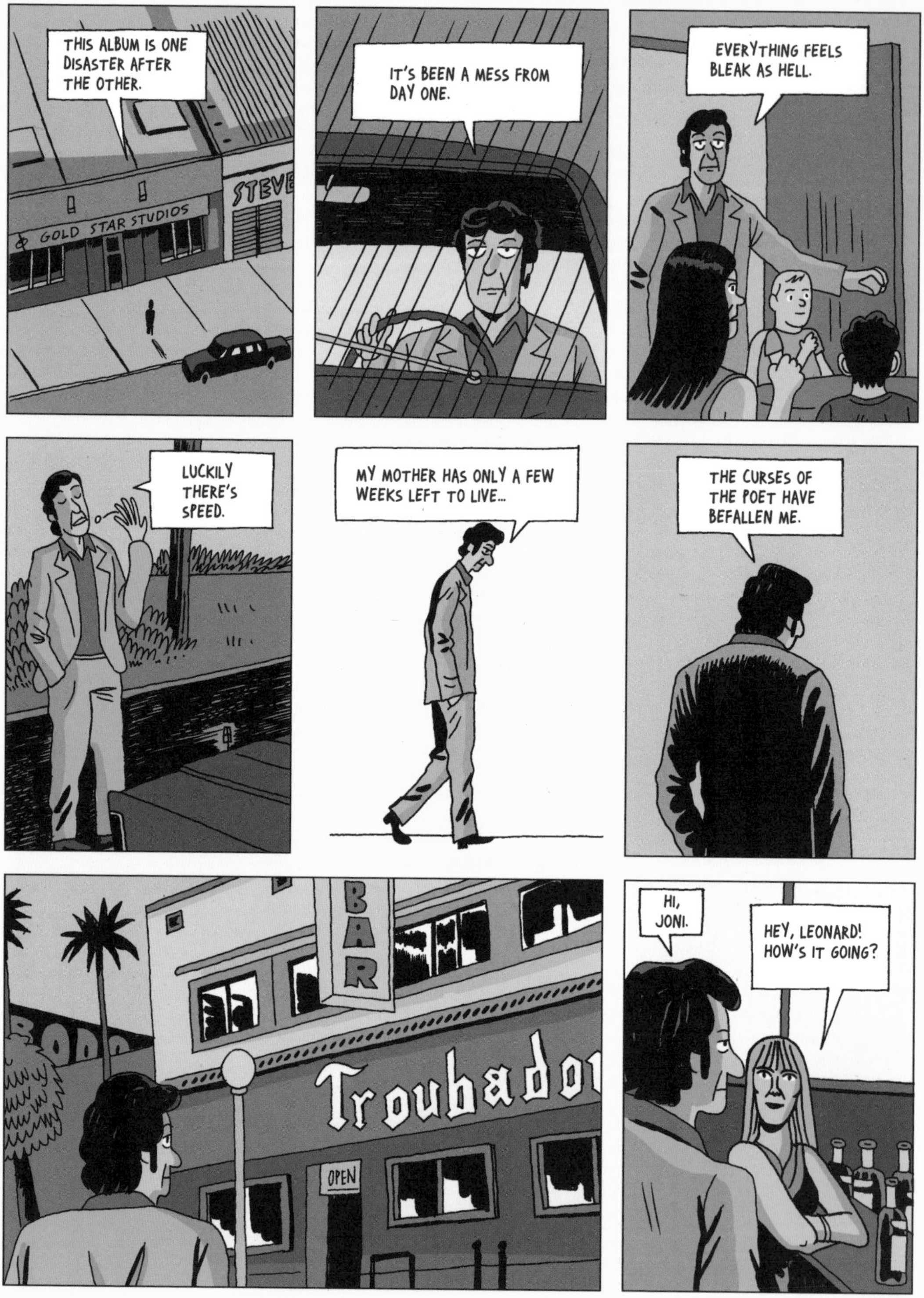
THIS ALBUM IS ONE DISASTER AFTER THE OTHER.
GOLD STAR STUDIOS
STEVE
IT'S BEEN A MESS FROM DAY ONE.
EVERYTHING FEELS BLEAK AS HELL.
LUCKILY THERE'S SPEED.
MY MOTHER HAS ONLY A FEW WEEKS LEFT TO LIVE...
THE CURSES OF THE POET HAVE BEFALLEN ME.
BAR
Troubado
OPEN
HI, JONI.
HEY, LEONARD! HOW'S IT GOING?

OOF...WHAT CAN I SAY THAT YOU HAVEN'T HEARD BEFORE?

MY MARRIAGE IS BROKEN... I'M BROKEN...

AND THERE YOU SIT WITH YOUR BEAUTIFUL QUESTIONS.

WITH ALL MY BETRAYALS, I FEEL LIKE A BIG PHONY.

I SWORE TO MYSELF THIS IS NOT THE MAN I WOULD BE.

EVERY LOVE STORY IS A WILD RIDE. MAYBE WE GET ON IT SO WE CAN WRITE THE MUSIC.

SOME PEOPLE WRITE GOOD SONGS FROM A PLACE OF TOTAL SERENITY.

LIKE WHO?

YEAH, YOU'RE RIGHT, NOBODY DOES.

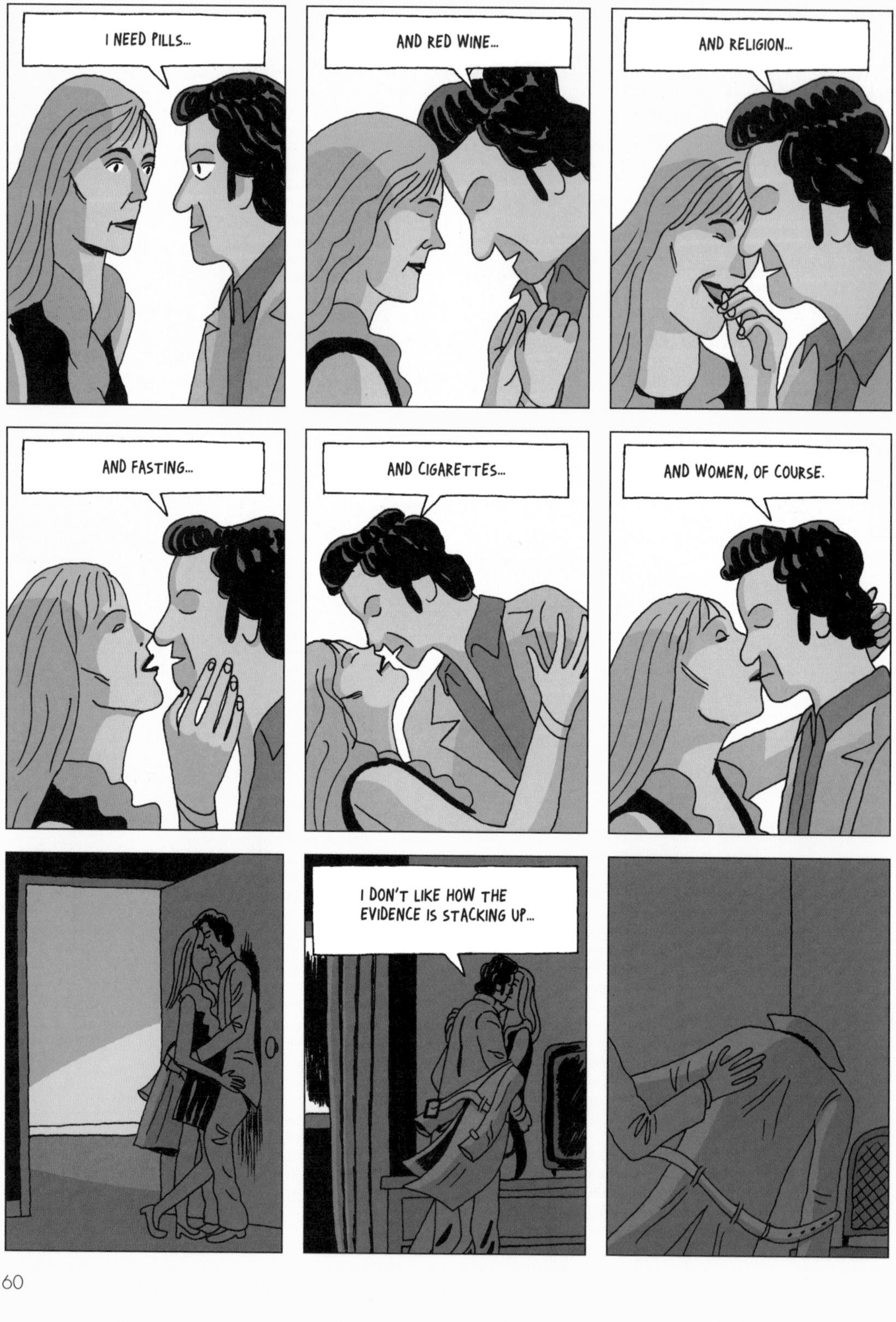
I NEED PILLS...
AND RED WINE...
AND RELIGION...
AND FASTING...
AND CIGARETTES...
AND WOMEN, OF COURSE.
I DON'T LIKE HOW THE EVIDENCE IS STACKING UP...

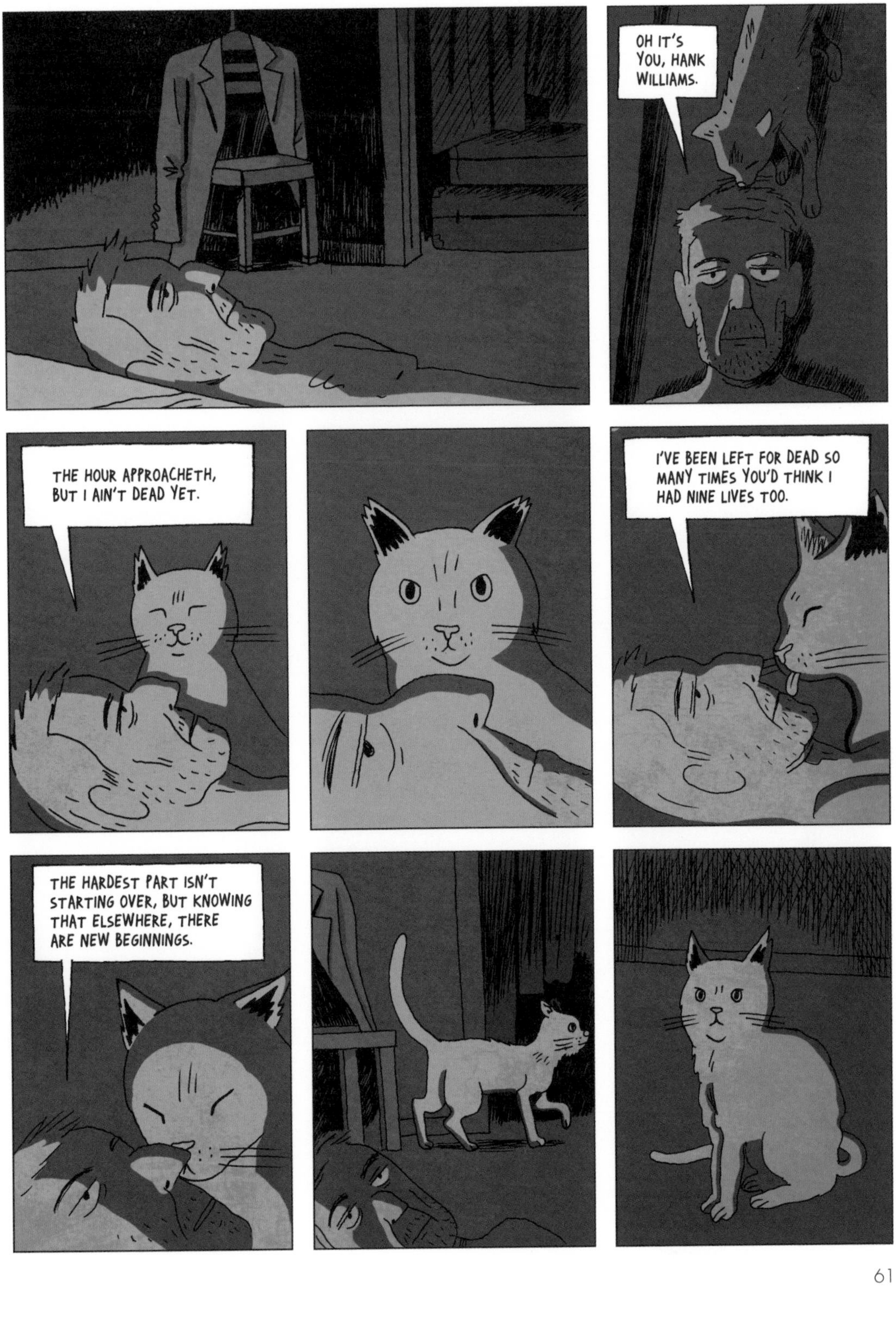
OH IT'S YOU, HANK WILLIAMS.
THE HOUR APPROACHETH, BUT I AIN'T DEAD YET.
I'VE BEEN LEFT FOR DEAD SO MANY TIMES YOU'D THINK I HAD NINE LIVES TOO.
THE HARDEST PART ISN'T STARTING OVER, BUT KNOWING THAT ELSEWHERE, THERE ARE NEW BEGINNINGS.

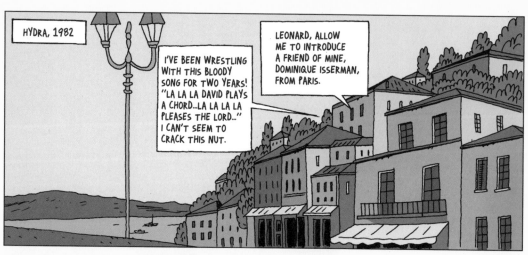

HYDRA, 1982

I'VE BEEN WRESTLING WITH THIS BLOODY SONG FOR TWO YEARS! "LA LA LA DAVID PLAYS A CHORD...LA LA LA LA PLEASES THE LORD..." I CAN'T SEEM TO CRACK THIS NUT.

LEONARD, ALLOW ME TO INTRODUCE A FRIEND OF MINE, DOMINIQUE ISSERMAN, FROM PARIS.

SORRY BUT MY FRENCH ISN'T GREAT. I CAN MANAGE, BUT NOT ENOUGH TO SPEAK OF MATTERS OF THE HEART.

DOMINIQUE IS AN OLD FRIEND OF MY WIFE, CAROLE.

ISSERMAN. THAT'S JEWISH ISN'T IT?

YES, MY FATHER IS JEWISH BUT NOT MY MOTHER.

WELL THAT MAKES YOU HALF NOT-JEWISH!

HA, EXACTLY RIGHT.

WHY DON'T YOU GUYS JOIN ME FOR DINNER TONIGHT?

I WILL MAKE MY SPECIAL WHITE BEAN SOUP.

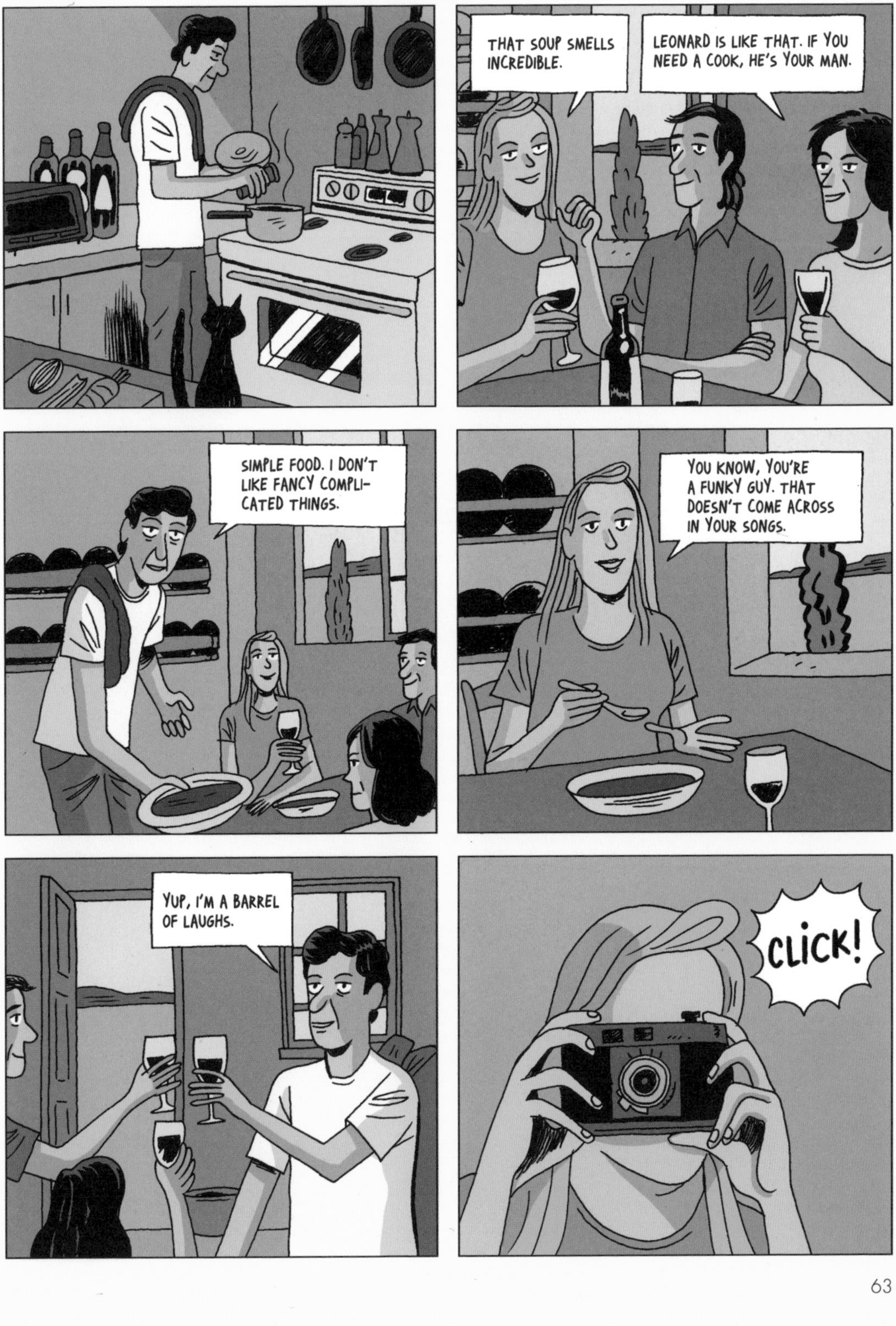
THAT SOUP SMELLS INCREDIBLE.
LEONARD IS LIKE THAT. IF YOU NEED A COOK, HE'S YOUR MAN.
SIMPLE FOOD. I DON'T LIKE FANCY COMPLI-CATED THINGS.
YOU KNOW, YOU'RE A FUNKY GUY. THAT DOESN'T COME ACROSS IN YOUR SONGS.
YUP, I'M A BARREL OF LAUGHS.
CLICK!

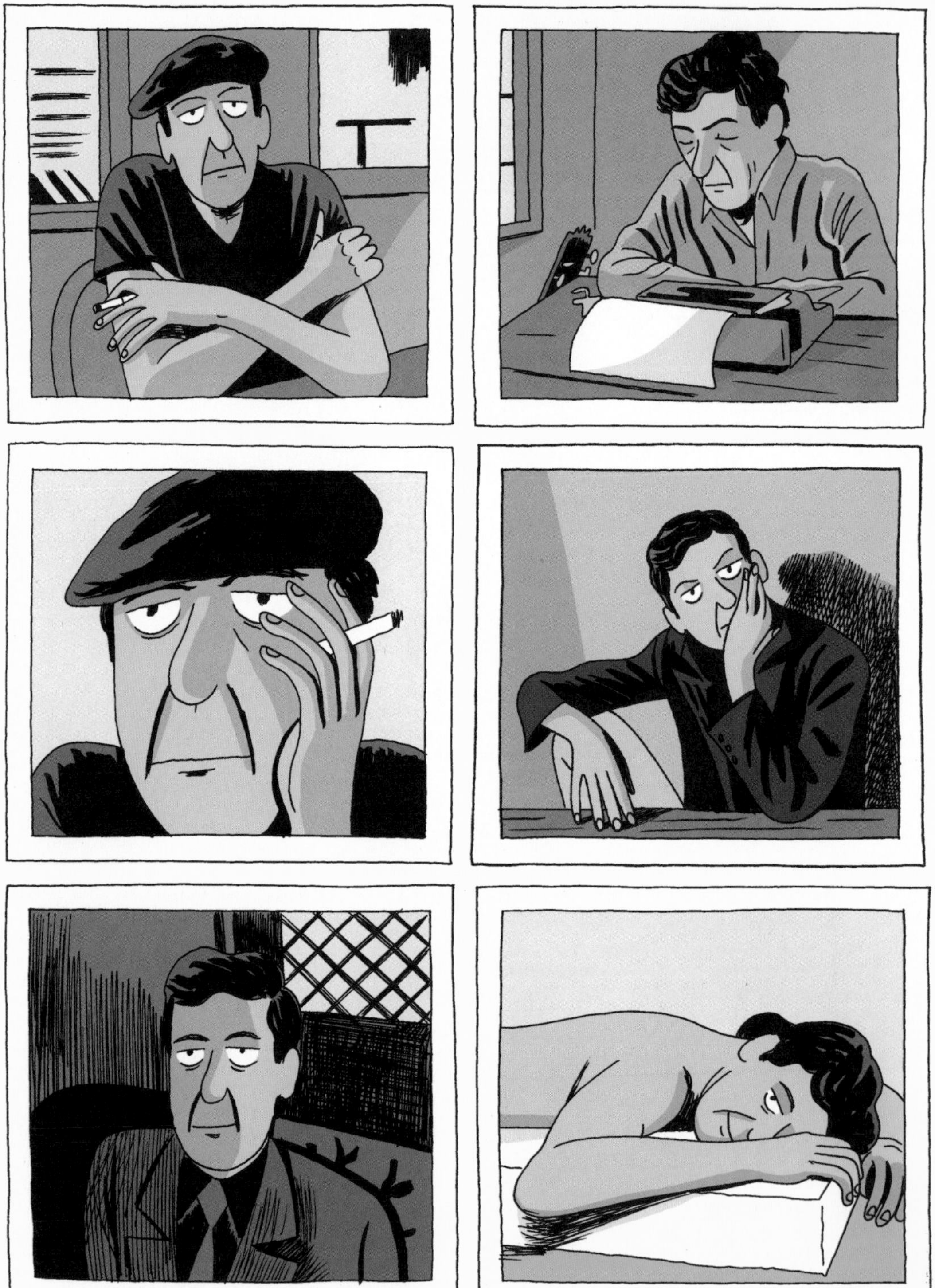

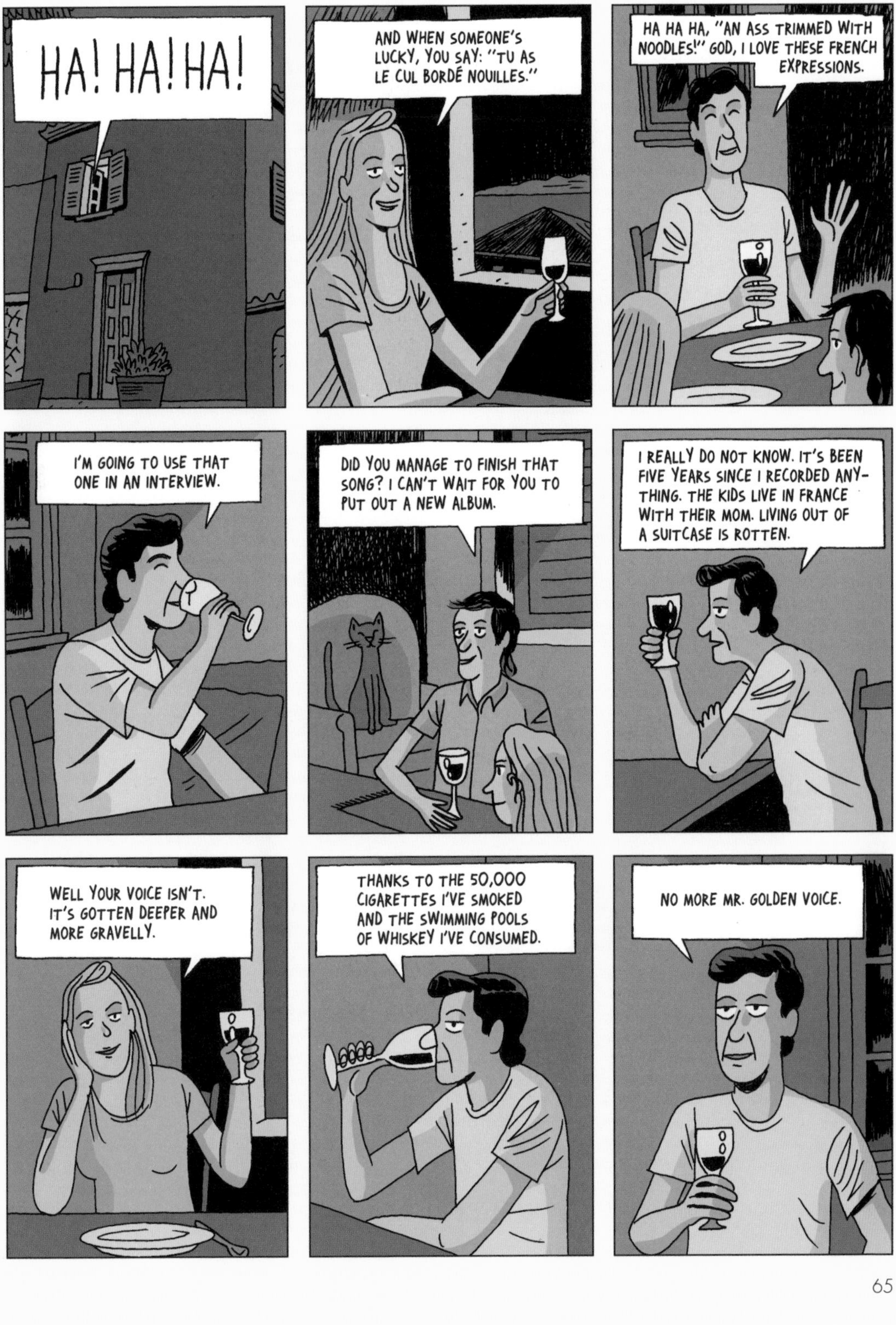
HA! HA! HA!
AND WHEN SOMEONE'S LUCKY, YOU SAY: "TU AS LE CUL BORDÉ NOUILLES."
HA HA HA, "AN ASS TRIMMED WITH NOODLES!" GOD, I LOVE THESE FRENCH EXPRESSIONS.
I'M GOING TO USE THAT ONE IN AN INTERVIEW.
DID YOU MANAGE TO FINISH THAT SONG? I CAN'T WAIT FOR YOU TO PUT OUT A NEW ALBUM.
I REALLY DO NOT KNOW. IT'S BEEN FIVE YEARS SINCE I RECORDED ANY-THING. THE KIDS LIVE IN FRANCE WITH THEIR MOM. LIVING OUT OF A SUITCASE IS ROTTEN.
WELL YOUR VOICE ISN'T. IT'S GOTTEN DEEPER AND MORE GRAVELLY.
THANKS TO THE 50,000 CIGARETTES I'VE SMOKED AND THE SWIMMING POOLS OF WHISKEY I'VE CONSUMED.
NO MORE MR. GOLDEN VOICE.

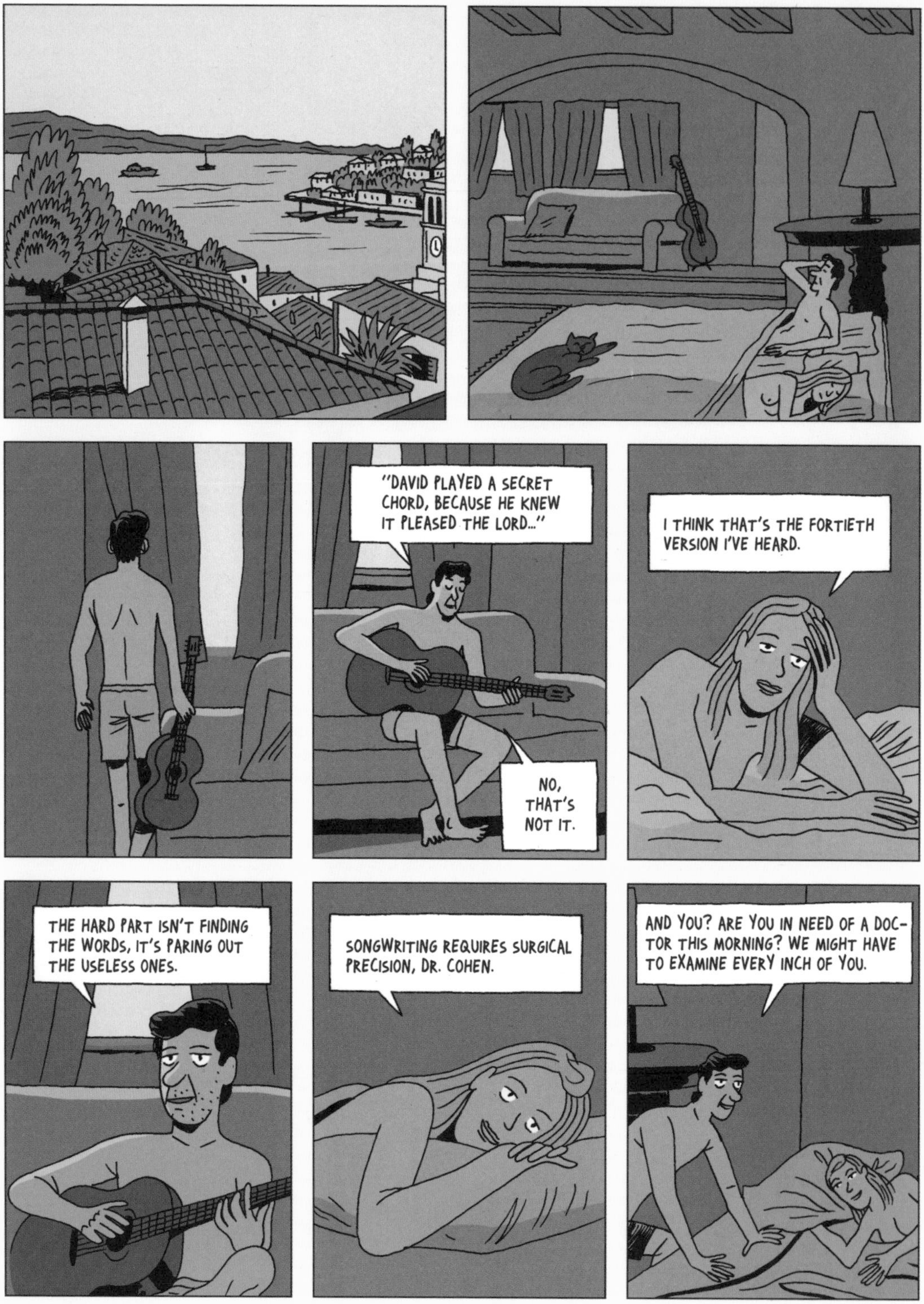
"DAVID PLAYED A SECRET CHORD, BECAUSE HE KNEW IT PLEASED THE LORD..."
NO, THAT'S NOT IT.
I THINK THAT'S THE FORTIETH VERSION I'VE HEARD.
THE HARD PART ISN'T FINDING THE WORDS, IT'S PARING OUT THE USELESS ONES.
SONGWRITING REQUIRES SURGICAL PRECISION, DR. COHEN.
AND YOU? ARE YOU IN NEED OF A DOCTOR THIS MORNING? WE MIGHT HAVE TO EXAMINE EVERY INCH OF YOU.

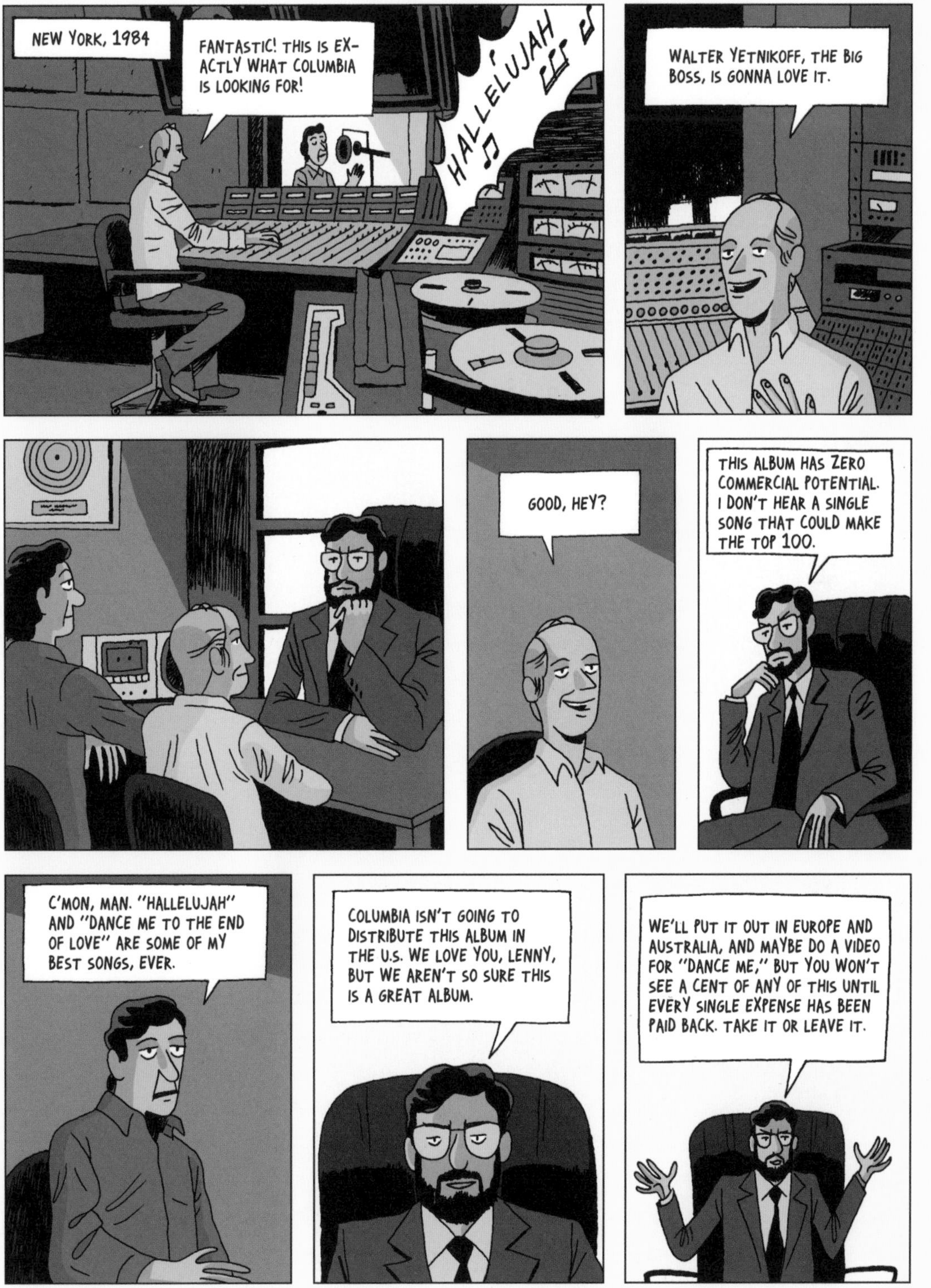
NEW YORK, 1984
FANTASTIC! THIS IS EXACTLY WHAT COLUMBIA IS LOOKING FOR!
HALLELUJAH
WALTER YETNIKOFF, THE BIG BOSS, IS GONNA LOVE IT.
GOOD, HEY?
THIS ALBUM HAS ZERO COMMERCIAL POTENTIAL. I DON'T HEAR A SINGLE SONG THAT COULD MAKE THE TOP 100.
C'MON, MAN. "HALLELUJAH" AND "DANCE ME TO THE END OF LOVE" ARE SOME OF MY BEST SONGS, EVER.
COLUMBIA ISN'T GOING TO DISTRIBUTE THIS ALBUM IN THE U.S. WE LOVE YOU, LENNY, BUT WE AREN'T SO SURE THIS IS A GREAT ALBUM.
WE'LL PUT IT OUT IN EUROPE AND AUSTRALIA, AND MAYBE DO A VIDEO FOR "DANCE ME," BUT YOU WON'T SEE A CENT OF ANY OF THIS UNTIL EVERY SINGLE EXPENSE HAS BEEN PAID BACK. TAKE IT OR LEAVE IT.

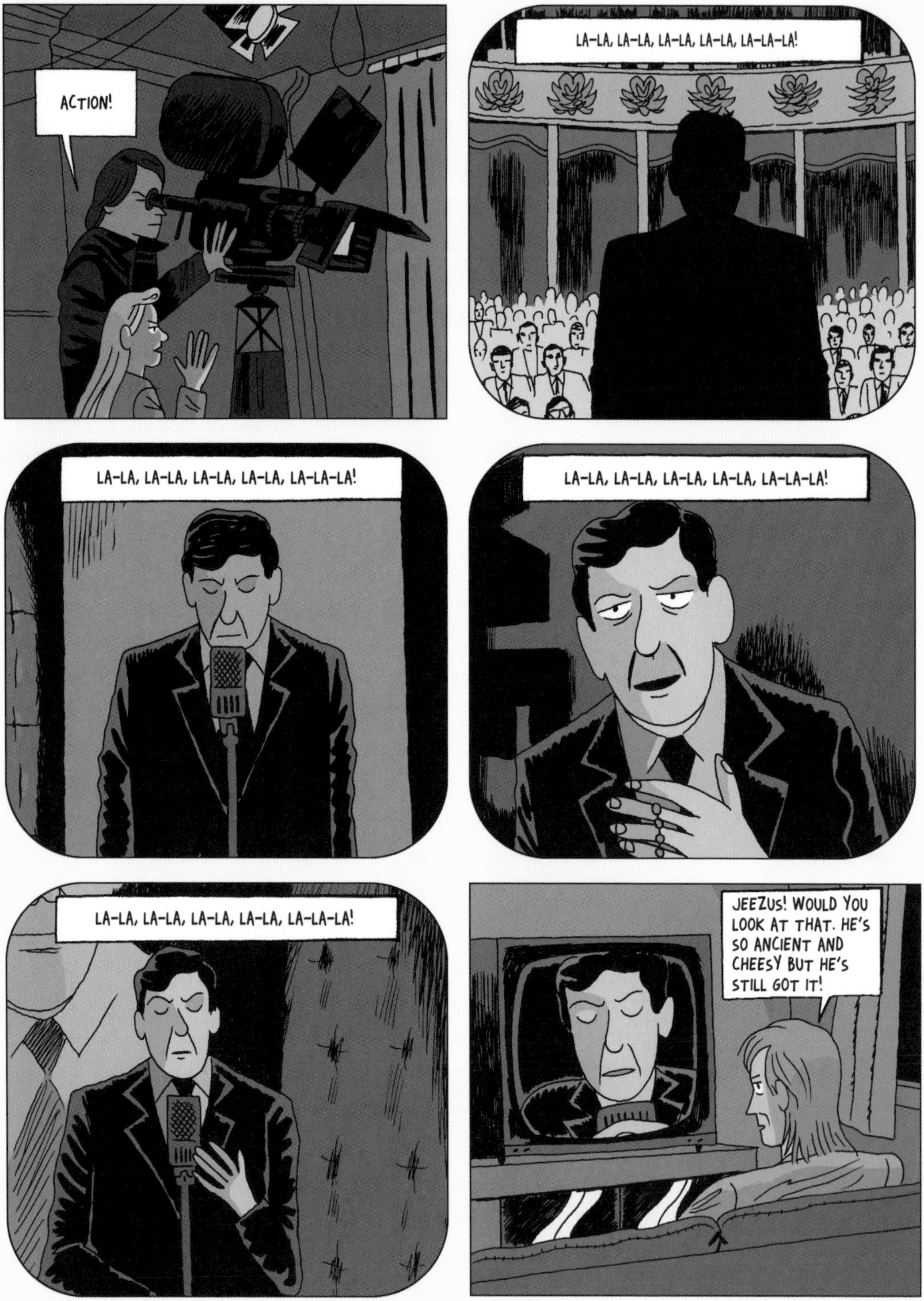
ACTION!
LA-LA, LA-LA, LA-LA, LA-LA, LA-LA-LA!
LA-LA, LA-LA, LA-LA, LA-LA, LA-LA-LA!
LA-LA, LA-LA, LA-LA, LA-LA, LA-LA-LA!
LA-LA, LA-LA, LA-LA, LA-LA, LA-LA-LA!
JEEZUS! WOULD YOU LOOK AT THAT. HE'S SO ANCIENT AND CHEESY BUT HE'S STILL GOT IT!

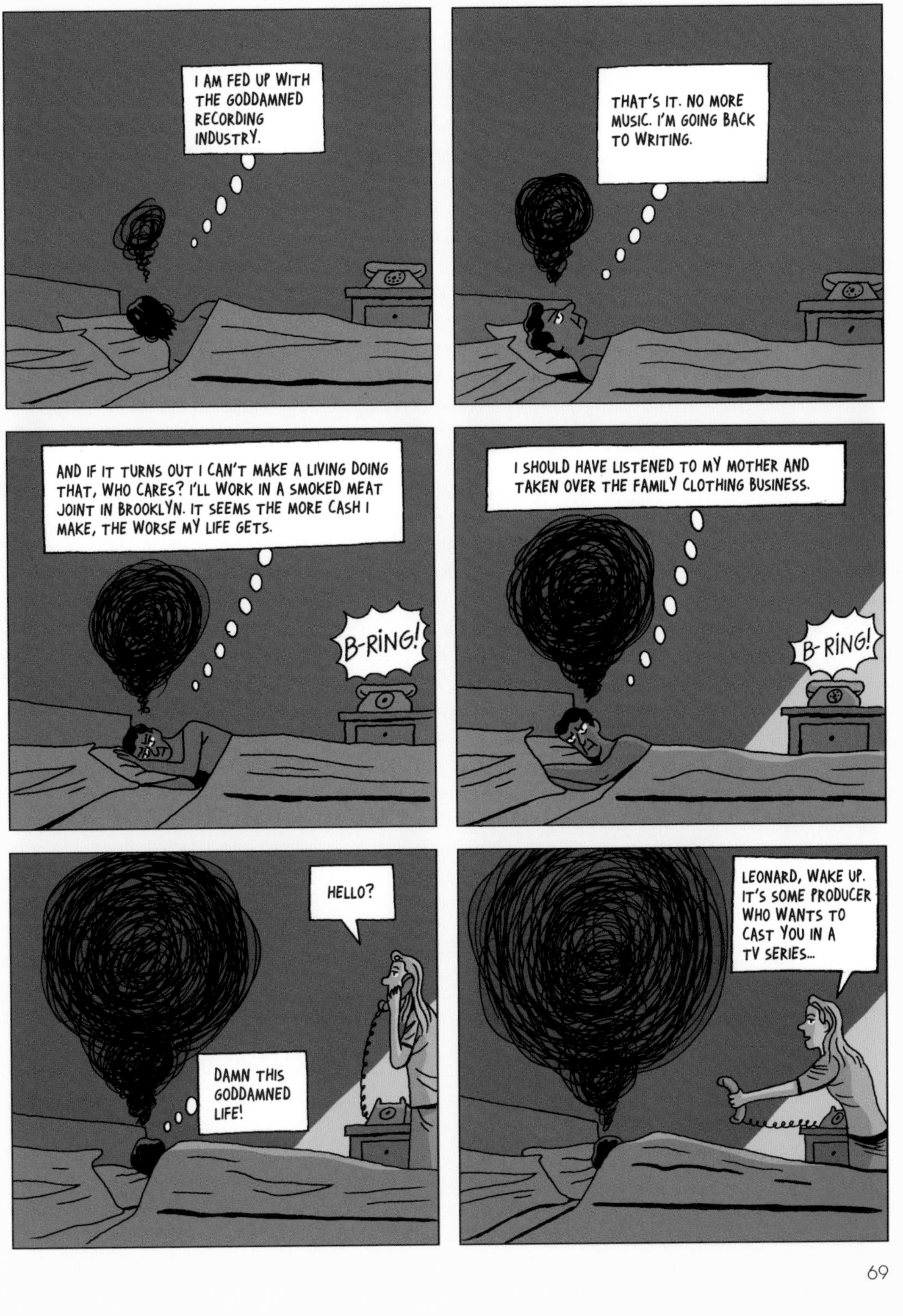

I AM FED UP WITH THE GODDAMNED RECORDING INDUSTRY.
THAT'S IT. NO MORE MUSIC. I'M GOING BACK TO WRITING.
AND IF IT TURNS OUT I CAN'T MAKE A LIVING DOING THAT, WHO CARES? I'LL WORK IN A SMOKED MEAT JOINT IN BROOKLYN. IT SEEMS THE MORE CASH I MAKE, THE WORSE MY LIFE GETS.
B-RING!
I SHOULD HAVE LISTENED TO MY MOTHER AND TAKEN OVER THE FAMILY CLOTHING BUSINESS.
B-RING!
HELLO?
DAMN THIS GODDAMNED LIFE!
LEONARD, WAKE UP. IT'S SOME PRODUCER WHO WANTS TO CAST YOU IN A TV SERIES...

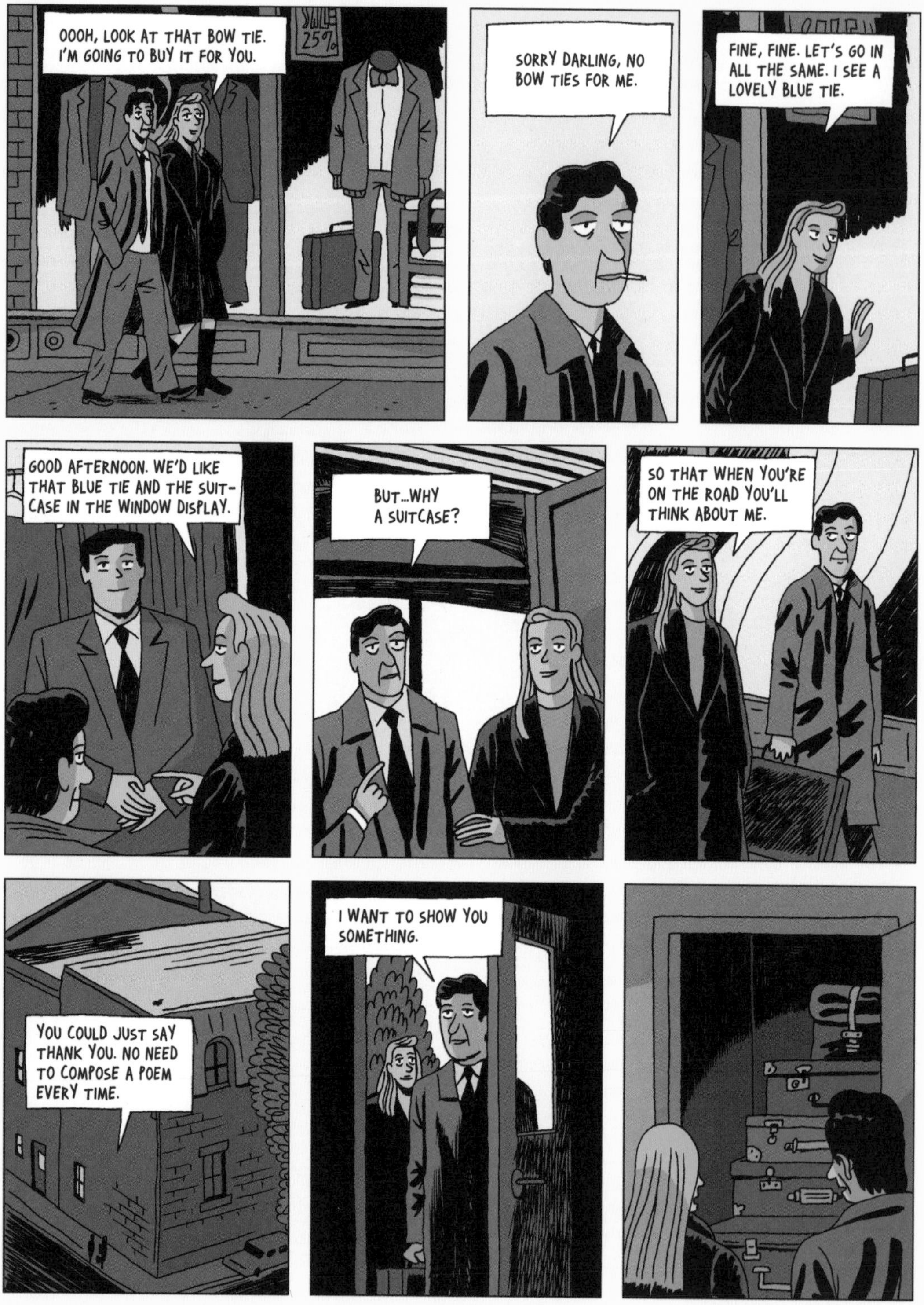
OOOH, LOOK AT THAT BOW TIE. I'M GOING TO BUY IT FOR YOU.
SALE 25%
SORRY DARLING, NO BOW TIES FOR ME.
FINE, FINE. LET'S GO IN ALL THE SAME. I SEE A LOVELY BLUE TIE.
GOOD AFTERNOON. WE'D LIKE THAT BLUE TIE AND THE SUIT-CASE IN THE WINDOW DISPLAY.
BUT...WHY A SUITCASE?
SO THAT WHEN YOU'RE ON THE ROAD YOU'LL THINK ABOUT ME.
YOU COULD JUST SAY THANK YOU. NO NEED TO COMPOSE A POEM EVERY TIME.
I WANT TO SHOW YOU SOMETHING.

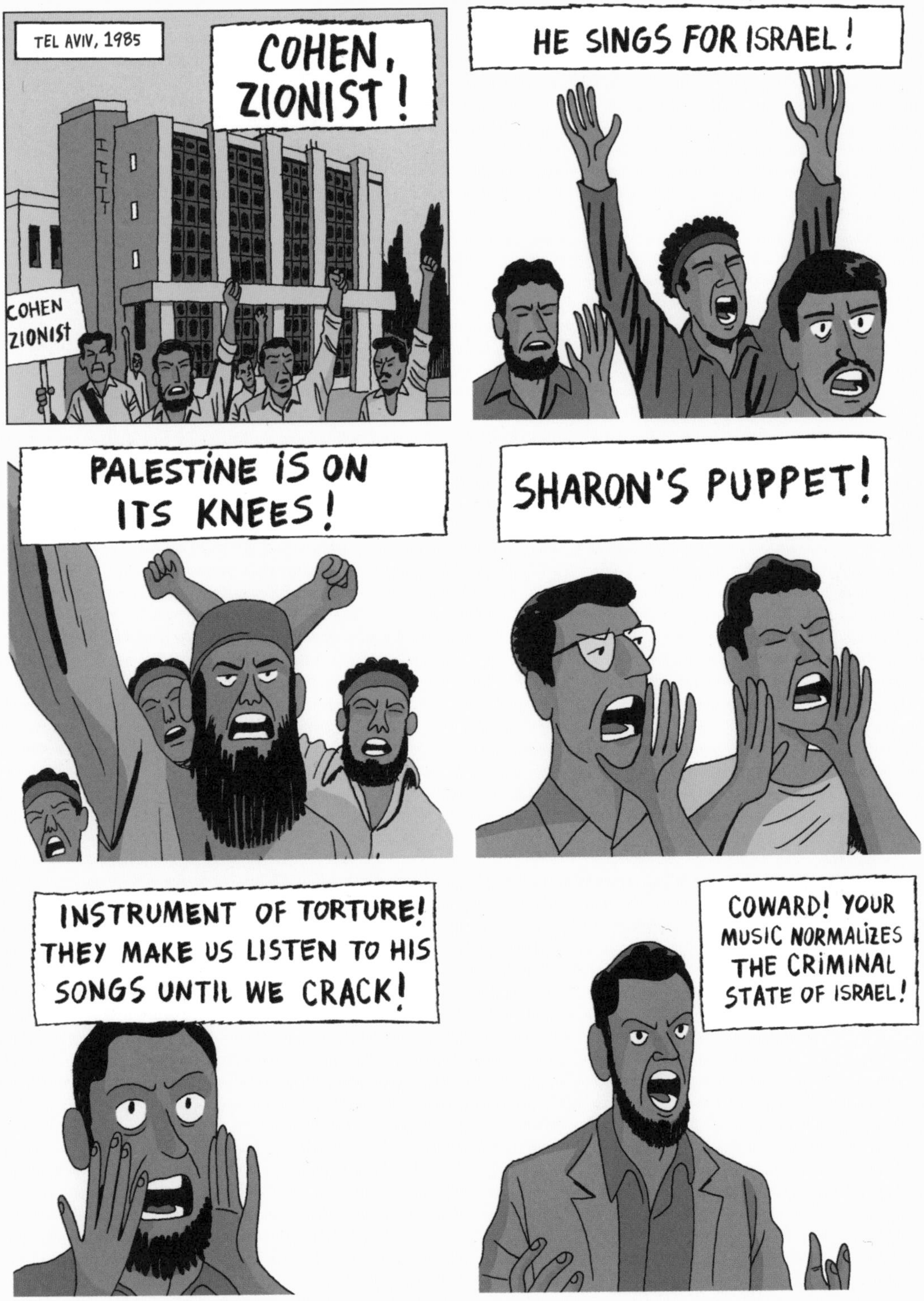
TEL AVIV, 1985
COHEN, ZIONIST!
COHEN ZIONIST
HE SINGS FOR ISRAEL!
PALESTINE IS ON ITS KNEES!
SHARON'S PUPPET!
INSTRUMENT OF TORTURE! THEY MAKE US LISTEN TO HIS SONGS UNTIL WE CRACK!
COWARD! YOUR MUSIC NORMALIZES THE CRIMINAL STATE OF ISRAEL!

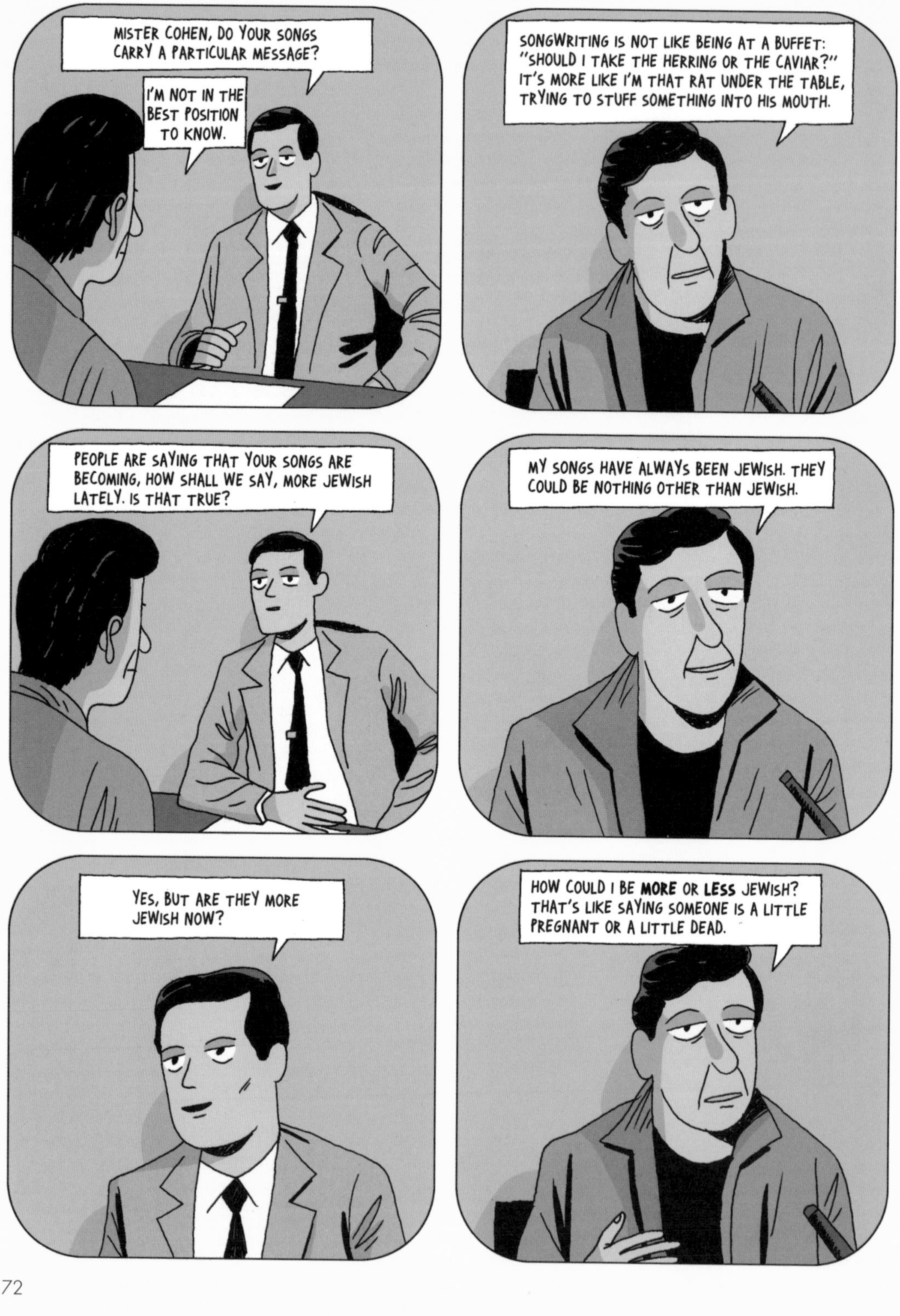
MISTER COHEN, DO YOUR SONGS CARRY A PARTICULAR MESSAGE?
I'M NOT IN THE BEST POSITION TO KNOW.
SONGWRITING IS NOT LIKE BEING AT A BUFFET: "SHOULD I TAKE THE HERRING OR THE CAVIAR?" IT'S MORE LIKE I'M THAT RAT UNDER THE TABLE, TRYING TO STUFF SOMETHING INTO HIS MOUTH.
PEOPLE ARE SAYING THAT YOUR SONGS ARE BECOMING, HOW SHALL WE SAY, MORE JEWISH LATELY. IS THAT TRUE?
MY SONGS HAVE ALWAYS BEEN JEWISH. THEY COULD BE NOTHING OTHER THAN JEWISH.
YES, BUT ARE THEY MORE JEWISH NOW?
HOW COULD I BE **MORE** OR **LESS** JEWISH? THAT'S LIKE SAYING SOMEONE IS A LITTLE PREGNANT OR A LITTLE DEAD.

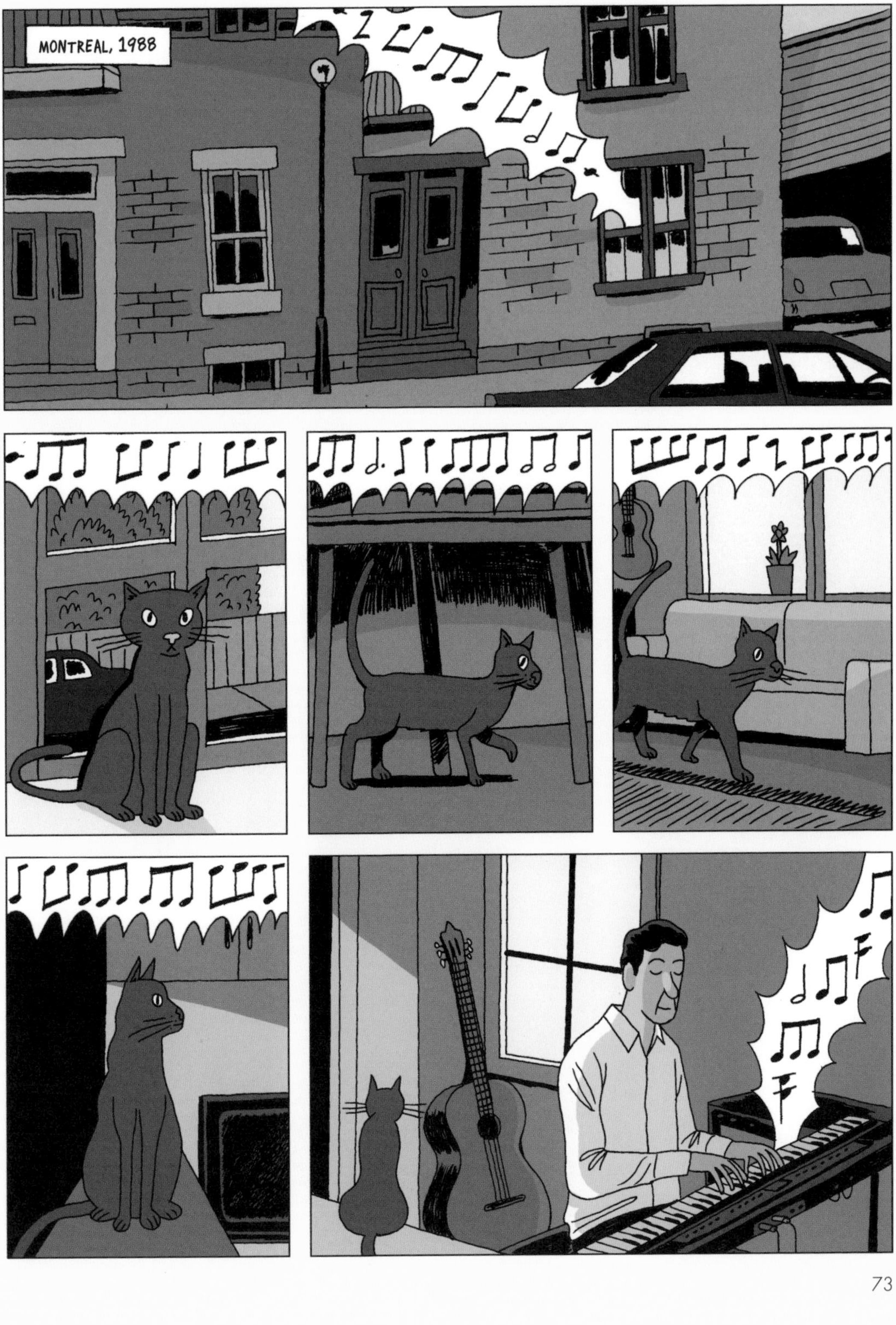
MONTREAL, 1988

HEY DAD, WHAT'S THAT YOU'VE BOUGHT?

IT'S A KIDDIE PIANO. COSTS NINETY-NINE DOLLARS AT EATONS. SOUNDING PRETTY GOOD!

IT'S NOT HARD CORE ROCK, BUT I KINDA LIKE IT. YOU KNOW YOU SOUND LIKE YOU'RE IN DEVO, RIGHT?

FOR A HAS-BEEN LIKE YOUR POPS, THAT IS A BIG COMPLIMENT.

MY LAST TWO ALBUMS WITH COLUMBIA WERE FLOPS. THEY REFUSE TO FUND ANY TOURING. I HAVE OFFICIALLY BECOME OLD-SCHOOL, MY DEAREST LORCA.

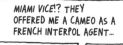

HA! YOU HAVE ALWAYS BEEN OLD-SCHOOL. THE ONLY THING THAT EVER CHANGES IS YOUR SHIRT.

ADAM, I'VE TOLD YOU A HUN-DRED TIMES. TURN DOWN THE VOLUME! WE CAN'T EVEN HEAR OURSELVES THINK.

C'MON. IT'S MIAMI VICE, MY FAVOURITE SHOW.

MIAMI VICE!? THEY OFFERED ME A CAMEO AS A FRENCH INTERPOL AGENT...

74

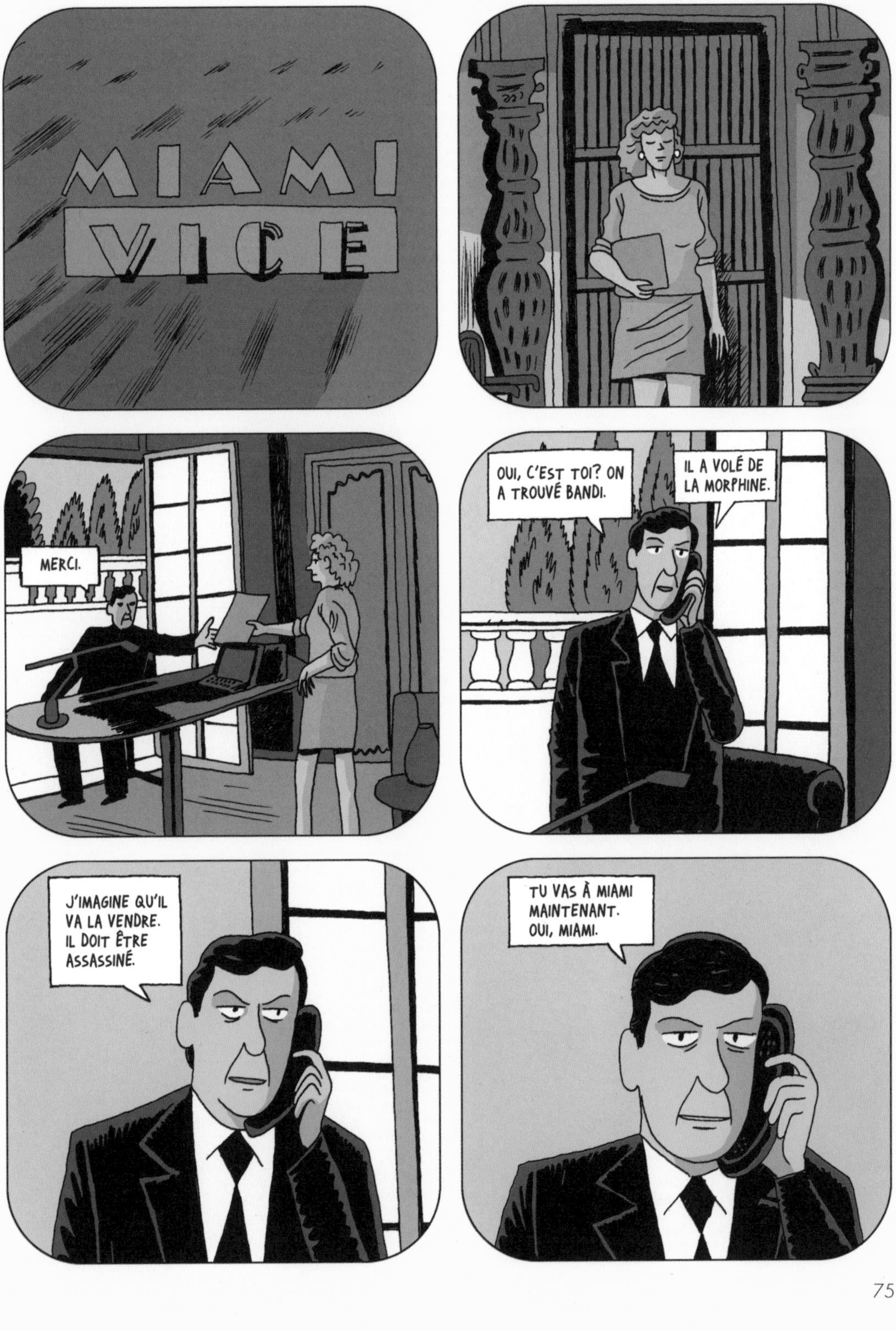
MIAMI
VICE
MERCI.
OUI, C'EST TOI? ON A TROUVÉ BANDI.
IL A VOLÉ DE LA MORPHINE.
J'IMAGINE QU'IL VA LA VENDRE. IL DOIT ÊTRE ASSASSINÉ.
TU VAS À MIAMI MAINTENANT. OUI, MIAMI.

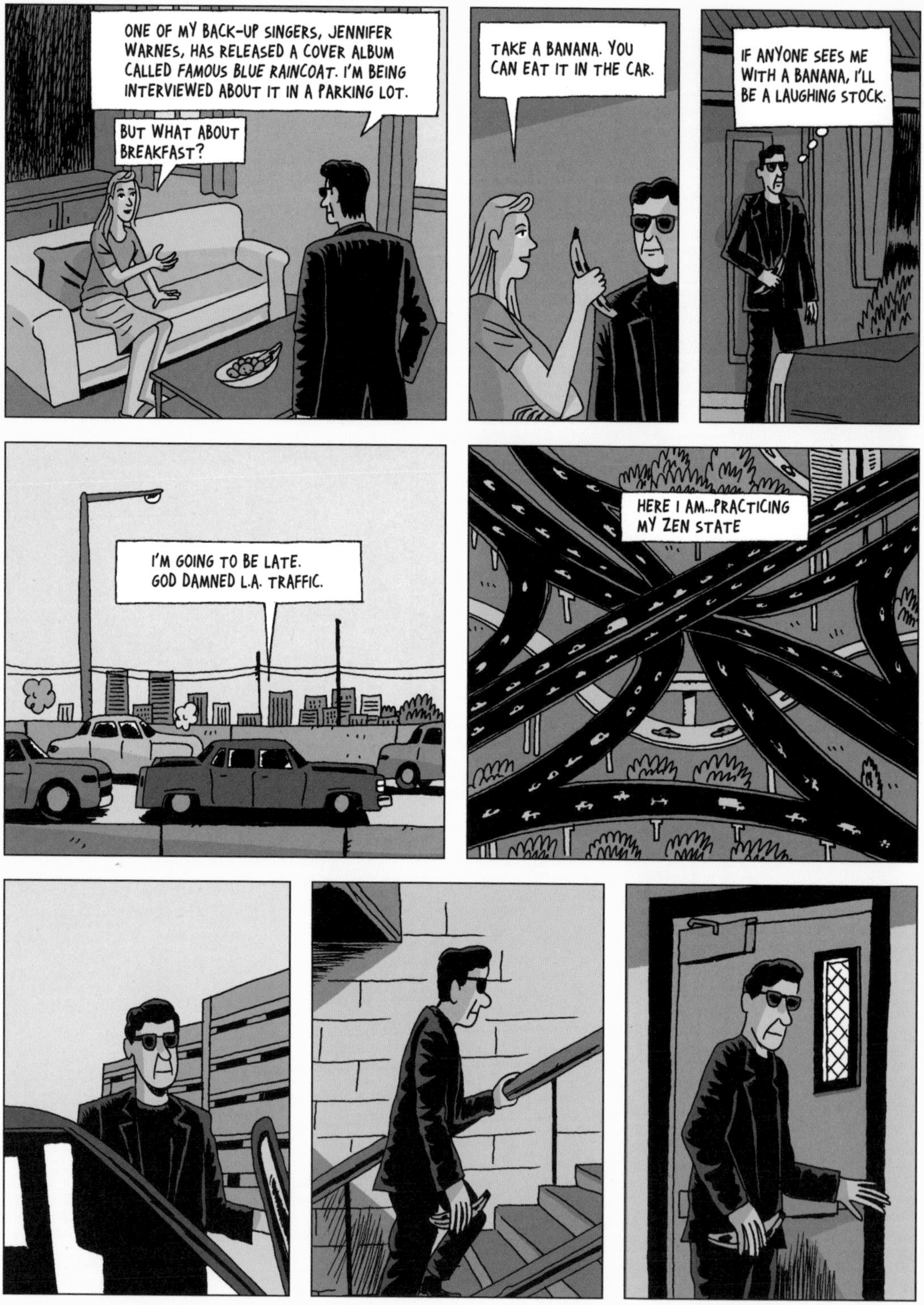
ONE OF MY BACK-UP SINGERS, JENNIFER WARNES, HAS RELEASED A COVER ALBUM CALLED FAMOUS BLUE RAINCOAT. I'M BEING INTERVIEWED ABOUT IT IN A PARKING LOT.
BUT WHAT ABOUT BREAKFAST?
TAKE A BANANA. YOU CAN EAT IT IN THE CAR.
IF ANYONE SEES ME WITH A BANANA, I'LL BE A LAUGHING STOCK.
I'M GOING TO BE LATE. GOD DAMNED L.A. TRAFFIC.
HERE I AM...PRACTICING MY ZEN STATE

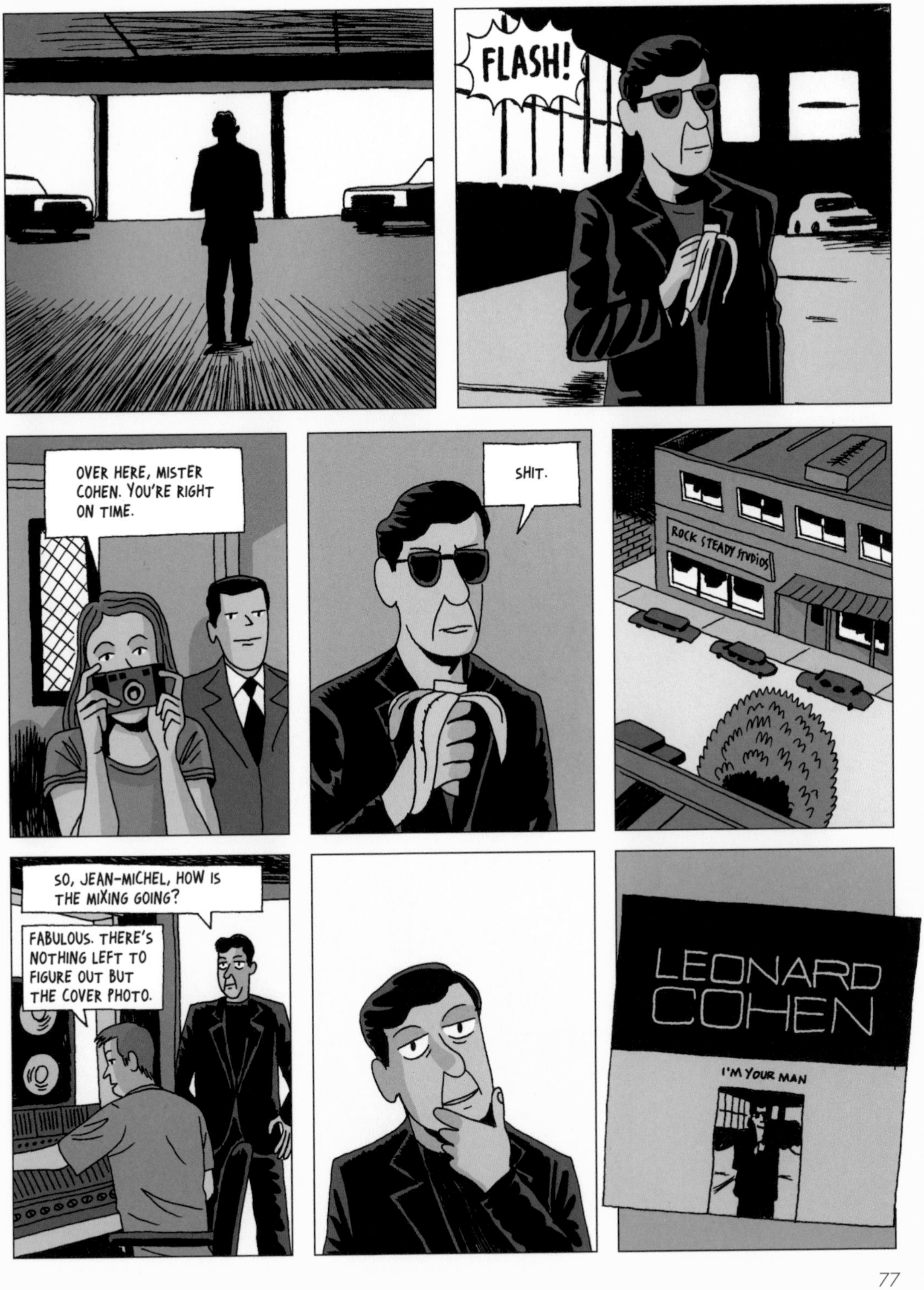
FLASH!
OVER HERE, MISTER COHEN. YOU'RE RIGHT ON TIME.
SHIT.
ROCK STEADY STUDIOS
SO, JEAN-MICHEL, HOW IS THE MIXING GOING?
FABULOUS. THERE'S NOTHING LEFT TO FIGURE OUT BUT THE COVER PHOTO.
LEONARD COHEN
I'M YOUR MAN

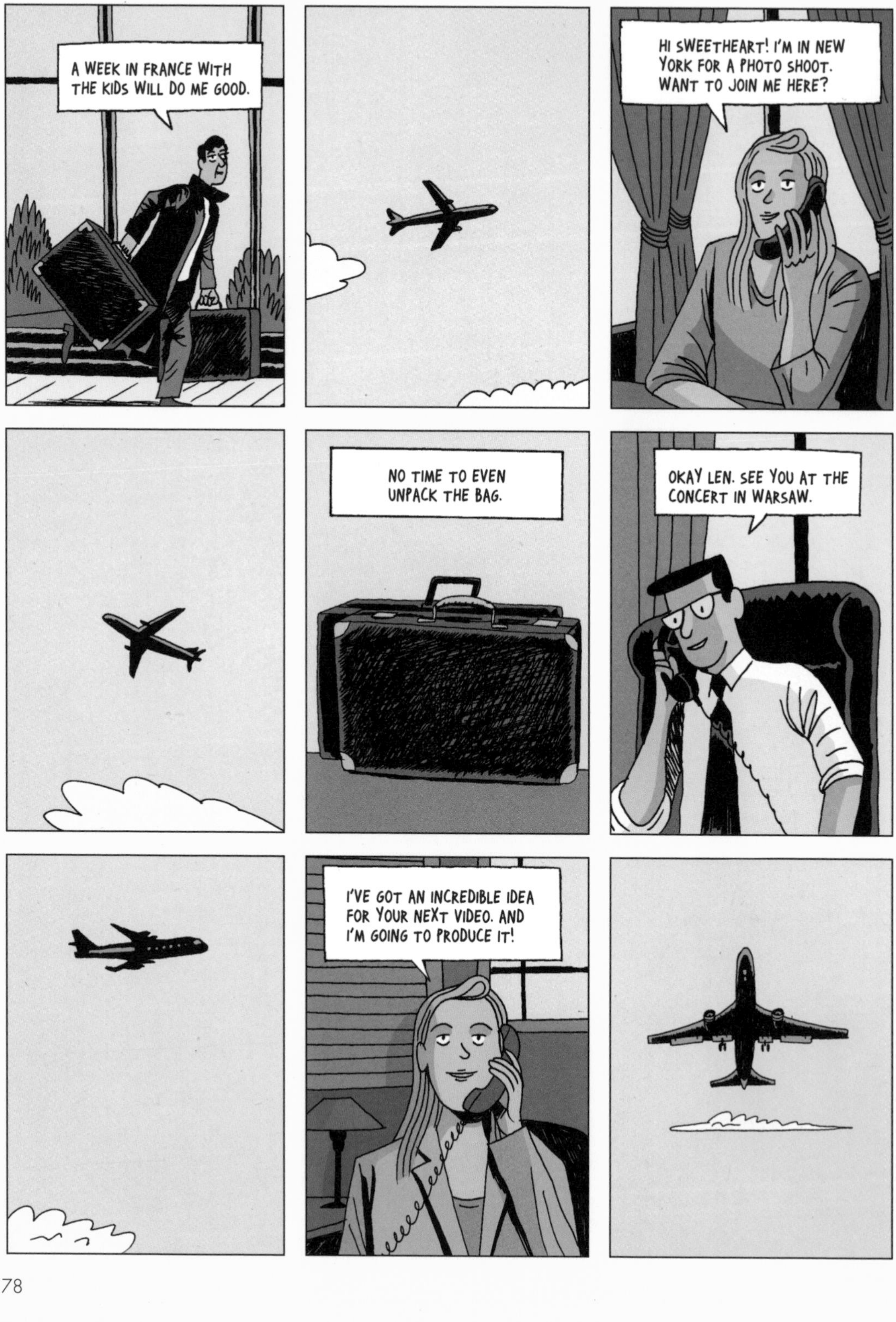
A WEEK IN FRANCE WITH THE KIDS WILL DO ME GOOD.
HI SWEETHEART! I'M IN NEW YORK FOR A PHOTO SHOOT. WANT TO JOIN ME HERE?
NO TIME TO EVEN UNPACK THE BAG.
OKAY LEN. SEE YOU AT THE CONCERT IN WARSAW.
I'VE GOT AN INCREDIBLE IDEA FOR YOUR NEXT VIDEO. AND I'M GOING TO PRODUCE IT!

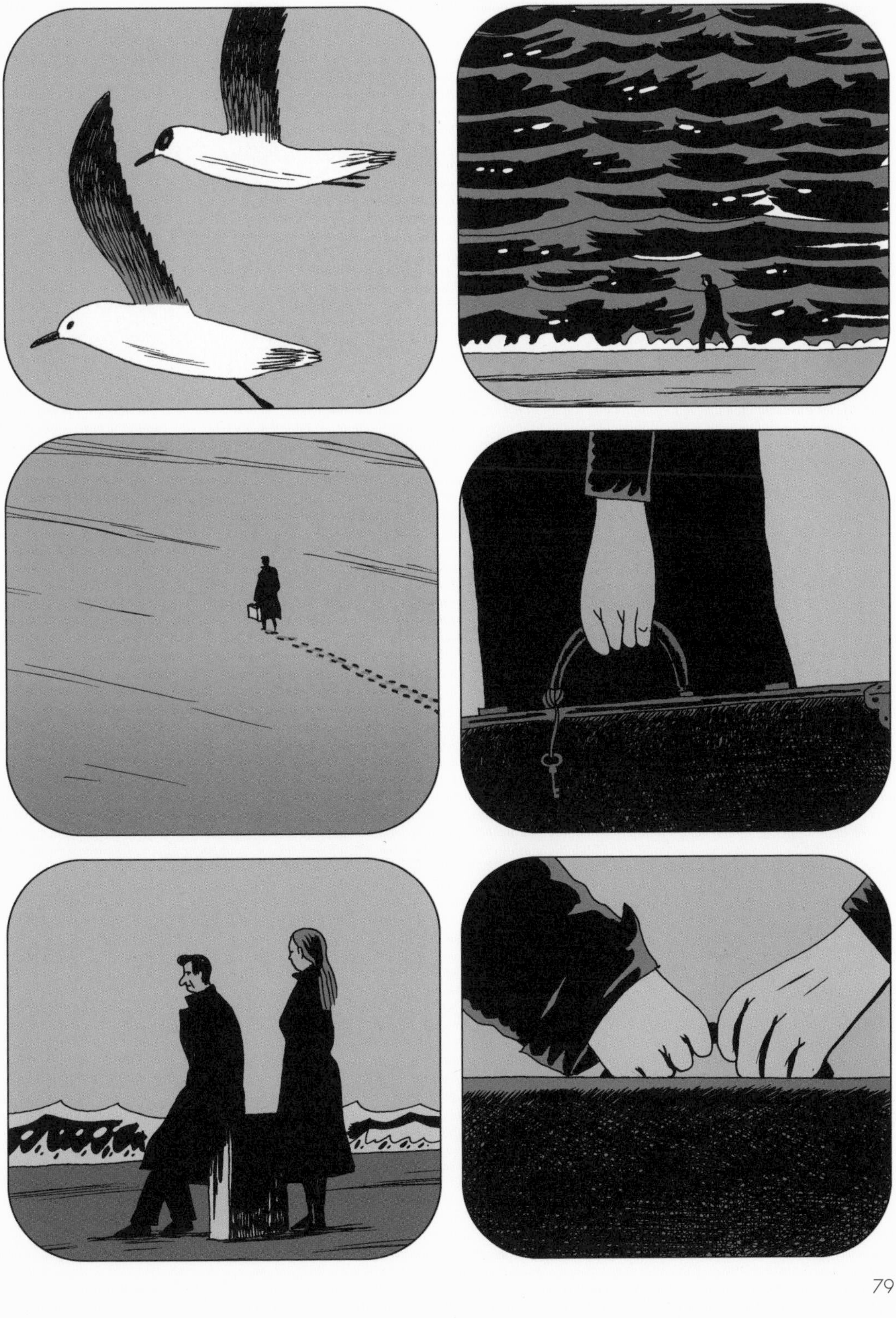

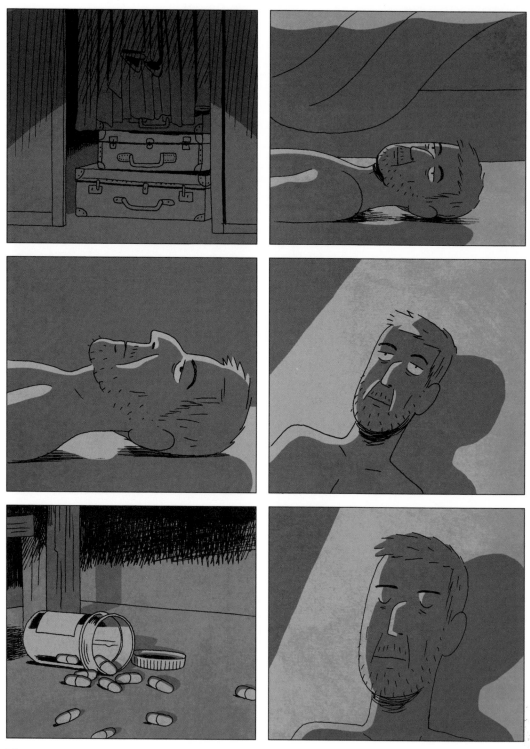

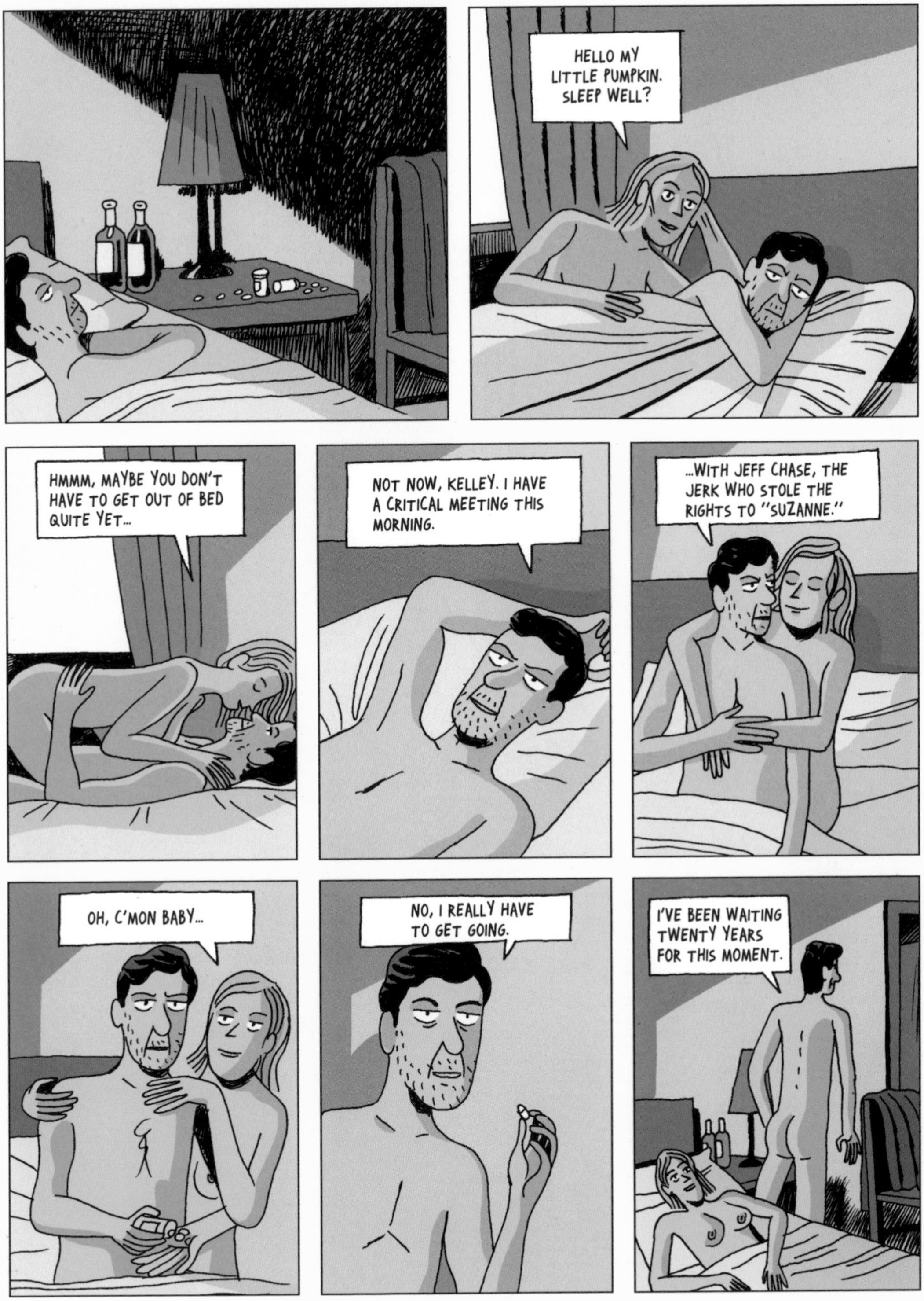
HELLO MY LITTLE PUMPKIN. SLEEP WELL?
HMMM, MAYBE YOU DON'T HAVE TO GET OUT OF BED QUITE YET...
NOT NOW, KELLEY. I HAVE A CRITICAL MEETING THIS MORNING.
...WITH JEFF CHASE, THE JERK WHO STOLE THE RIGHTS TO "SUZANNE."
OH, C'MON BABY...
NO, I REALLY HAVE TO GET GOING.
I'VE BEEN WAITING TWENTY YEARS FOR THIS MOMENT.

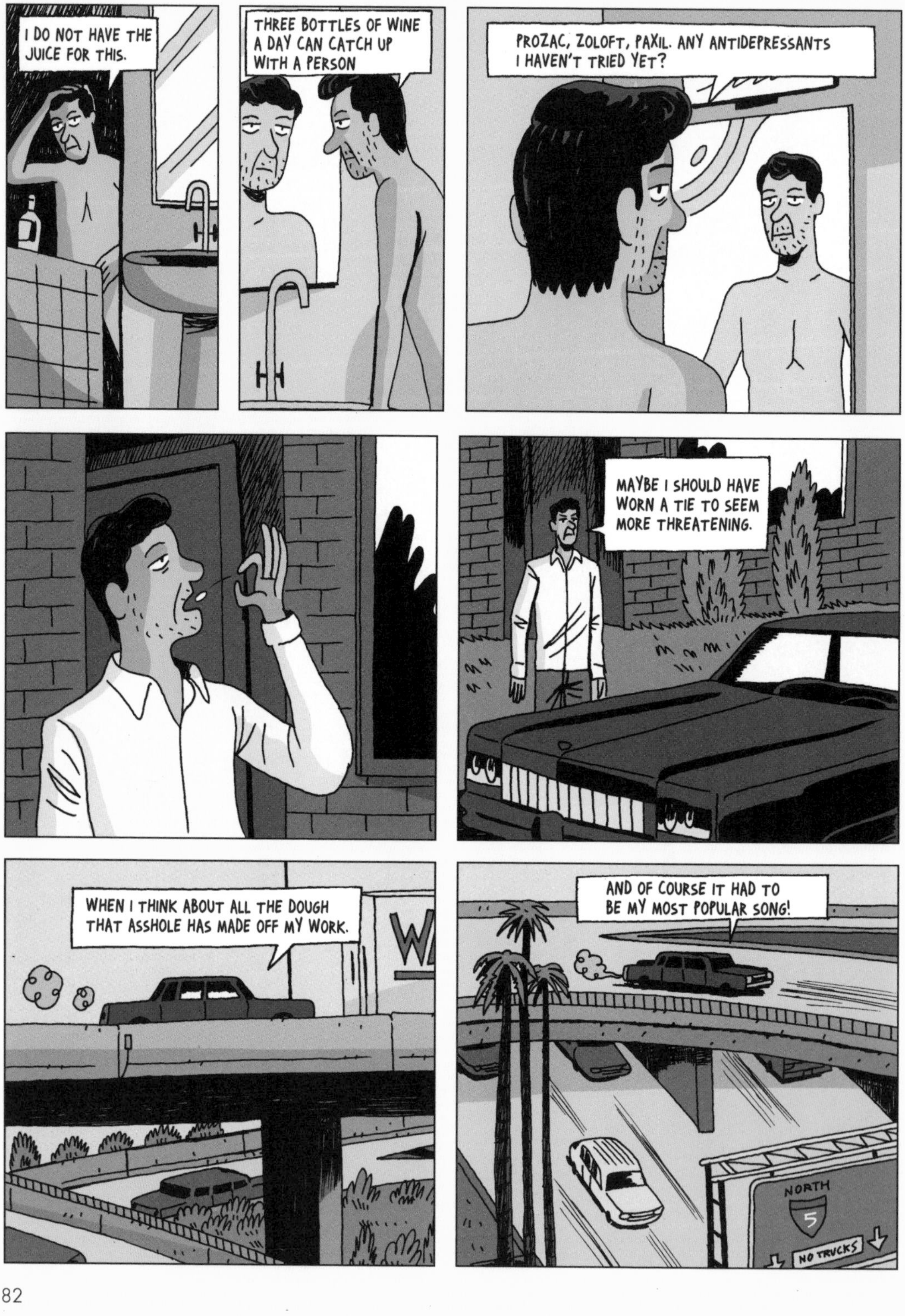
I DO NOT HAVE THE JUICE FOR THIS.
THREE BOTTLES OF WINE A DAY CAN CATCH UP WITH A PERSON
PROZAC, ZOLOFT, PAXIL. ANY ANTIDEPRESSANTS I HAVEN'T TRIED YET?
MAYBE I SHOULD HAVE WORN A TIE TO SEEM MORE THREATENING.
WHEN I THINK ABOUT ALL THE DOUGH THAT ASSHOLE HAS MADE OFF MY WORK.
AND OF COURSE IT HAD TO BE MY MOST POPULAR SONG!
NORTH
5
NO TRUCKS

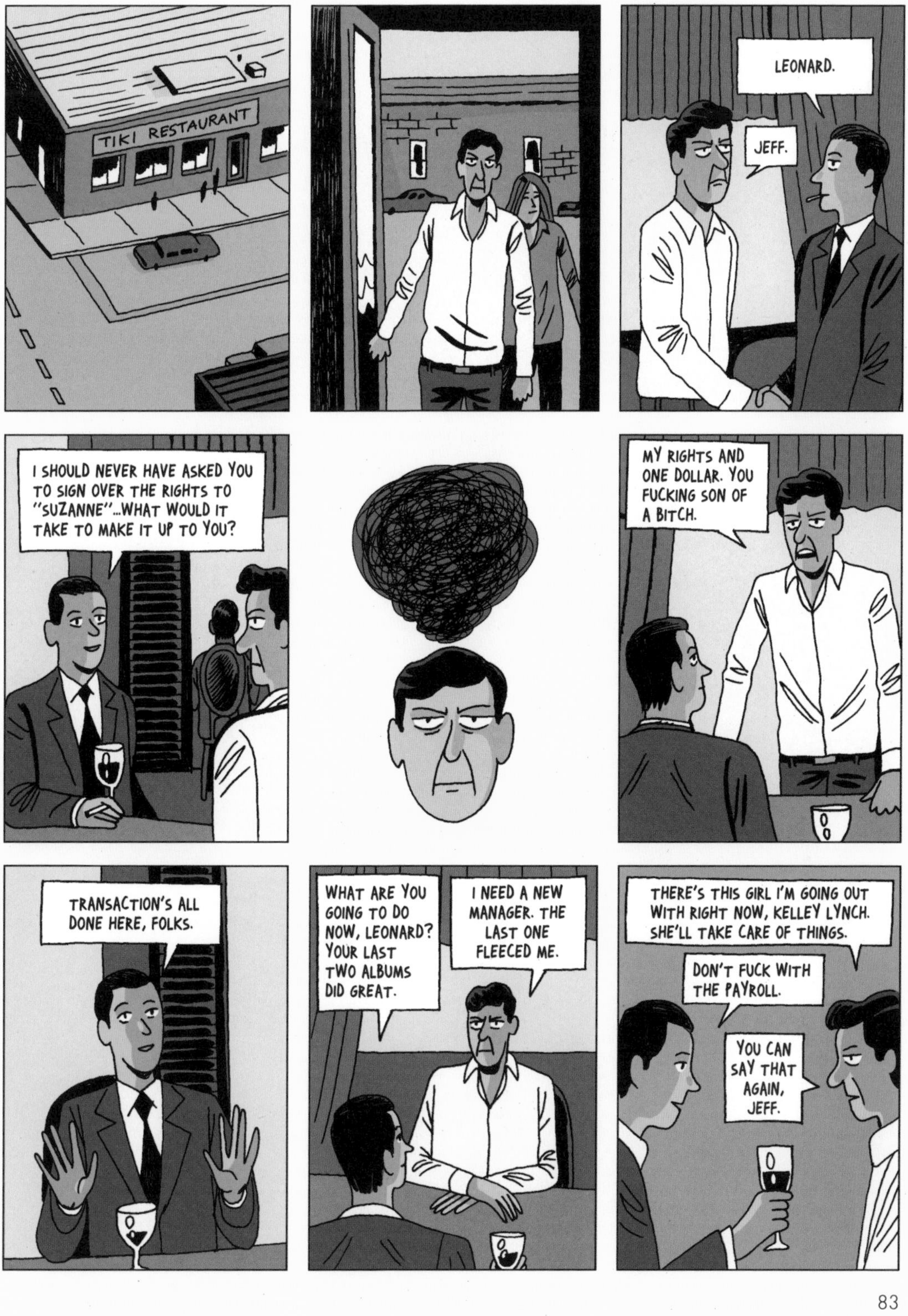
TIKI RESTAURANT
LEONARD.
JEFF.
I SHOULD NEVER HAVE ASKED YOU TO SIGN OVER THE RIGHTS TO "SUZANNE"...WHAT WOULD IT TAKE TO MAKE IT UP TO YOU?
MY RIGHTS AND ONE DOLLAR. YOU FUCKING SON OF A BITCH.
TRANSACTION'S ALL DONE HERE, FOLKS.
WHAT ARE YOU GOING TO DO NOW, LEONARD? YOUR LAST TWO ALBUMS DID GREAT.
I NEED A NEW MANAGER. THE LAST ONE FLEECED ME.
THERE'S THIS GIRL I'M GOING OUT WITH RIGHT NOW, KELLEY LYNCH. SHE'LL TAKE CARE OF THINGS.
DON'T FUCK WITH THE PAYROLL.
YOU CAN SAY THAT AGAIN, JEFF.

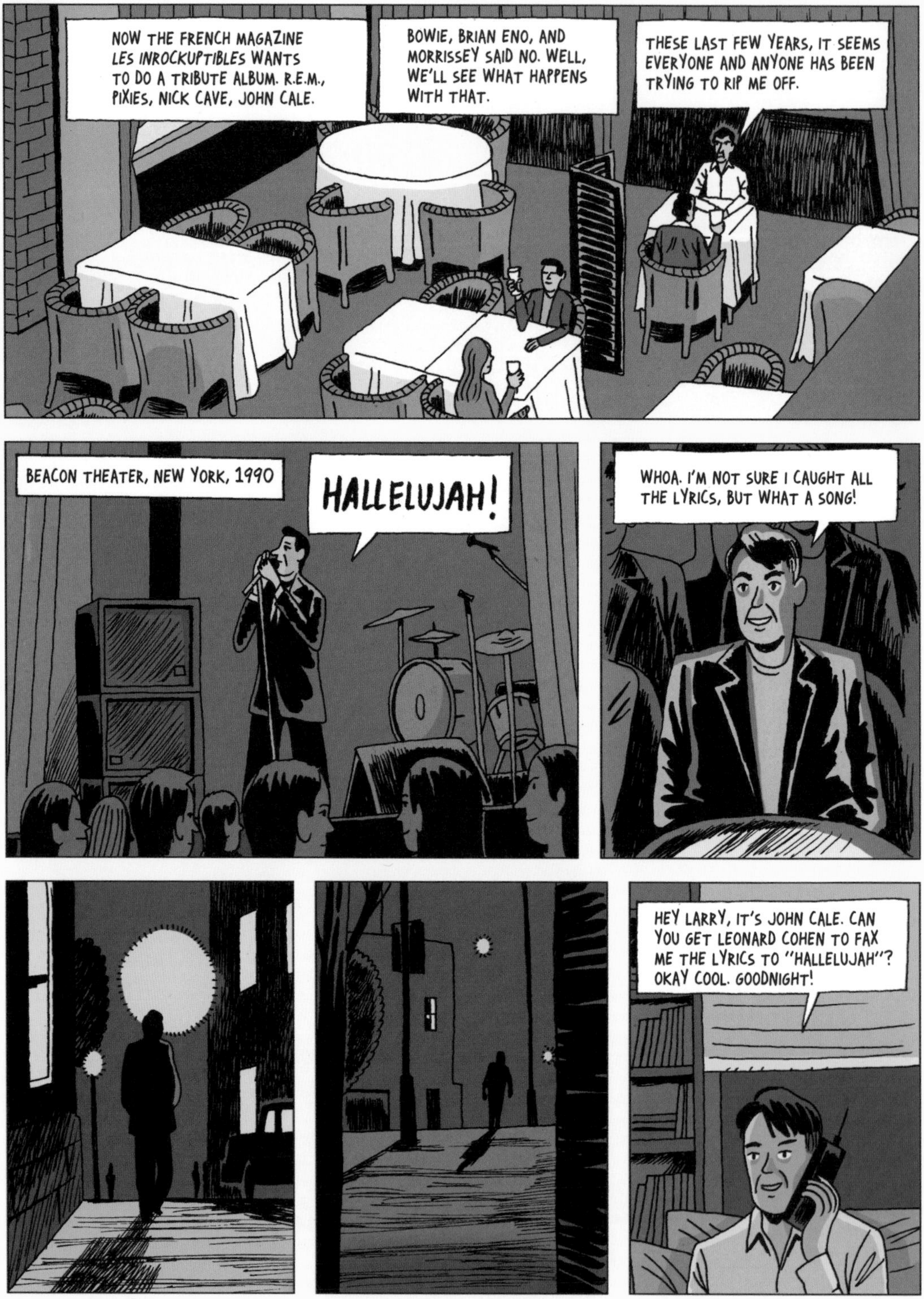
NOW THE FRENCH MAGAZINE LES INROCKUPTIBLES WANTS TO DO A TRIBUTE ALBUM. R.E.M., PIXIES, NICK CAVE, JOHN CALE.
BOWIE, BRIAN ENO, AND MORRISSEY SAID NO. WELL, WE'LL SEE WHAT HAPPENS WITH THAT.
THESE LAST FEW YEARS, IT SEEMS EVERYONE AND ANYONE HAS BEEN TRYING TO RIP ME OFF.
BEACON THEATER, NEW YORK, 1990
HALLELUJAH!
WHOA. I'M NOT SURE I CAUGHT ALL THE LYRICS, BUT WHAT A SONG!
HEY LARRY, IT'S JOHN CALE. CAN YOU GET LEONARD COHEN TO FAX ME THE LYRICS TO "HALLELUJAH"? OKAY COOL. GOODNIGHT!

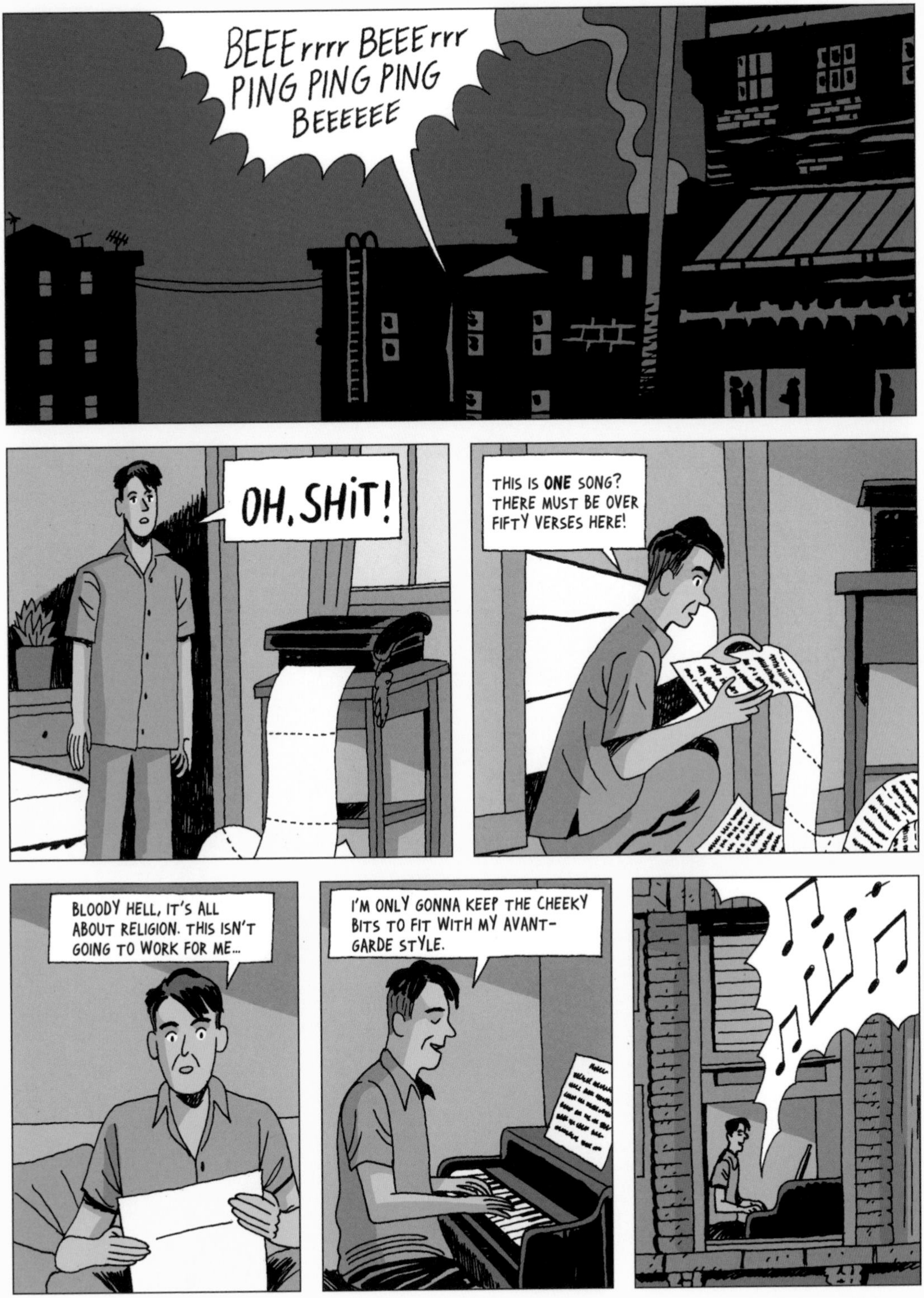
BEEErrrr BEEErrr
PING PING PING
BEEEEEE
OH, SHIT!
THIS IS **ONE** SONG? THERE MUST BE OVER FIFTY VERSES HERE!
BLOODY HELL, IT'S ALL ABOUT RELIGION. THIS ISN'T GOING TO WORK FOR ME...
I'M ONLY GONNA KEEP THE CHEEKY BITS TO FIT WITH MY AVANT-GARDE STYLE.

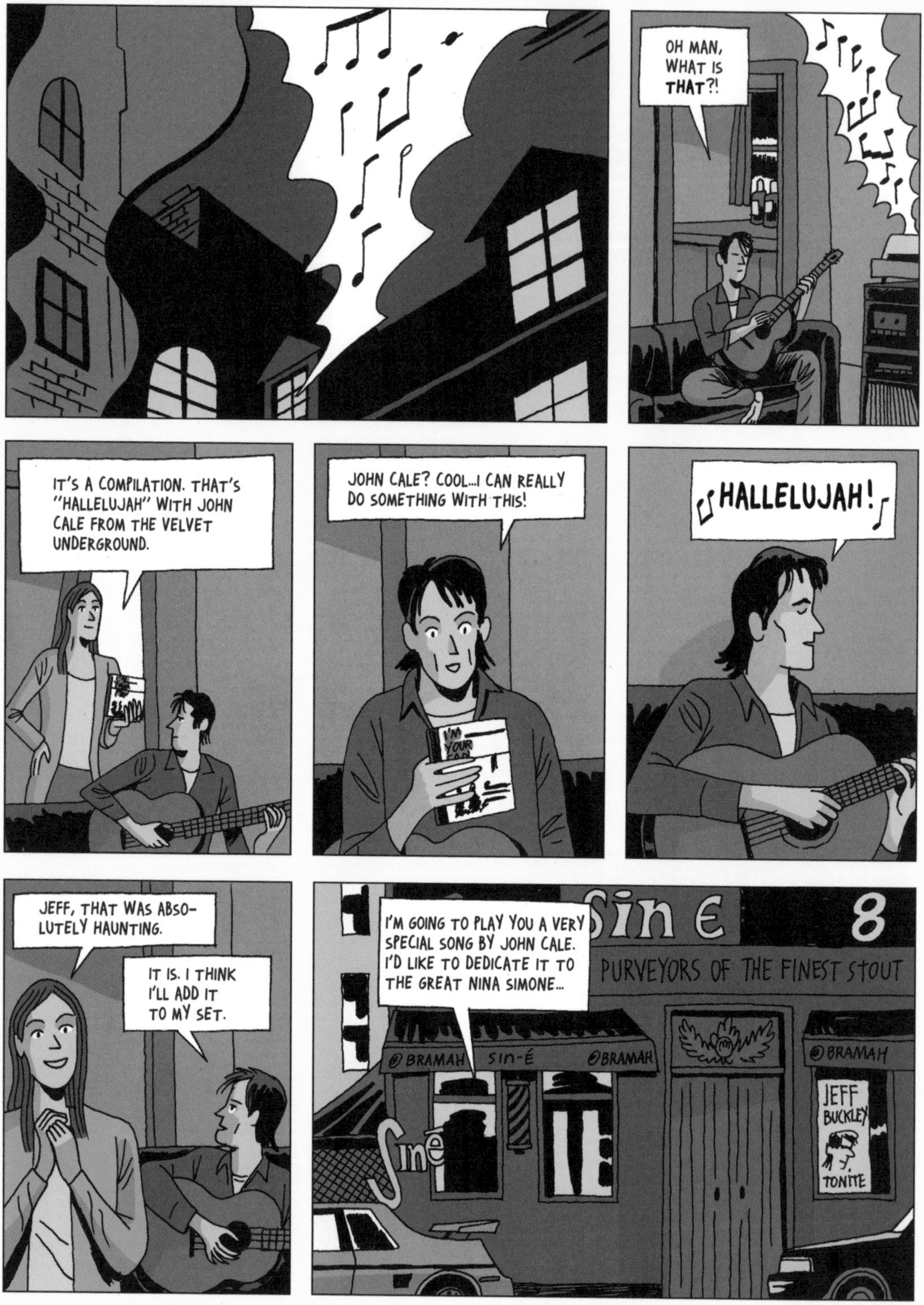
OH MAN, WHAT IS THAT?!
IT'S A COMPILATION. THAT'S "HALLELUJAH" WITH JOHN CALE FROM THE VELVET UNDERGROUND.
JOHN CALE? COOL...I CAN REALLY DO SOMETHING WITH THIS!
HALLELUJAH!
JEFF, THAT WAS ABSOLUTELY HAUNTING.
IT IS. I THINK I'LL ADD IT TO MY SET.
Sin É
8
PURVEYORS OF THE FINEST STOUT
I'M GOING TO PLAY YOU A VERY SPECIAL SONG BY JOHN CALE. I'D LIKE TO DEDICATE IT TO THE GREAT NINA SIMONE...
BRAMAH
Sin-É
BRAMAH
BRAMAH
JEFF BUCKLEY TONITE
Sinè

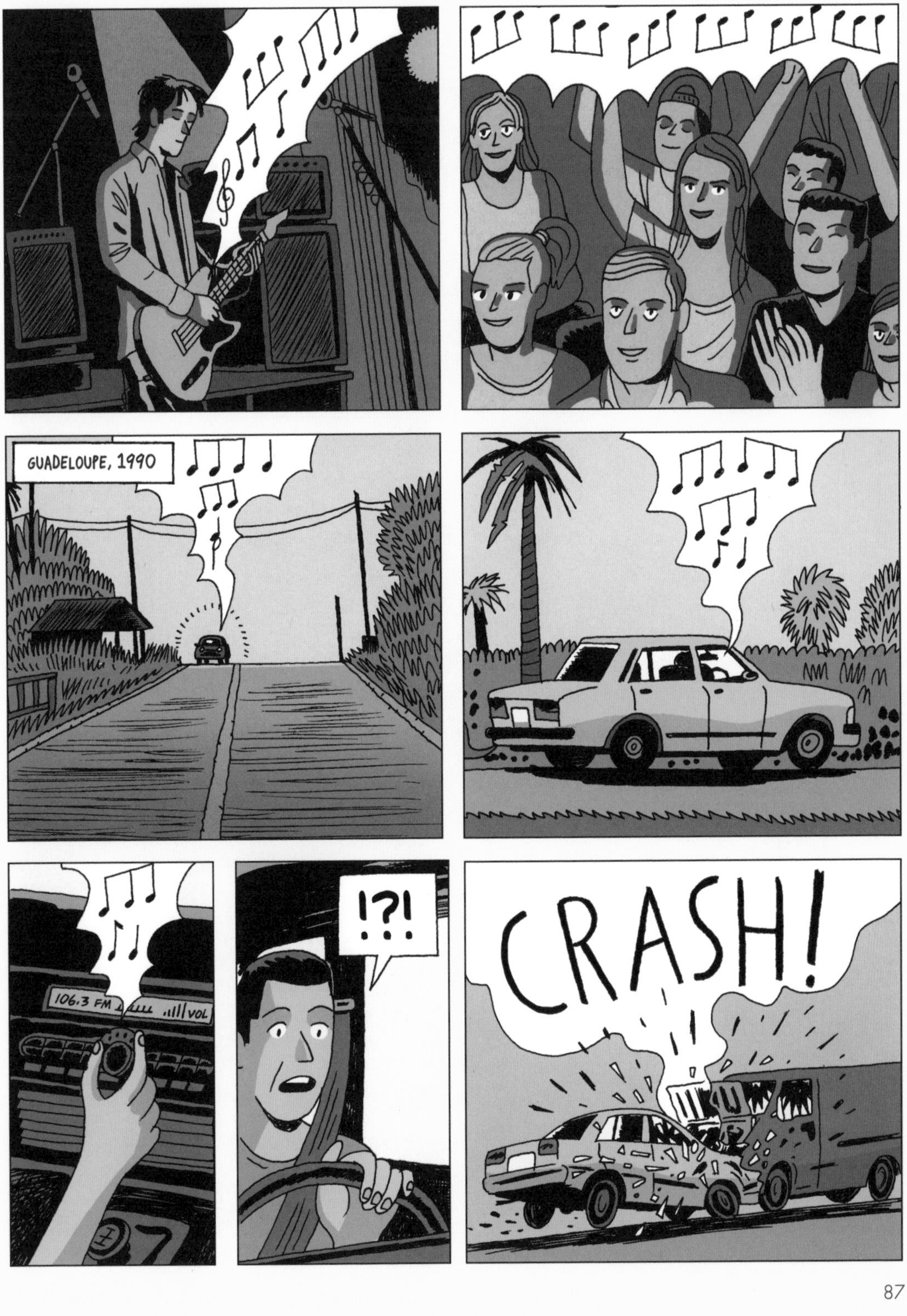
GUADELOUPE, 1990
106.3 FM
VOL
!?!
CRASH!

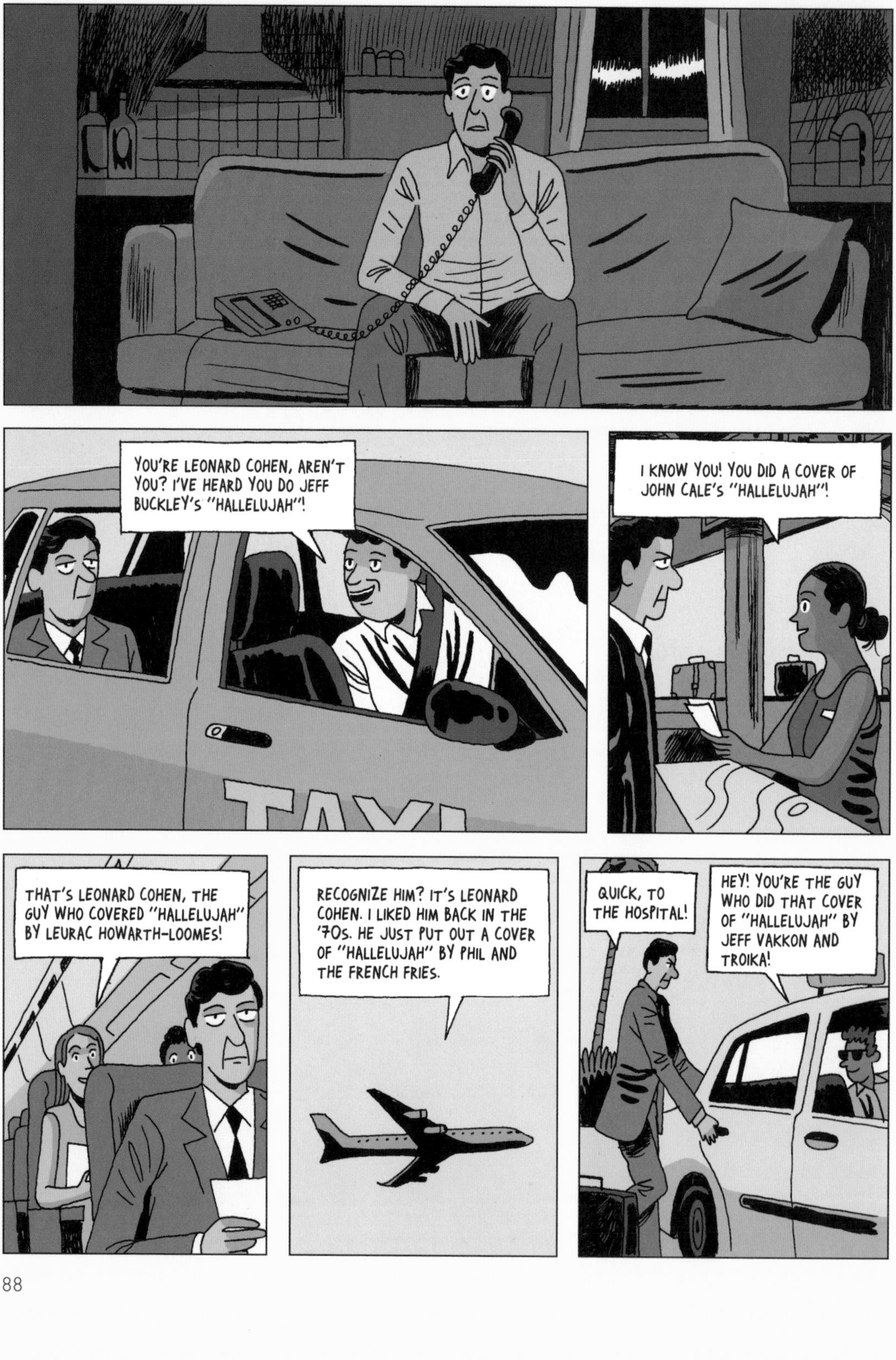
YOU'RE LEONARD COHEN, AREN'T YOU? I'VE HEARD YOU DO JEFF BUCKLEY'S "HALLELUJAH"!
TAXI
I KNOW YOU! YOU DID A COVER OF JOHN CALE'S "HALLELUJAH"!
THAT'S LEONARD COHEN, THE GUY WHO COVERED "HALLELUJAH" BY LEURAC HOWARTH-LOOMES!
RECOGNIZE HIM? IT'S LEONARD COHEN. I LIKED HIM BACK IN THE '70S. HE JUST PUT OUT A COVER OF "HALLELUJAH" BY PHIL AND THE FRENCH FRIES.
QUICK, TO THE HOSPITAL!
HEY! YOU'RE THE GUY WHO DID THAT COVER OF "HALLELUJAH" BY JEFF VAKKON AND TROIKA!

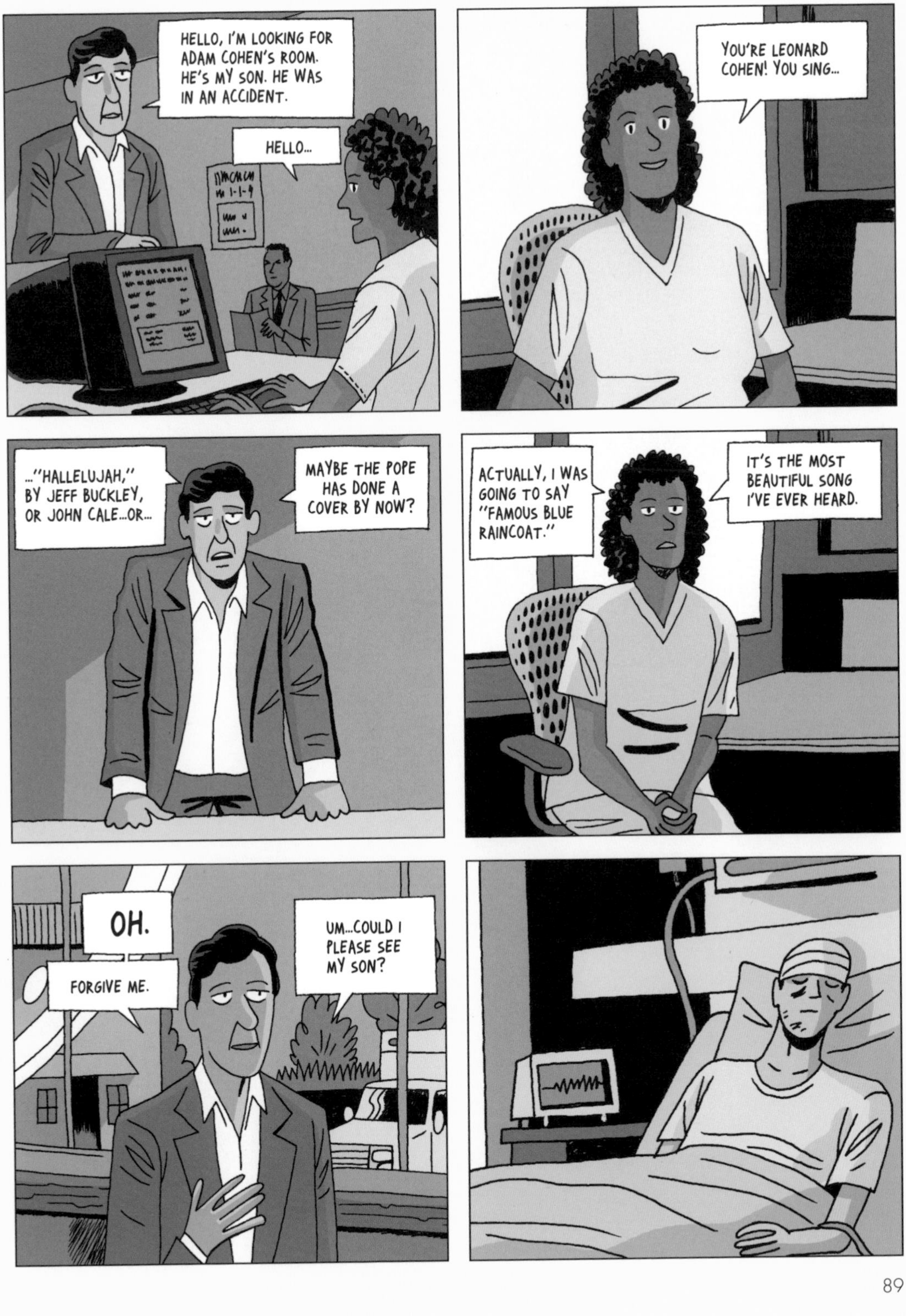
HELLO, I'M LOOKING FOR ADAM COHEN'S ROOM. HE'S MY SON. HE WAS IN AN ACCIDENT.
HELLO...
YOU'RE LEONARD COHEN! YOU SING...
..."HALLELUJAH," BY JEFF BUCKLEY, OR JOHN CALE...OR...
MAYBE THE POPE HAS DONE A COVER BY NOW?
ACTUALLY, I WAS GOING TO SAY "FAMOUS BLUE RAINCOAT."
IT'S THE MOST BEAUTIFUL SONG I'VE EVER HEARD.
OH.
FORGIVE ME.
UM...COULD I PLEASE SEE MY SON?

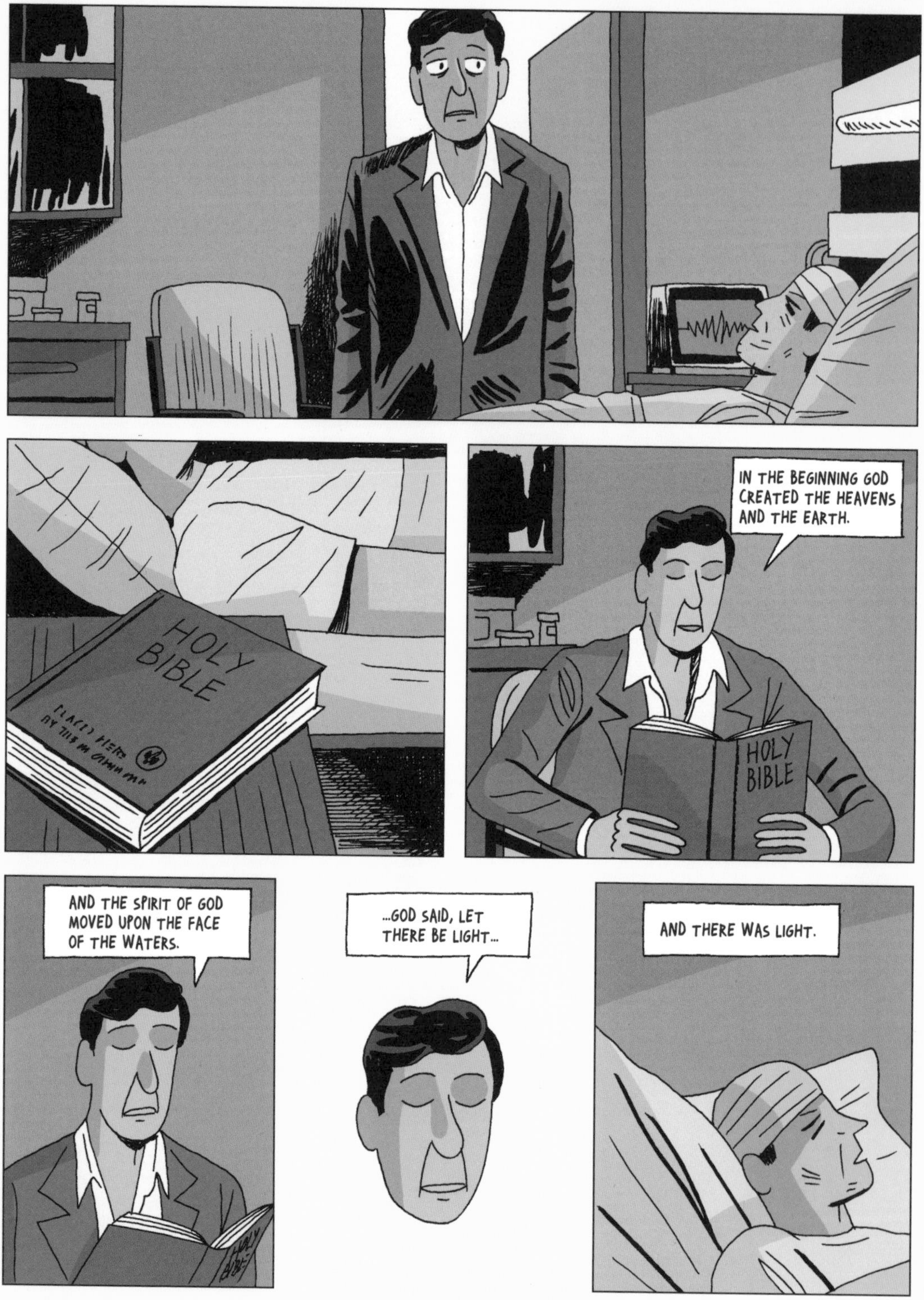
HOLY BIBLE
IN THE BEGINNING GOD CREATED THE HEAVENS AND THE EARTH.
HOLY BIBLE
AND THE SPIRIT OF GOD MOVED UPON THE FACE OF THE WATERS.
...GOD SAID, LET THERE BE LIGHT...
AND THERE WAS LIGHT.

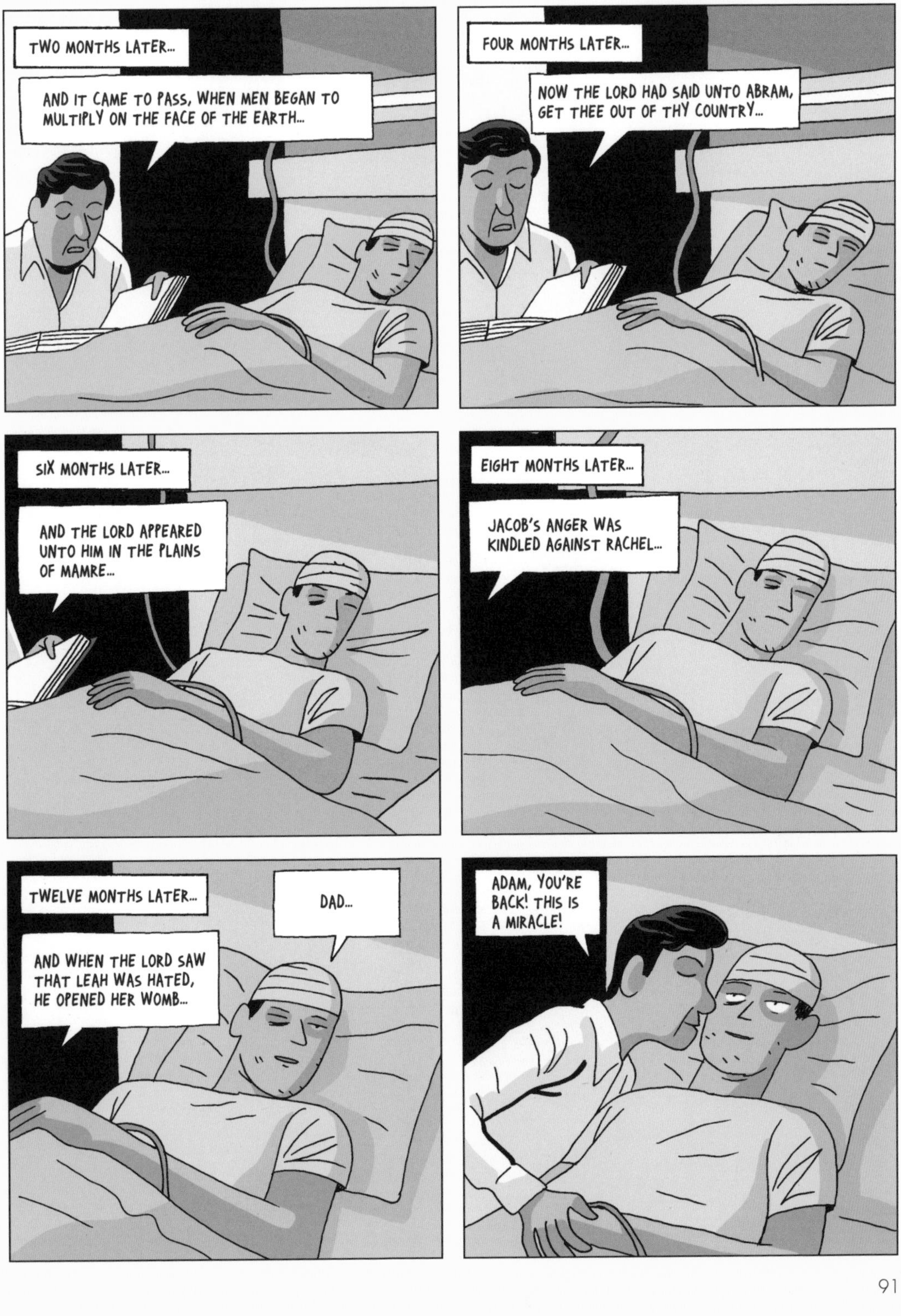
TWO MONTHS LATER...
AND IT CAME TO PASS, WHEN MEN BEGAN TO MULTIPLY ON THE FACE OF THE EARTH...
FOUR MONTHS LATER...
NOW THE LORD HAD SAID UNTO ABRAM, GET THEE OUT OF THY COUNTRY...
SIX MONTHS LATER...
AND THE LORD APPEARED UNTO HIM IN THE PLAINS OF MAMRE...
EIGHT MONTHS LATER...
JACOB'S ANGER WAS KINDLED AGAINST RACHEL...
TWELVE MONTHS LATER...
AND WHEN THE LORD SAW THAT LEAH WAS HATED, HE OPENED HER WOMB...
DAD...
ADAM, YOU'RE BACK! THIS IS A MIRACLE!

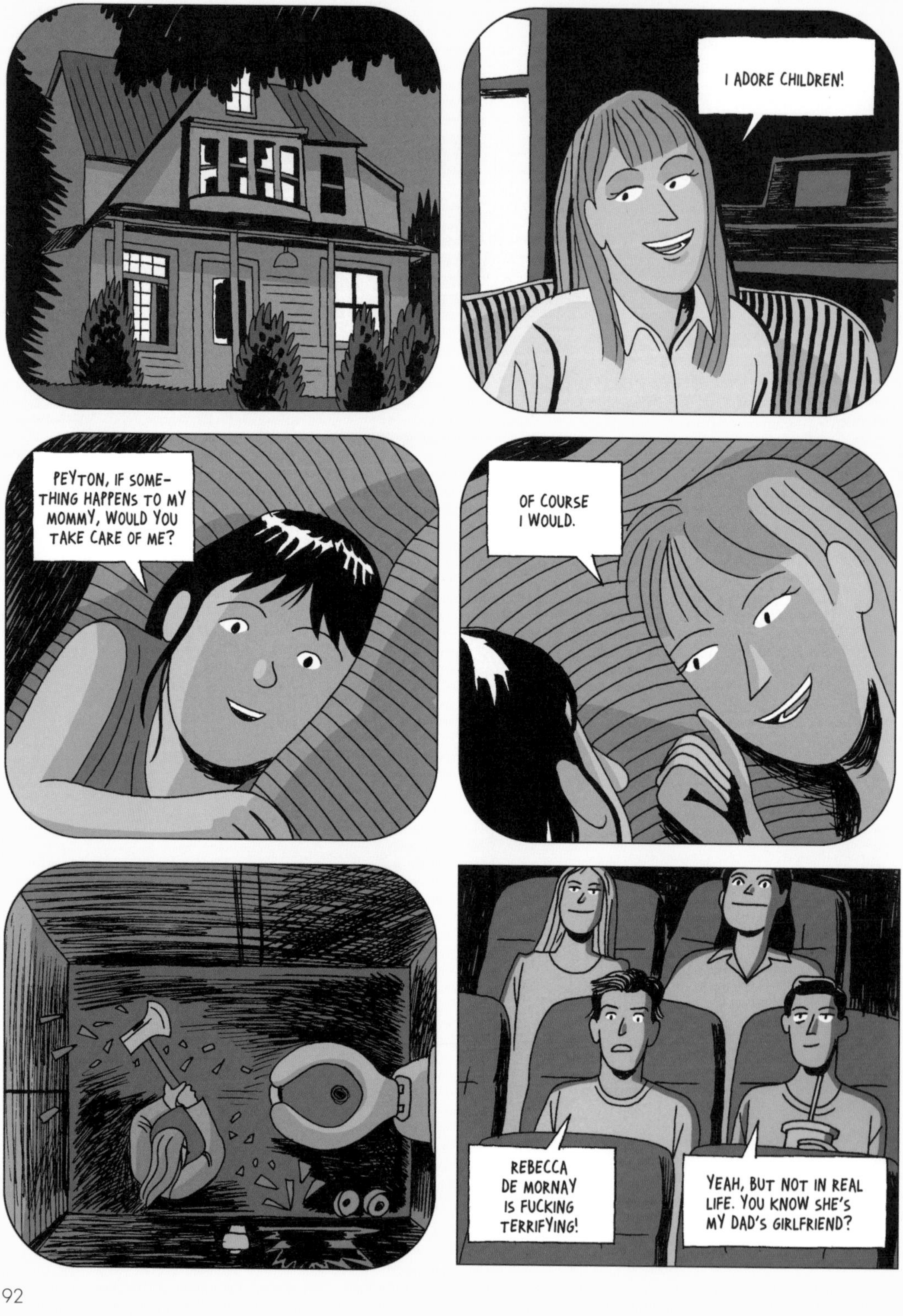
I ADORE CHILDREN!
PEYTON, IF SOMETHING HAPPENS TO MY MOMMY, WOULD YOU TAKE CARE OF ME?
OF COURSE I WOULD.
REBECCA DE MORNAY IS FUCKING TERRIFYING!
YEAH, BUT NOT IN REAL LIFE. YOU KNOW SHE'S MY DAD'S GIRLFRIEND?

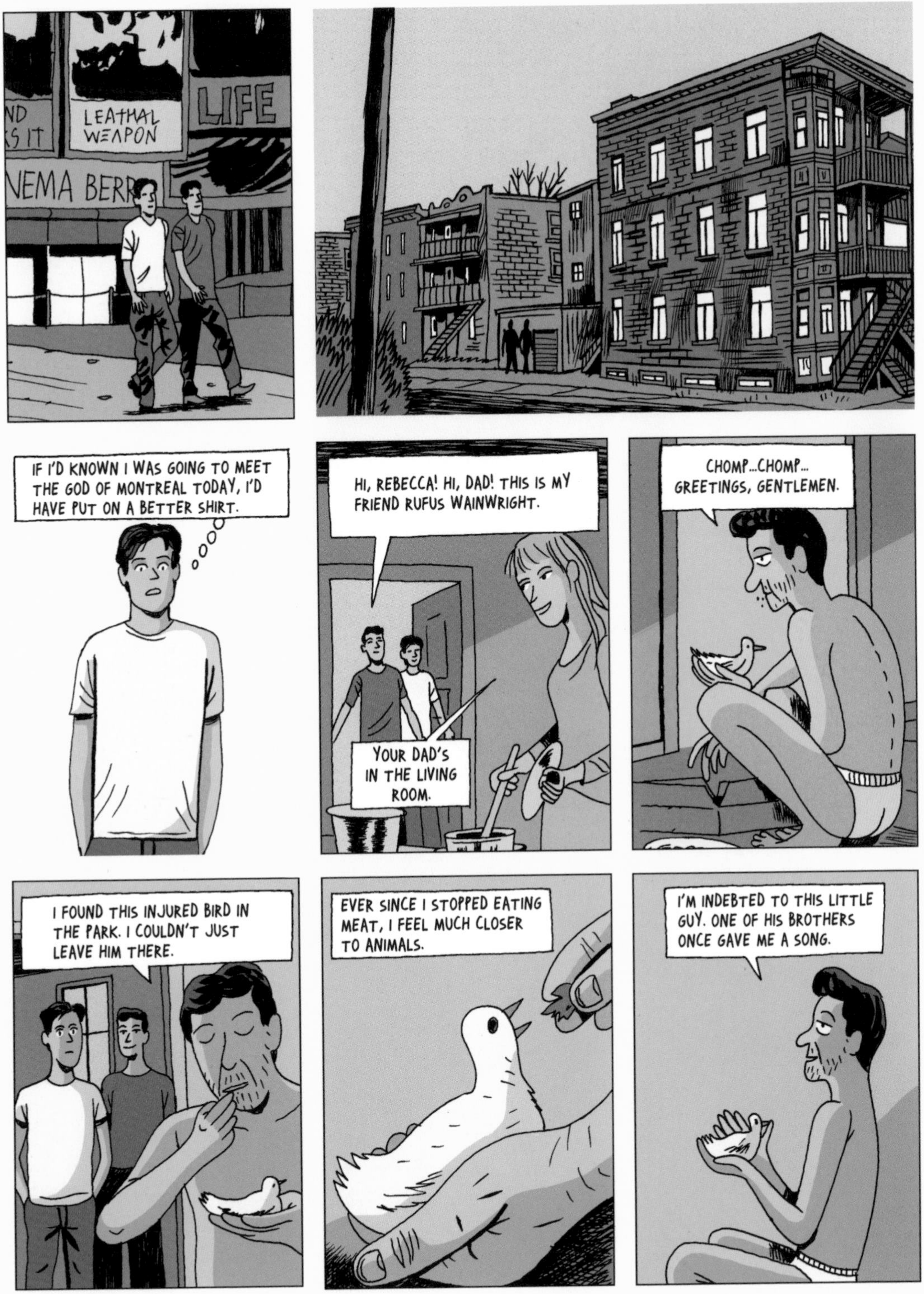
ND
S IT
LEATHAL WEAPON
LIFE
NEMA BERR
IF I'D KNOWN I WAS GOING TO MEET THE GOD OF MONTREAL TODAY, I'D HAVE PUT ON A BETTER SHIRT.
HI, REBECCA! HI, DAD! THIS IS MY FRIEND RUFUS WAINWRIGHT.
YOUR DAD'S IN THE LIVING ROOM.
CHOMP...CHOMP... GREETINGS, GENTLEMEN.
I FOUND THIS INJURED BIRD IN THE PARK. I COULDN'T JUST LEAVE HIM THERE.
EVER SINCE I STOPPED EATING MEAT, I FEEL MUCH CLOSER TO ANIMALS.
I'M INDEBTED TO THIS LITTLE GUY. ONE OF HIS BROTHERS ONCE GAVE ME A SONG.

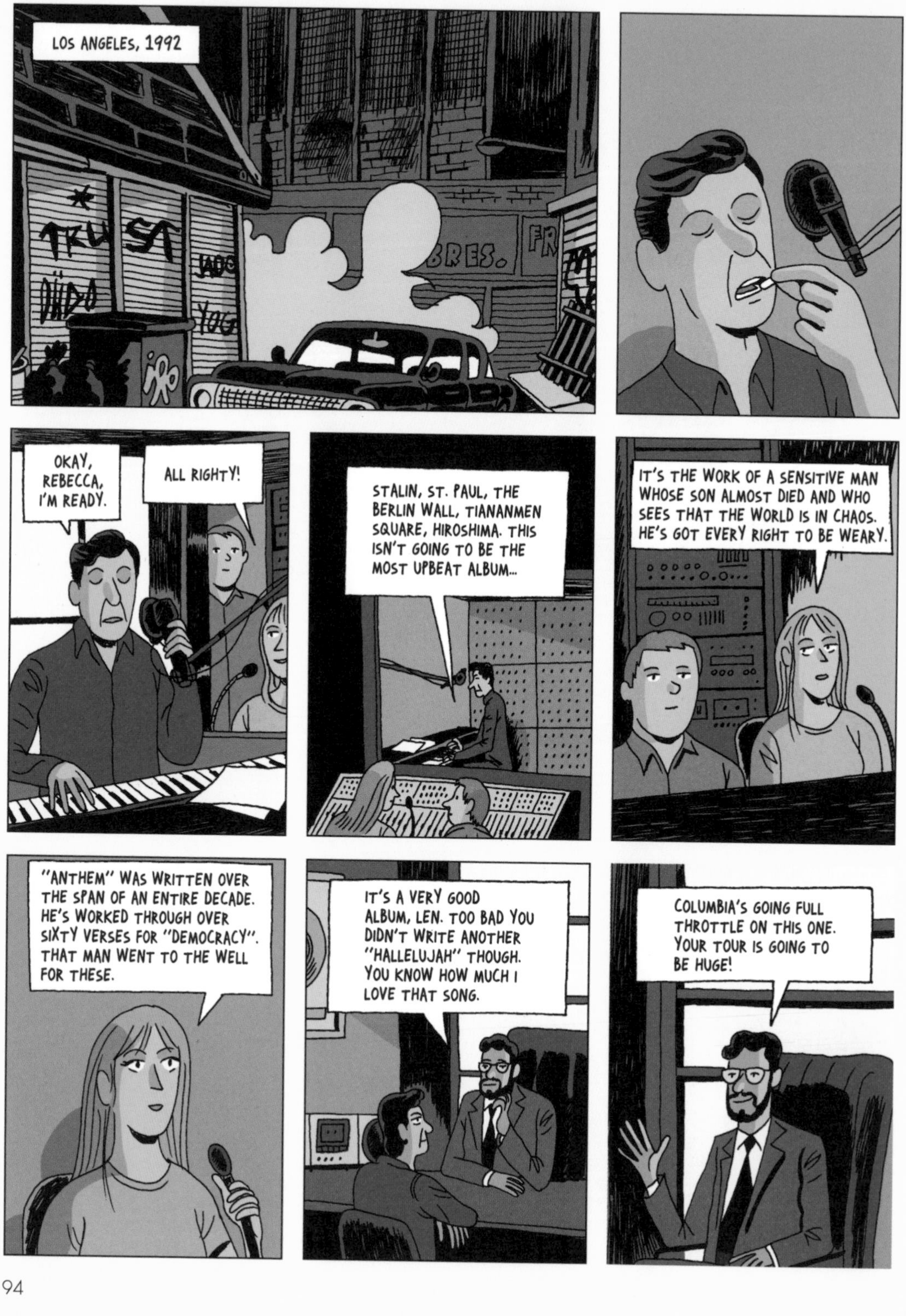
LOS ANGELES, 1992
OKAY, REBECCA, I'M READY.
ALL RIGHTY!
STALIN, ST. PAUL, THE BERLIN WALL, TIANANMEN SQUARE, HIROSHIMA. THIS ISN'T GOING TO BE THE MOST UPBEAT ALBUM...
IT'S THE WORK OF A SENSITIVE MAN WHOSE SON ALMOST DIED AND WHO SEES THAT THE WORLD IS IN CHAOS. HE'S GOT EVERY RIGHT TO BE WEARY.
"ANTHEM" WAS WRITTEN OVER THE SPAN OF AN ENTIRE DECADE. HE'S WORKED THROUGH OVER SIXTY VERSES FOR "DEMOCRACY". THAT MAN WENT TO THE WELL FOR THESE.
IT'S A VERY GOOD ALBUM, LEN. TOO BAD YOU DIDN'T WRITE ANOTHER "HALLELUJAH" THOUGH. YOU KNOW HOW MUCH I LOVE THAT SONG.
COLUMBIA'S GOING FULL THROTTLE ON THIS ONE. YOUR TOUR IS GOING TO BE HUGE!

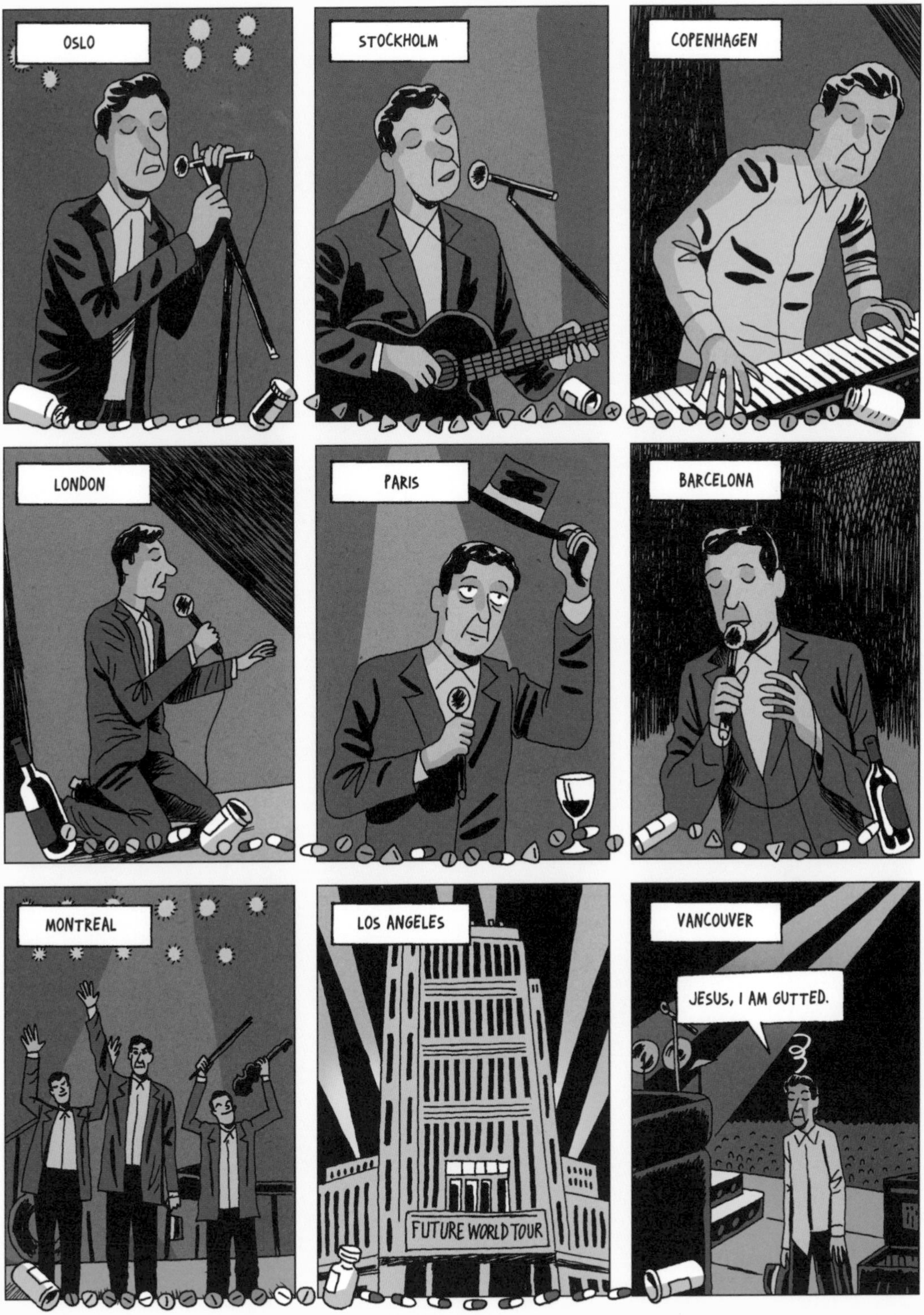
OSLO
STOCKHOLM
COPENHAGEN
LONDON
PARIS
BARCELONA
MONTREAL
LOS ANGELES
FUTURE WORLD TOUR
VANCOUVER
JESUS, I AM GUTTED.

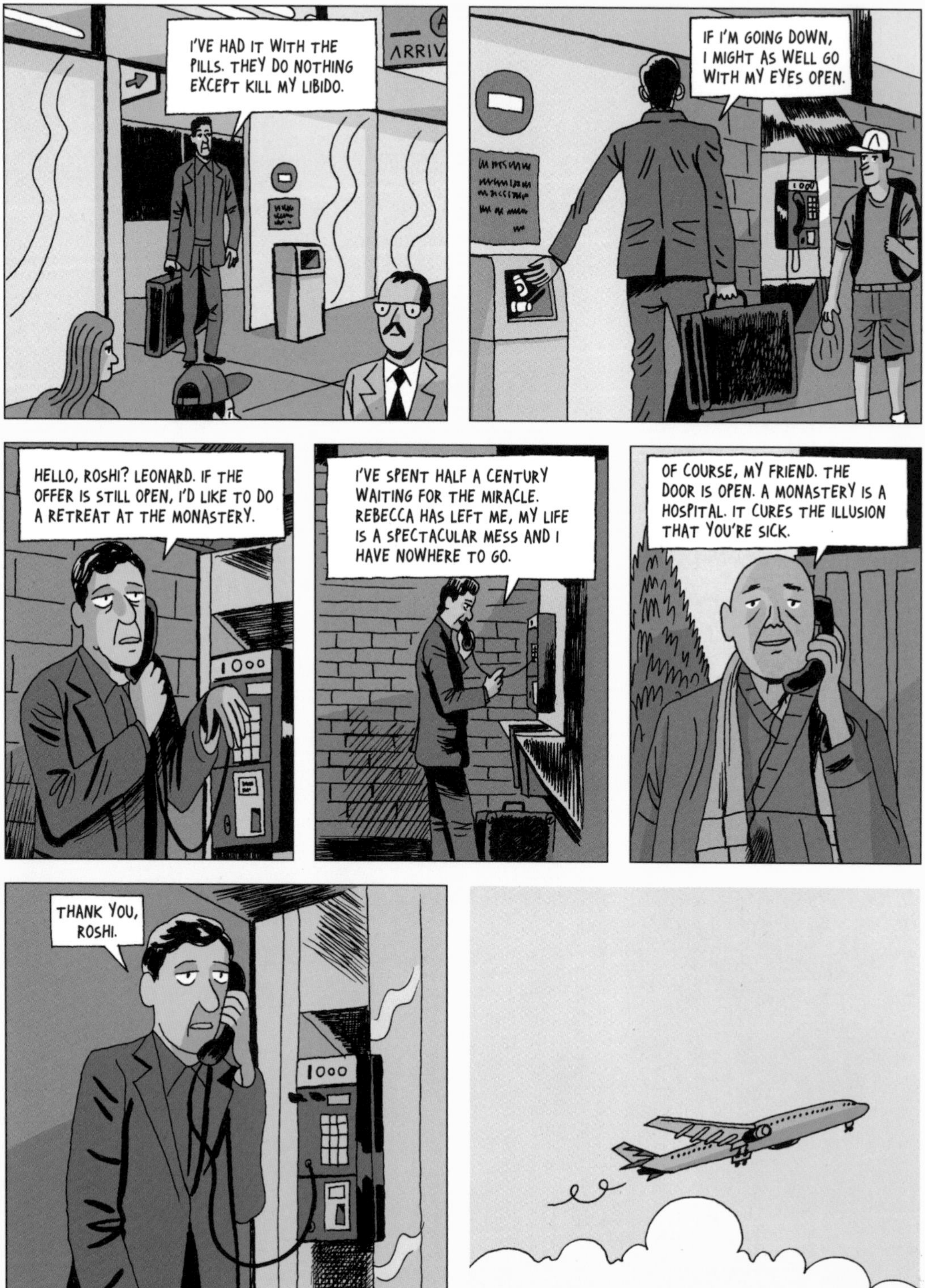
I'VE HAD IT WITH THE PILLS. THEY DO NOTHING EXCEPT KILL MY LIBIDO.
ARRIV
IF I'M GOING DOWN, I MIGHT AS WELL GO WITH MY EYES OPEN.
HELLO, ROSHI? LEONARD. IF THE OFFER IS STILL OPEN, I'D LIKE TO DO A RETREAT AT THE MONASTERY.
I'VE SPENT HALF A CENTURY WAITING FOR THE MIRACLE. REBECCA HAS LEFT ME, MY LIFE IS A SPECTACULAR MESS AND I HAVE NOWHERE TO GO.
OF COURSE, MY FRIEND. THE DOOR IS OPEN. A MONASTERY IS A HOSPITAL. IT CURES THE ILLUSION THAT YOU'RE SICK.
THANK YOU, ROSHI.

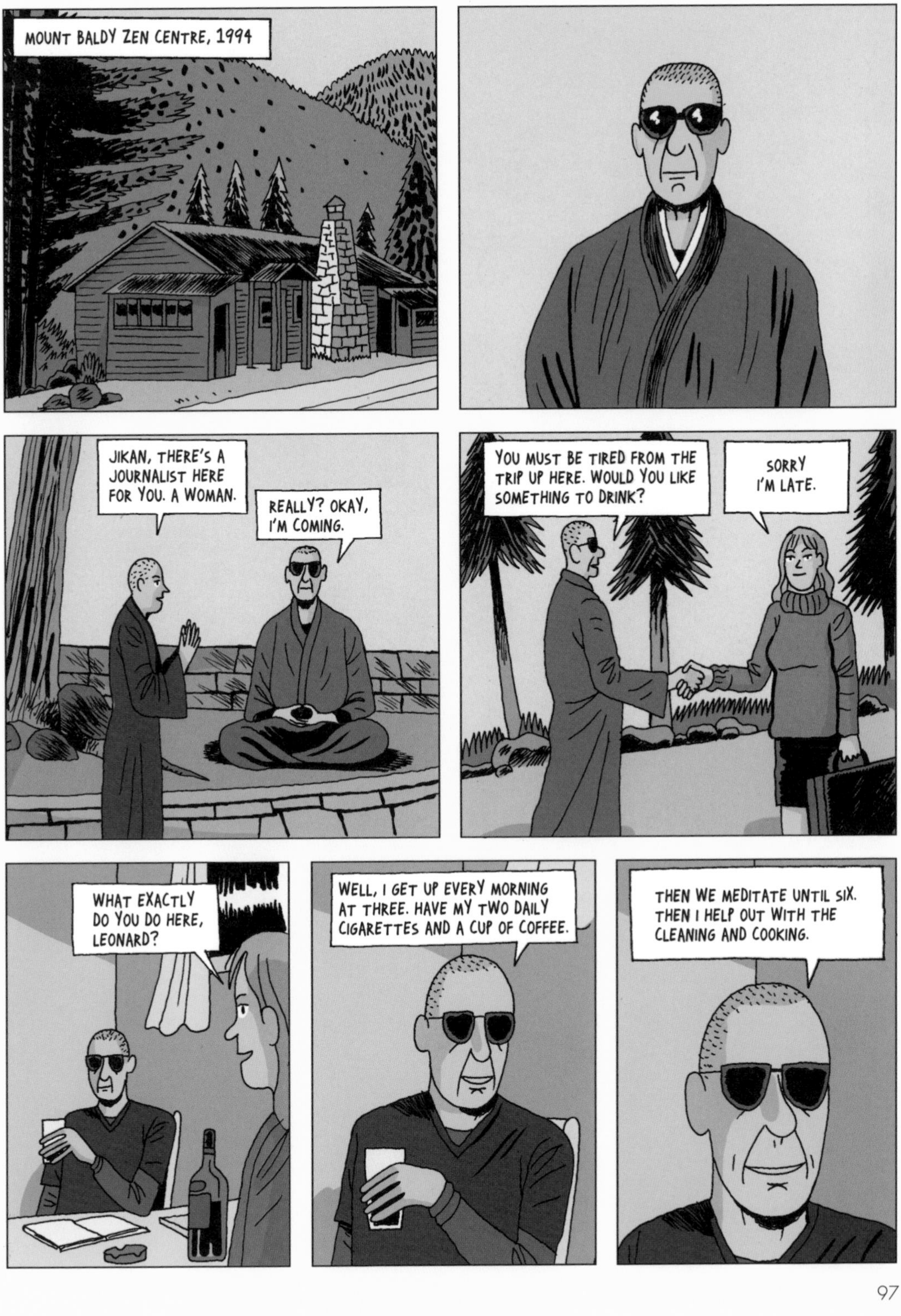
MOUNT BALDY ZEN CENTRE, 1994
JIKAN, THERE'S A JOURNALIST HERE FOR YOU. A WOMAN.
REALLY? OKAY, I'M COMING.
YOU MUST BE TIRED FROM THE TRIP UP HERE. WOULD YOU LIKE SOMETHING TO DRINK?
SORRY I'M LATE.
WHAT EXACTLY DO YOU DO HERE, LEONARD?
WELL, I GET UP EVERY MORNING AT THREE. HAVE MY TWO DAILY CIGARETTES AND A CUP OF COFFEE.
THEN WE MEDITATE UNTIL SIX. THEN I HELP OUT WITH THE CLEANING AND COOKING.

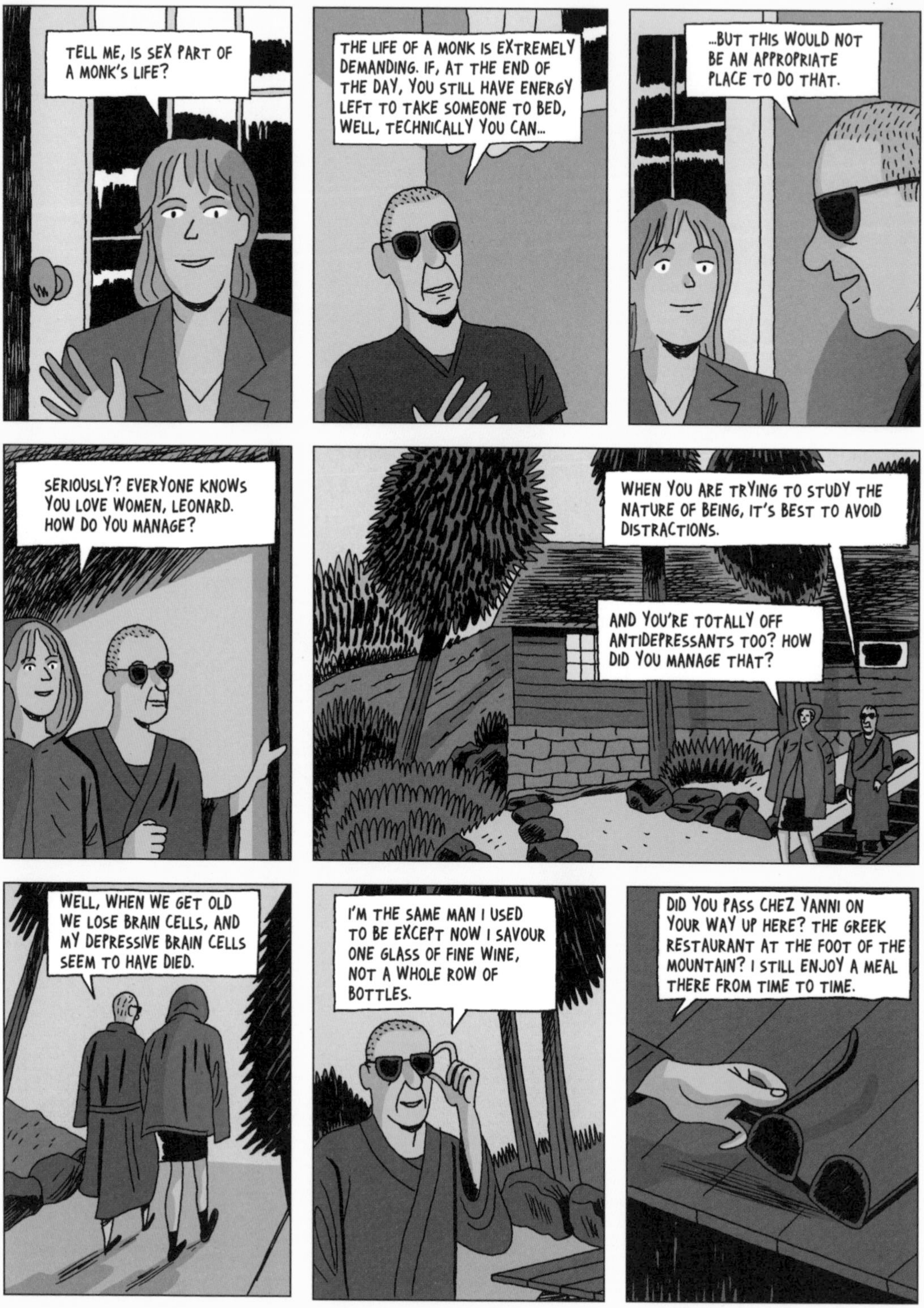
TELL ME, IS SEX PART OF A MONK'S LIFE?
THE LIFE OF A MONK IS EXTREMELY DEMANDING. IF, AT THE END OF THE DAY, YOU STILL HAVE ENERGY LEFT TO TAKE SOMEONE TO BED, WELL, TECHNICALLY YOU CAN...
...BUT THIS WOULD NOT BE AN APPROPRIATE PLACE TO DO THAT.
SERIOUSLY? EVERYONE KNOWS YOU LOVE WOMEN, LEONARD. HOW DO YOU MANAGE?
WHEN YOU ARE TRYING TO STUDY THE NATURE OF BEING, IT'S BEST TO AVOID DISTRACTIONS.
AND YOU'RE TOTALLY OFF ANTIDEPRESSANTS TOO? HOW DID YOU MANAGE THAT?
WELL, WHEN WE GET OLD WE LOSE BRAIN CELLS, AND MY DEPRESSIVE BRAIN CELLS SEEM TO HAVE DIED.
I'M THE SAME MAN I USED TO BE EXCEPT NOW I SAVOUR ONE GLASS OF FINE WINE, NOT A WHOLE ROW OF BOTTLES.
DID YOU PASS CHEZ YANNI ON YOUR WAY UP HERE? THE GREEK RESTAURANT AT THE FOOT OF THE MOUNTAIN? I STILL ENJOY A MEAL THERE FROM TIME TO TIME.

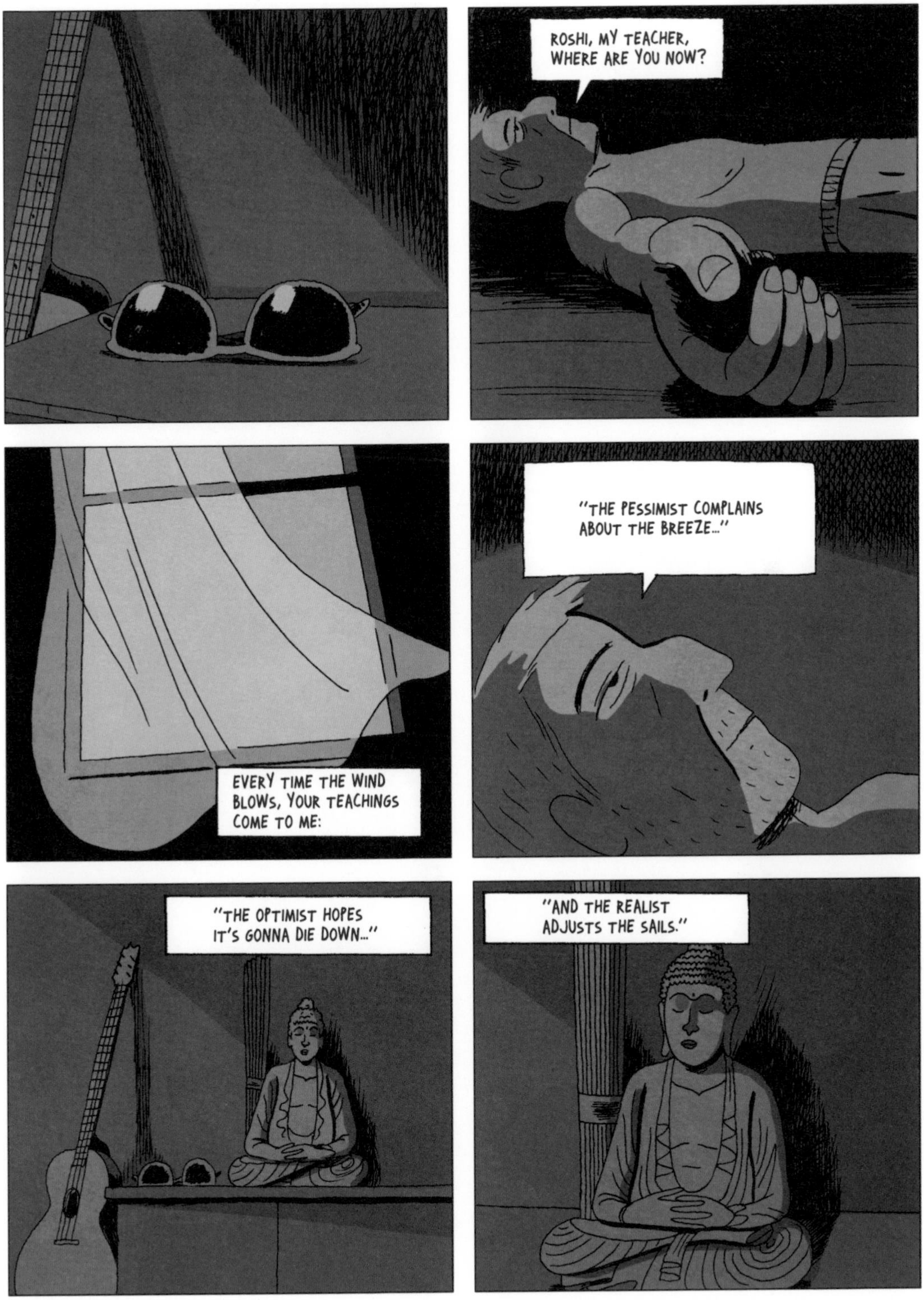

ROSHI, MY TEACHER, WHERE ARE YOU NOW?
EVERY TIME THE WIND BLOWS, YOUR TEACHINGS COME TO ME:
"THE PESSIMIST COMPLAINS ABOUT THE BREEZE..."
"THE OPTIMIST HOPES IT'S GONNA DIE DOWN..."
"AND THE REALIST ADJUSTS THE SAILS."

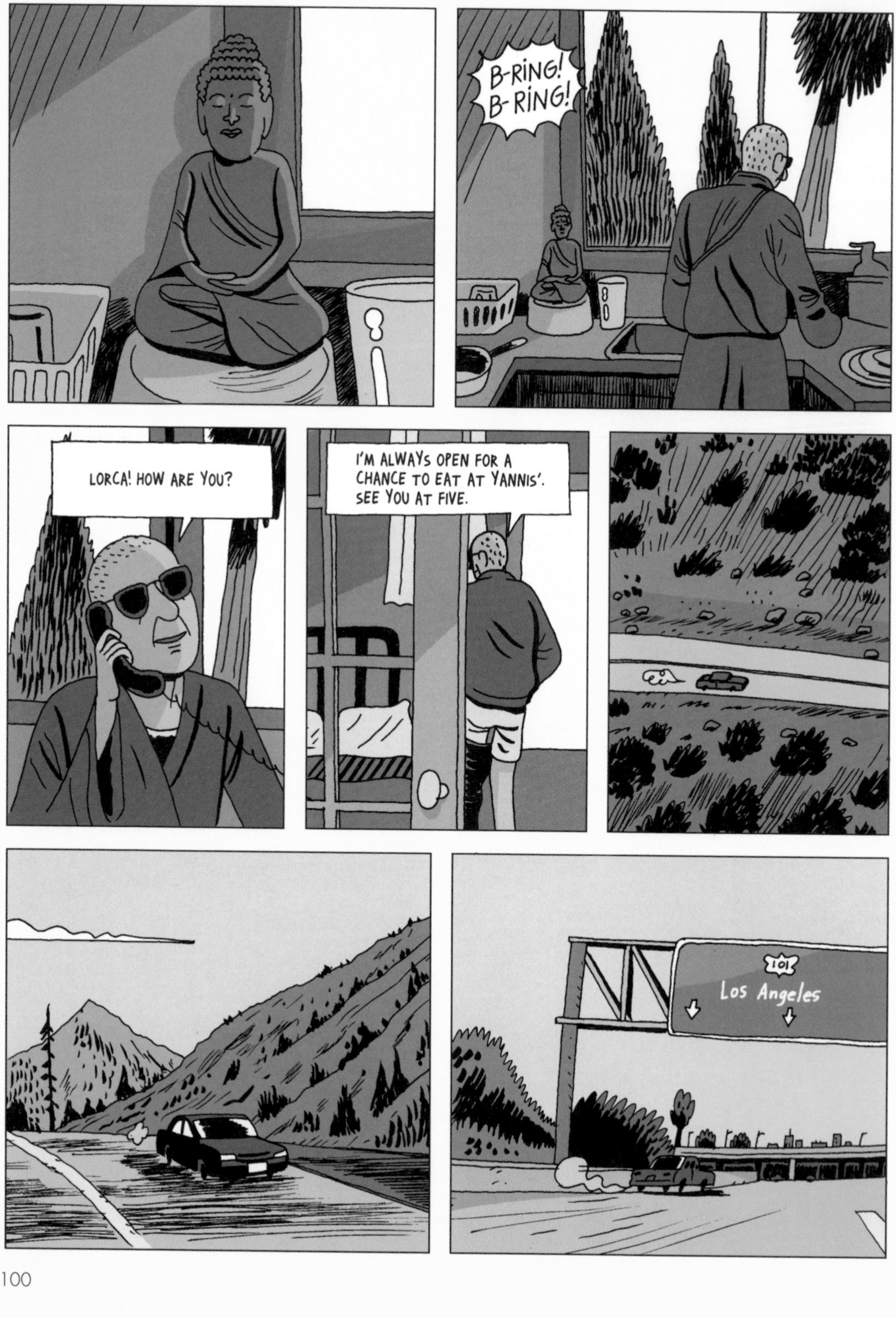
B-RING! B-RING!
LORCA! HOW ARE YOU?
I'M ALWAYS OPEN FOR A CHANCE TO EAT AT YANNIS'. SEE YOU AT FIVE.
101
Los Angeles

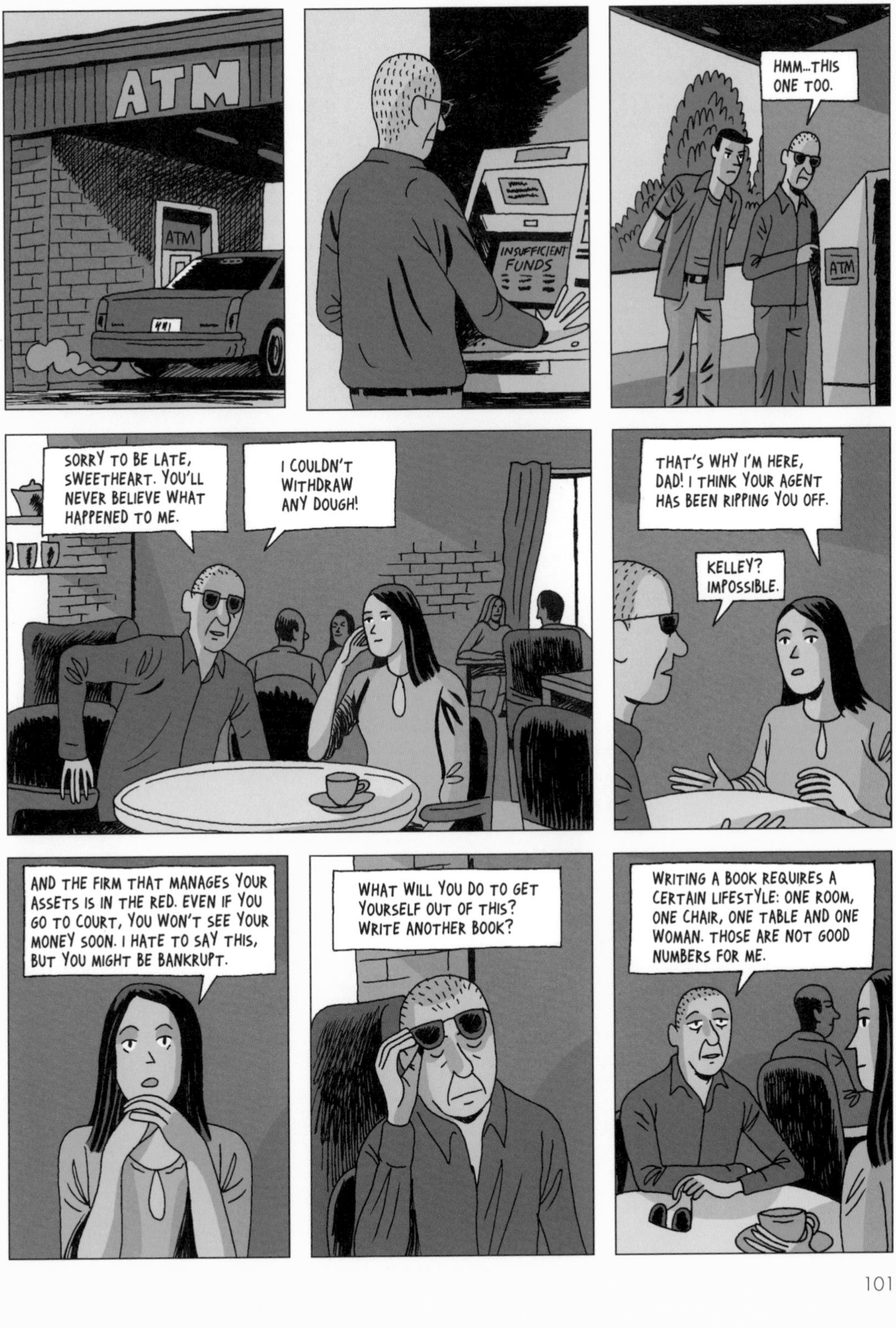
ATM
ATM
INSUFFICIENT FUNDS
HMM...THIS ONE TOO.
ATM
SORRY TO BE LATE, SWEETHEART. YOU'LL NEVER BELIEVE WHAT HAPPENED TO ME.
I COULDN'T WITHDRAW ANY DOUGH!
THAT'S WHY I'M HERE, DAD! I THINK YOUR AGENT HAS BEEN RIPPING YOU OFF.
KELLEY? IMPOSSIBLE.
AND THE FIRM THAT MANAGES YOUR ASSETS IS IN THE RED. EVEN IF YOU GO TO COURT, YOU WON'T SEE YOUR MONEY SOON. I HATE TO SAY THIS, BUT YOU MIGHT BE BANKRUPT.
WHAT WILL YOU DO TO GET YOURSELF OUT OF THIS? WRITE ANOTHER BOOK?
WRITING A BOOK REQUIRES A CERTAIN LIFESTYLE: ONE ROOM, ONE CHAIR, ONE TABLE AND ONE WOMAN. THOSE ARE NOT GOOD NUMBERS FOR ME.

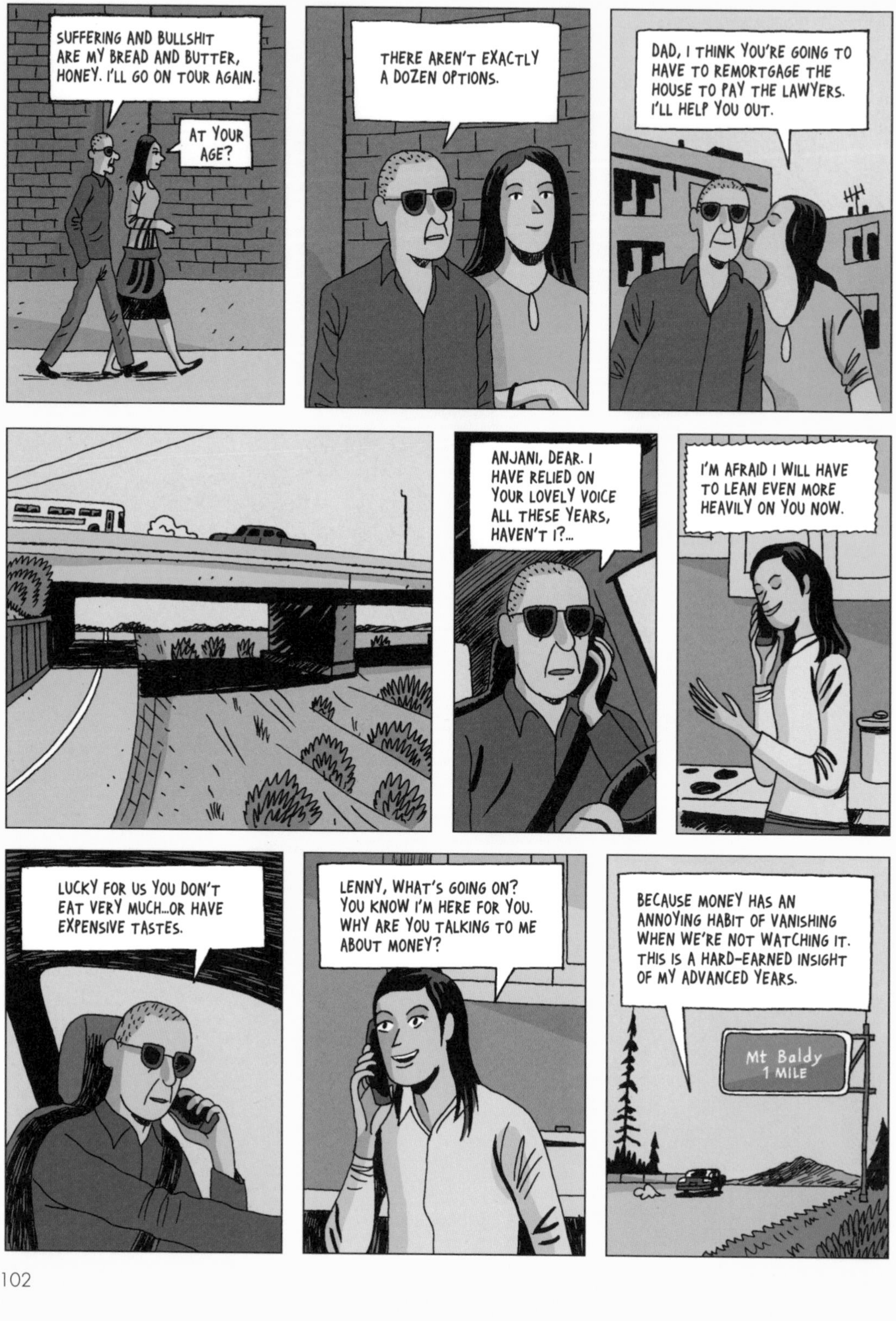
SUFFERING AND BULLSHIT ARE MY BREAD AND BUTTER, HONEY. I'LL GO ON TOUR AGAIN.
AT YOUR AGE?
THERE AREN'T EXACTLY A DOZEN OPTIONS.
DAD, I THINK YOU'RE GOING TO HAVE TO REMORTGAGE THE HOUSE TO PAY THE LAWYERS. I'LL HELP YOU OUT.
ANJANI, DEAR. I HAVE RELIED ON YOUR LOVELY VOICE ALL THESE YEARS, HAVEN'T I?...
I'M AFRAID I WILL HAVE TO LEAN EVEN MORE HEAVILY ON YOU NOW.
LUCKY FOR US YOU DON'T EAT VERY MUCH...OR HAVE EXPENSIVE TASTES.
LENNY, WHAT'S GOING ON? YOU KNOW I'M HERE FOR YOU. WHY ARE YOU TALKING TO ME ABOUT MONEY?
BECAUSE MONEY HAS AN ANNOYING HABIT OF VANISHING WHEN WE'RE NOT WATCHING IT. THIS IS A HARD-EARNED INSIGHT OF MY ADVANCED YEARS.
Mt Baldy
1 MILE

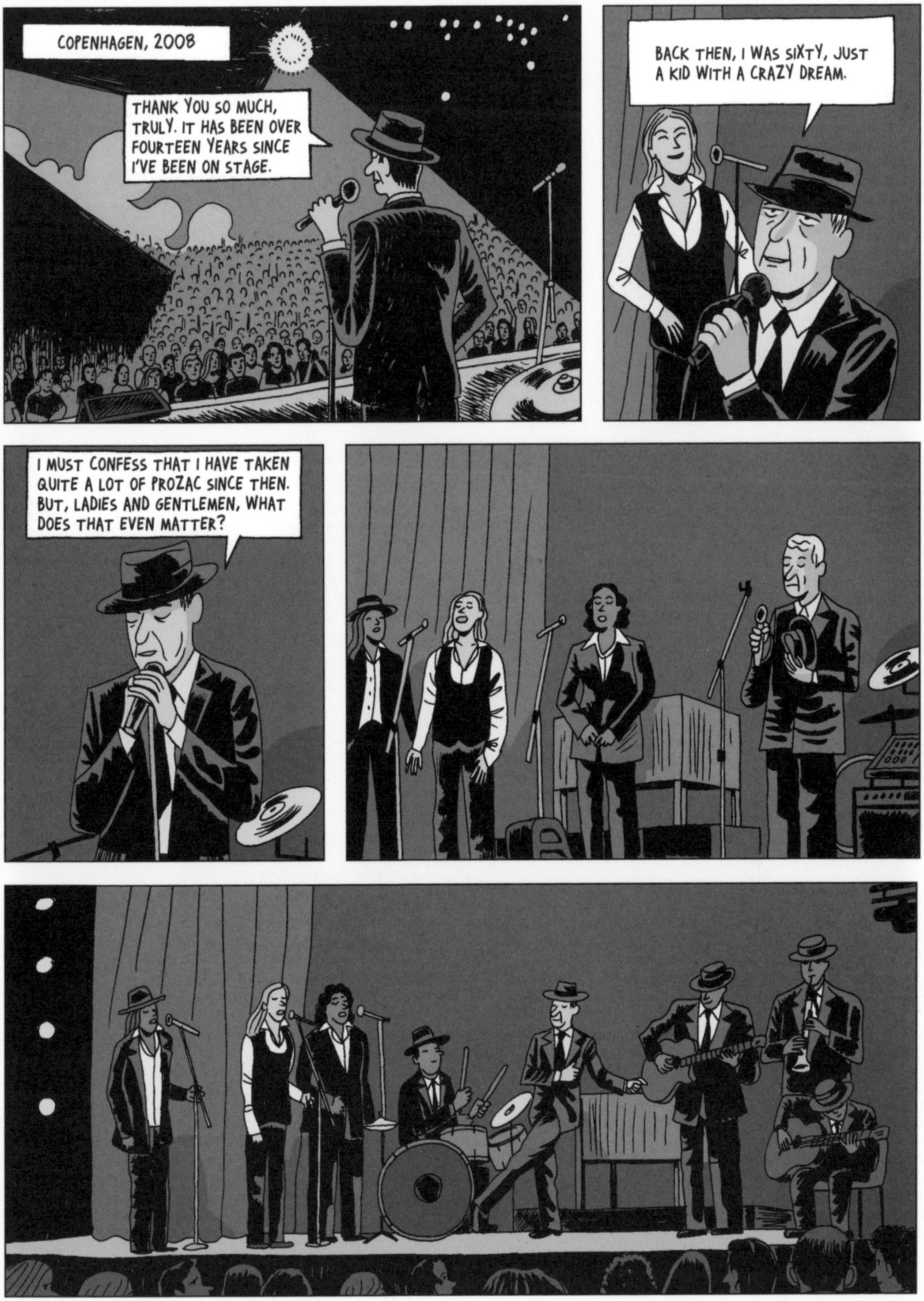
COPENHAGEN, 2008
THANK YOU SO MUCH, TRULY. IT HAS BEEN OVER FOURTEEN YEARS SINCE I'VE BEEN ON STAGE.
BACK THEN, I WAS SIXTY, JUST A KID WITH A CRAZY DREAM.
I MUST CONFESS THAT I HAVE TAKEN QUITE A LOT OF PROZAC SINCE THEN. BUT, LADIES AND GENTLEMEN, WHAT DOES THAT EVEN MATTER?

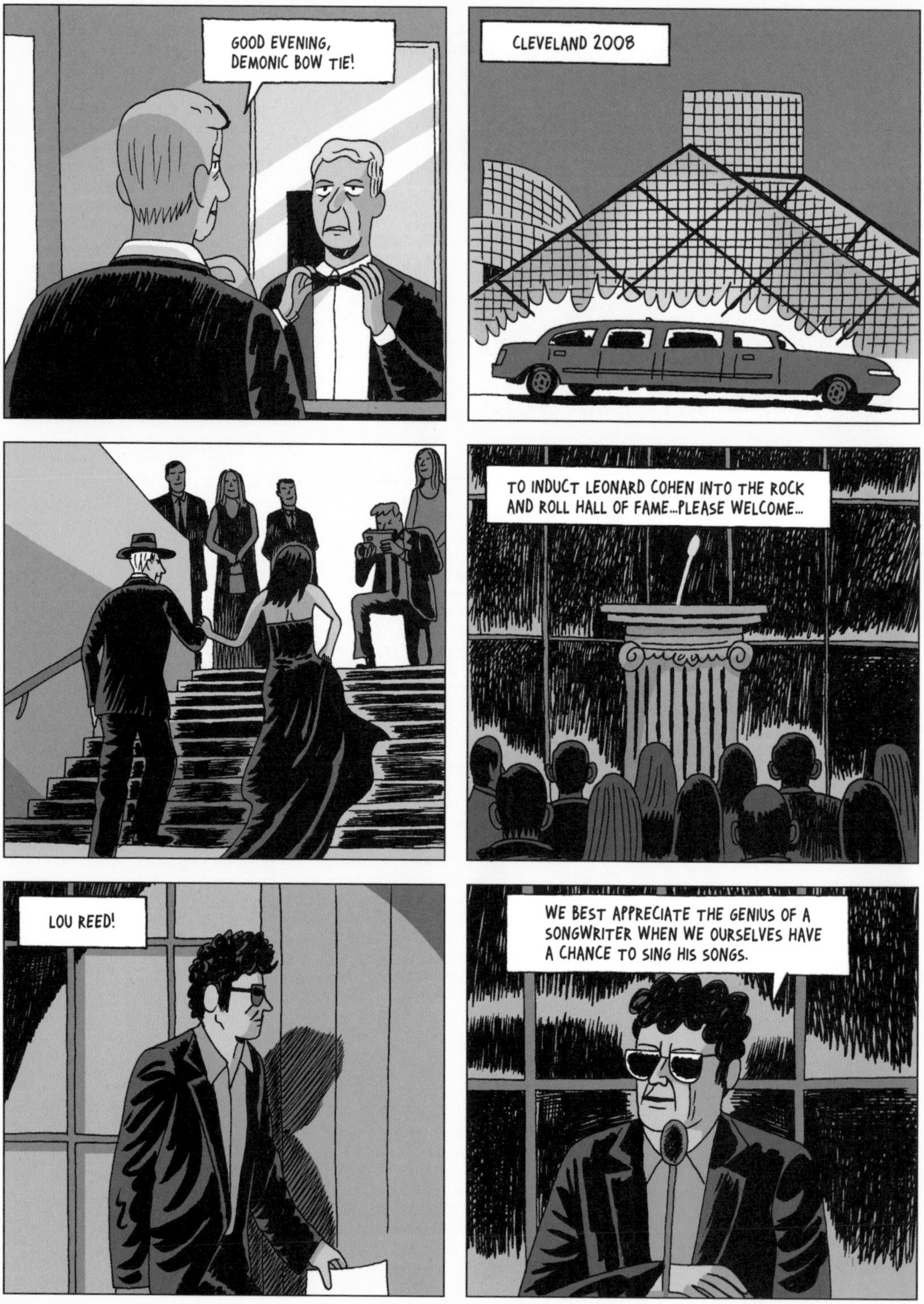
GOOD EVENING, DEMONIC BOW TIE!
CLEVELAND 2008
TO INDUCT LEONARD COHEN INTO THE ROCK AND ROLL HALL OF FAME...PLEASE WELCOME...
LOU REED!
WE BEST APPRECIATE THE GENIUS OF A SONGWRITER WHEN WE OURSELVES HAVE A CHANCE TO SING HIS SONGS.

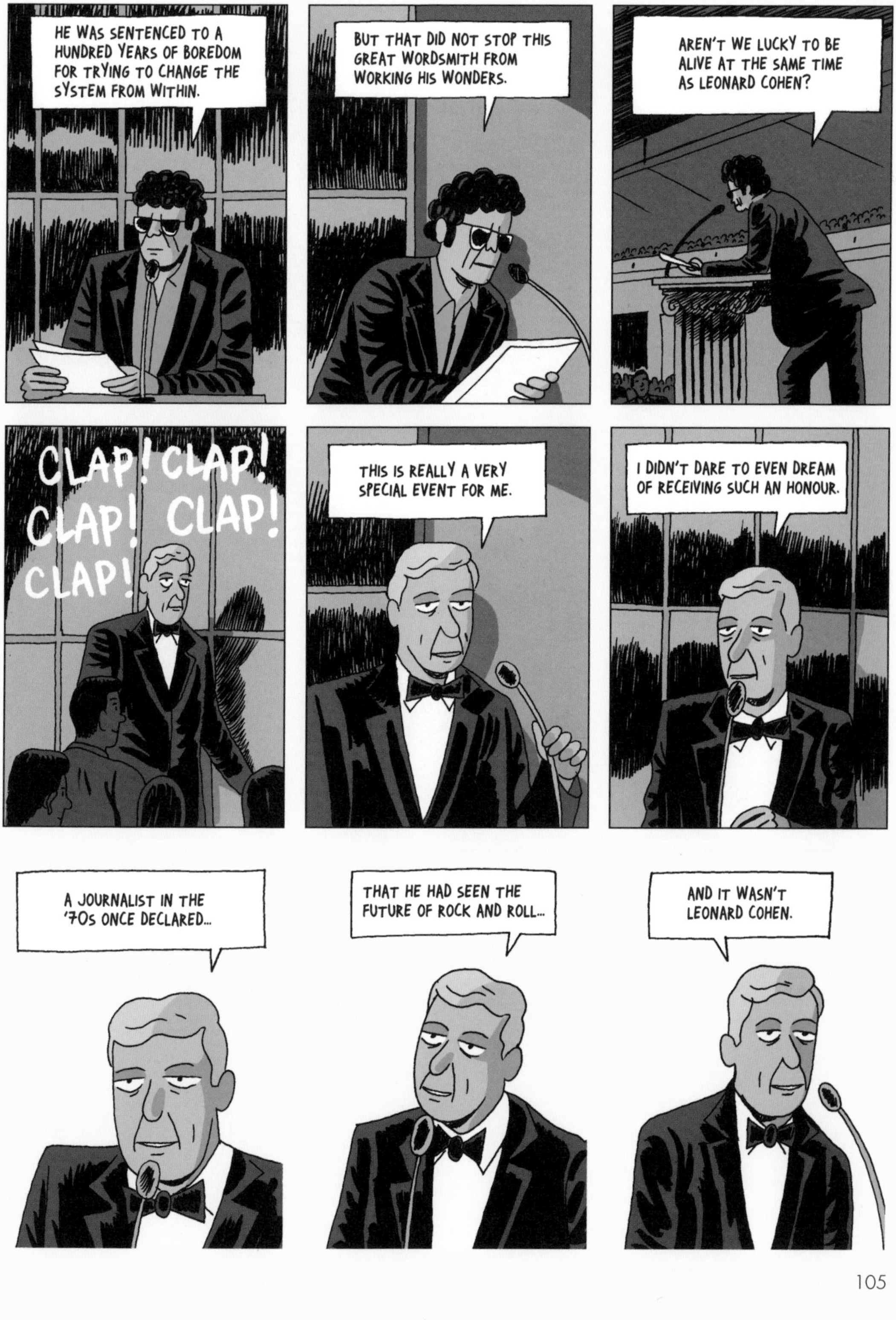
HE WAS SENTENCED TO A HUNDRED YEARS OF BOREDOM FOR TRYING TO CHANGE THE SYSTEM FROM WITHIN.
BUT THAT DID NOT STOP THIS GREAT WORDSMITH FROM WORKING HIS WONDERS.
AREN'T WE LUCKY TO BE ALIVE AT THE SAME TIME AS LEONARD COHEN?
CLAP! CLAP! CLAP! CLAP! CLAP!
THIS IS REALLY A VERY SPECIAL EVENT FOR ME.
I DIDN'T DARE TO EVEN DREAM OF RECEIVING SUCH AN HONOUR.
A JOURNALIST IN THE '70s ONCE DECLARED...
THAT HE HAD SEEN THE FUTURE OF ROCK AND ROLL...
AND IT WASN'T LEONARD COHEN.

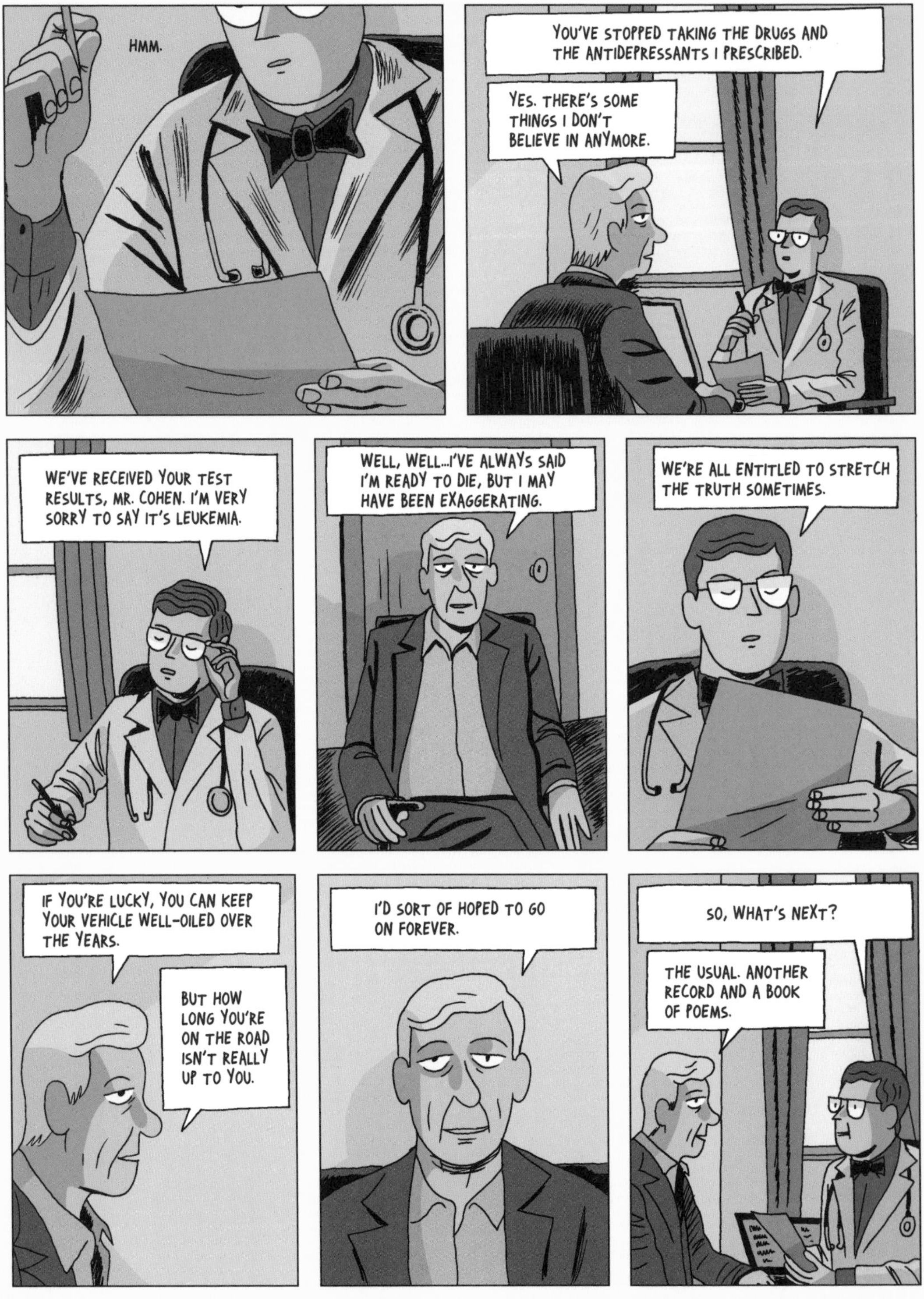
HMM.
YOU'VE STOPPED TAKING THE DRUGS AND THE ANTIDEPRESSANTS I PRESCRIBED.
YES. THERE'S SOME THINGS I DON'T BELIEVE IN ANYMORE.
WE'VE RECEIVED YOUR TEST RESULTS, MR. COHEN. I'M VERY SORRY TO SAY IT'S LEUKEMIA.
WELL, WELL...I'VE ALWAYS SAID I'M READY TO DIE, BUT I MAY HAVE BEEN EXAGGERATING.
WE'RE ALL ENTITLED TO STRETCH THE TRUTH SOMETIMES.
IF YOU'RE LUCKY, YOU CAN KEEP YOUR VEHICLE WELL-OILED OVER THE YEARS.
BUT HOW LONG YOU'RE ON THE ROAD ISN'T REALLY UP TO YOU.
I'D SORT OF HOPED TO GO ON FOREVER.
SO, WHAT'S NEXT?
THE USUAL. ANOTHER RECORD AND A BOOK OF POEMS.

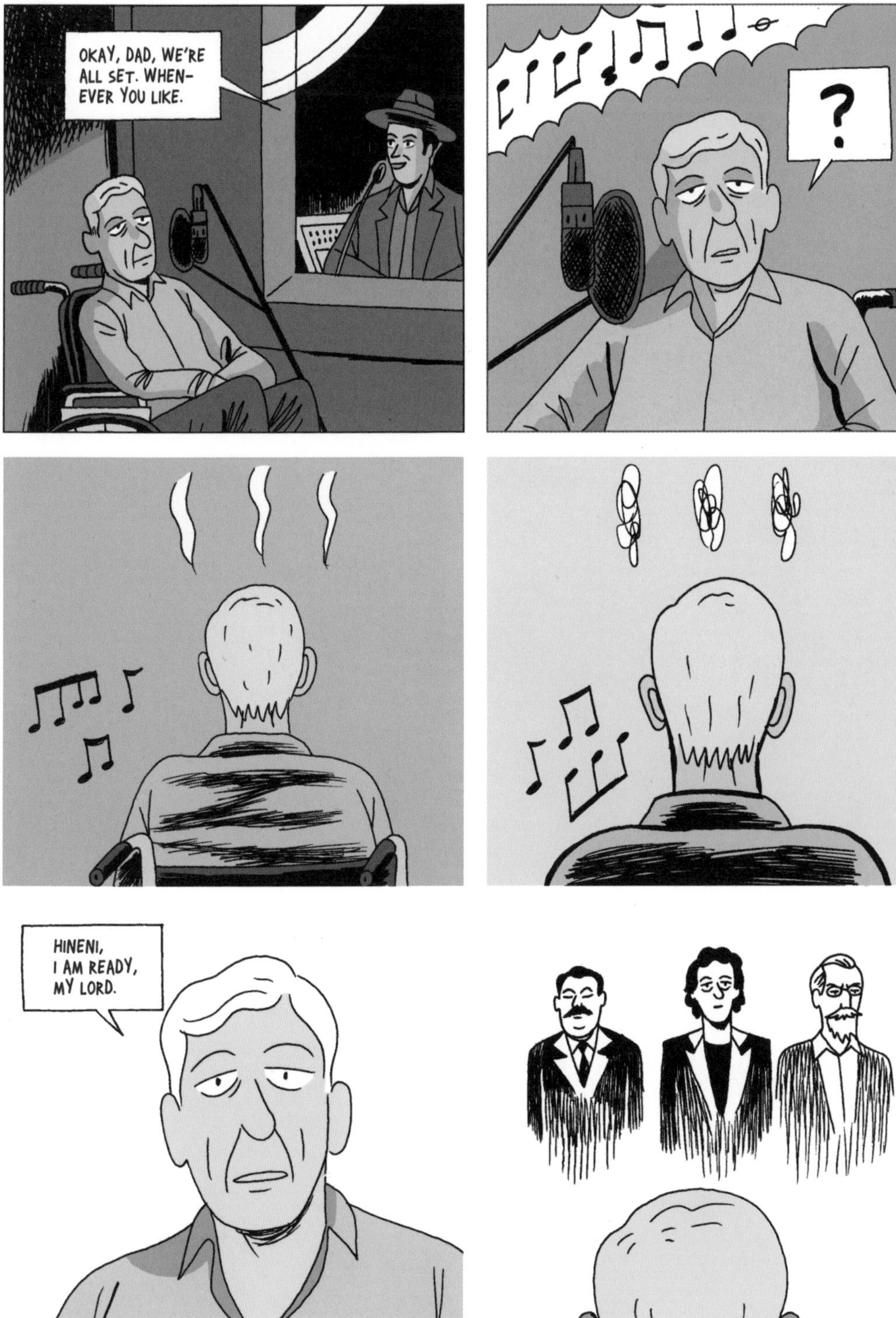
OKAY, DAD, WE'RE ALL SET. WHEN-EVER YOU LIKE.
?
HINENI, I AM READY, MY LORD.

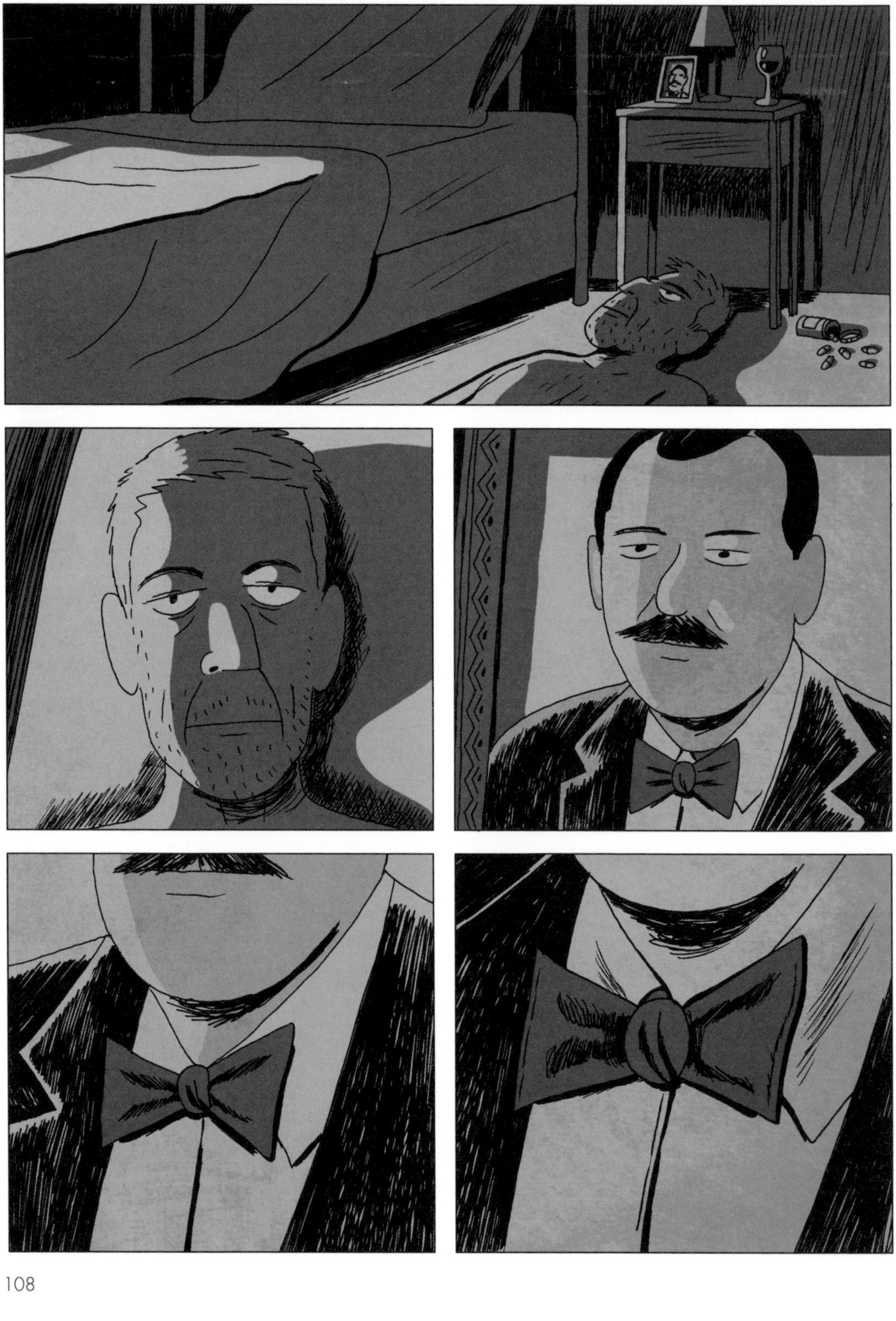

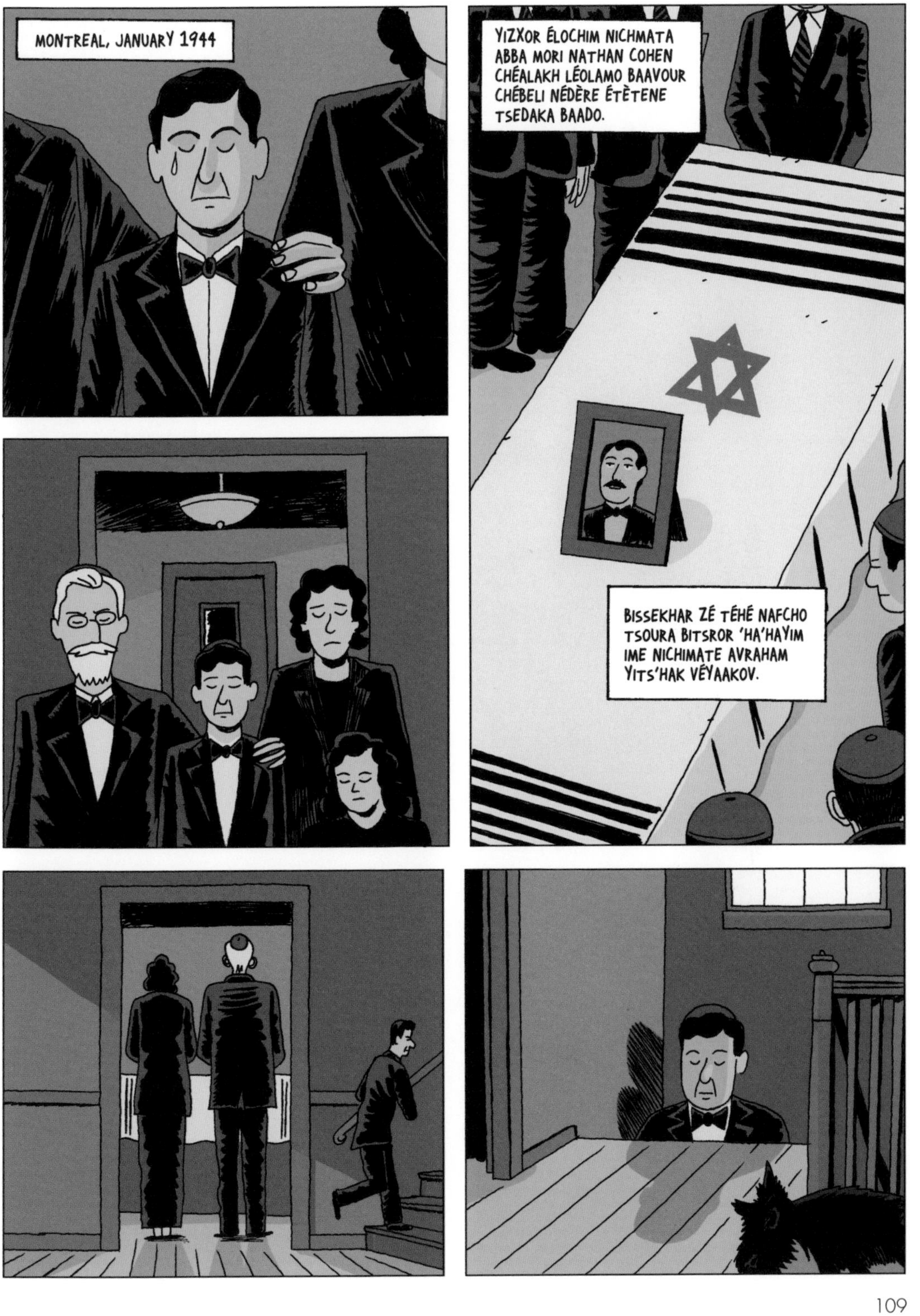
MONTREAL, JANUARY 1944
YIZXOR ÉLOCHIM NICHMATA ABBA MORI NATHAN COHEN CHÉALAKH LÉOLAMO BAAVOUR CHÉBELI NÉDÈRE ÉTÈTENE TSEDAKA BAADO.
BISSEKHAR ZÉ TÉHÉ NAFCHO TSOURA BITSROR 'HA'HAYIM IME NICHIMATE AVRAHAM YITS'HAK VÉYAAKOV.

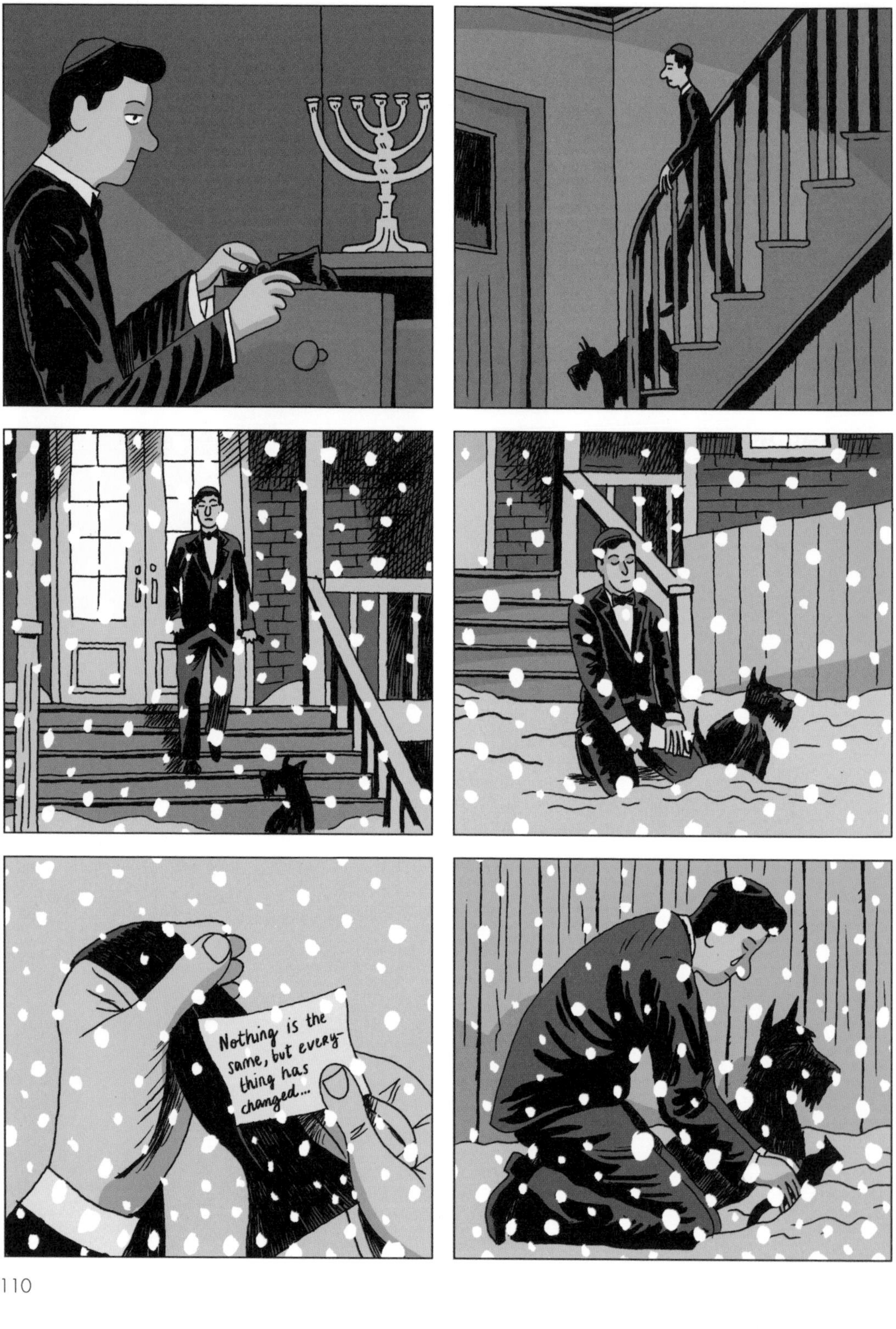
Nothing is the same, but everything has changed...

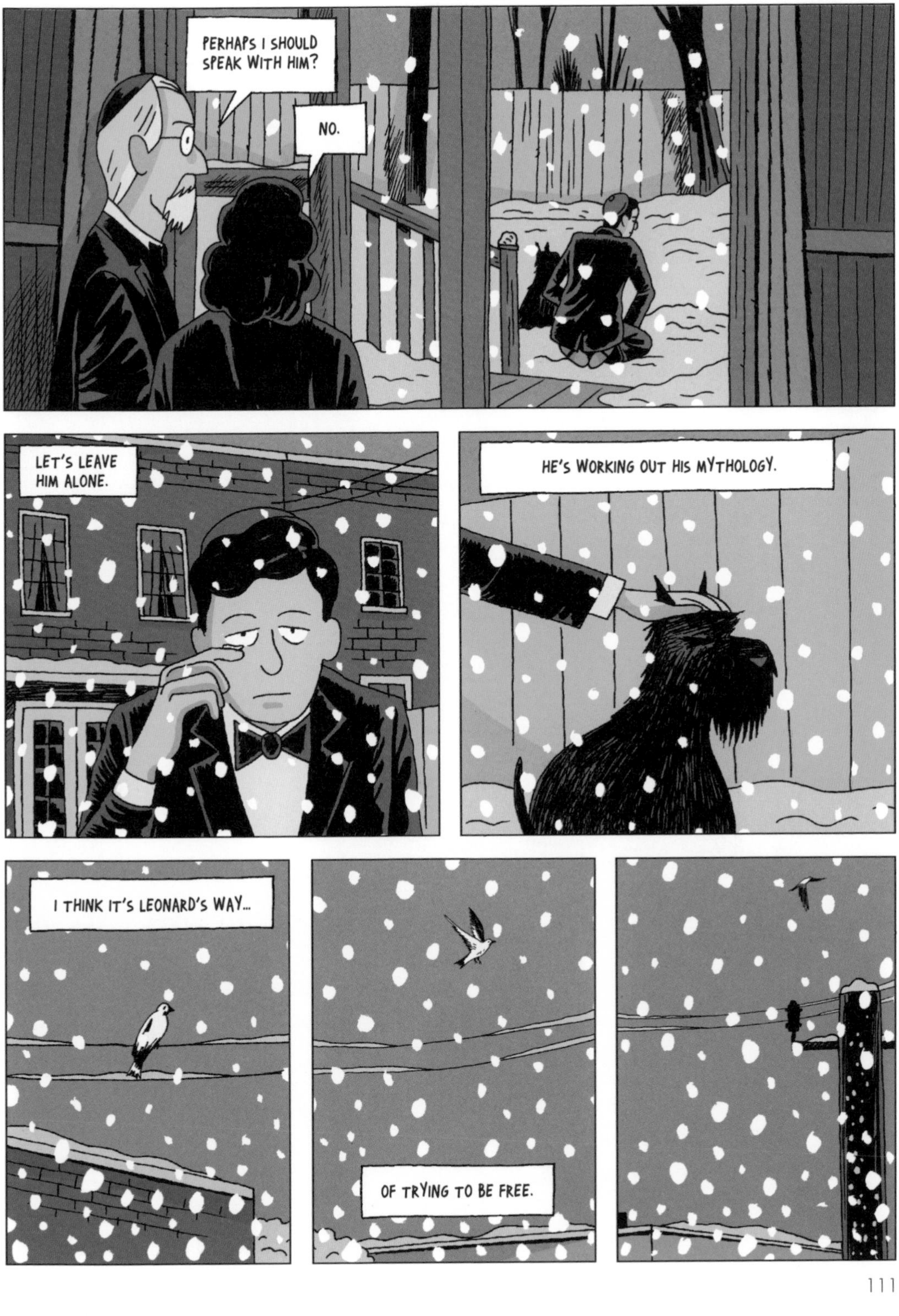
PERHAPS I SHOULD SPEAK WITH HIM?
NO.
LET'S LEAVE HIM ALONE.
HE'S WORKING OUT HIS MYTHOLOGY.
I THINK IT'S LEONARD'S WAY...
OF TRYING TO BE FREE.

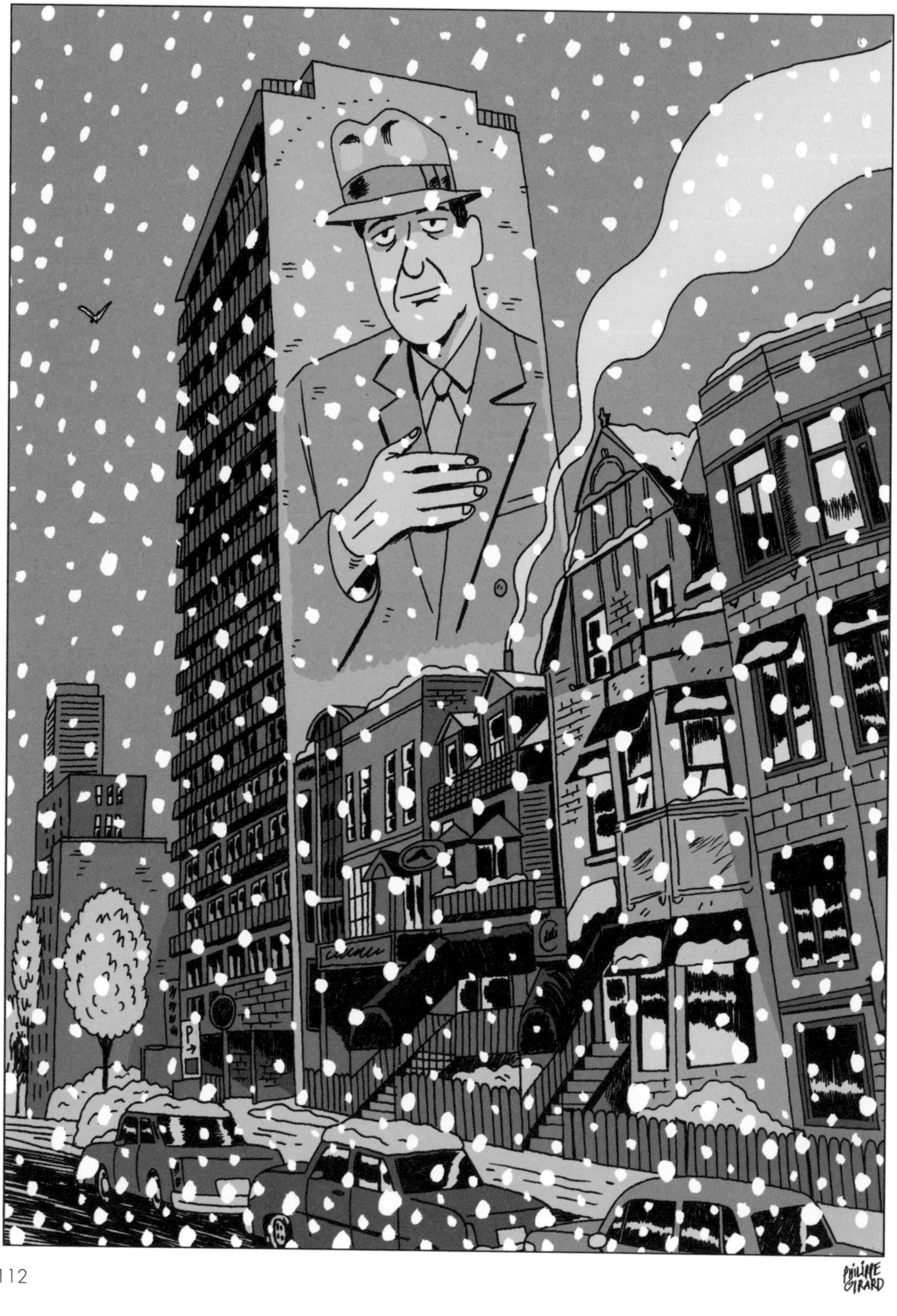
P

PHILIPPE GIRARD

Rogues' Gallery

ARMAND VAILLANCOURT: PAINTER AND SCULPTOR, KEY FIGURE IN THE HISTORY OF QUEBEC ART. INTERNATIONALLY KNOWN FOR THE *QUÉBEC LIBRE!* FOUNTAIN IN SAN FRANCISCO.

JUDY COLLINS: A POPULAR SINGER-SONGWRITER WHOSE COVERS OF SONGS BY JONI MITCHELL, RANDY NEWMAN, AND COHEN HELPED LAUNCH THEIR CAREERS.

JOHN HAMMOND: AMERICAN MUSIC PRODUCER AND TALENT SCOUT, CREDITED WITH DISCOVERING BOB DYLAN AND BRUCE SPRINGSTEEN.

LOU REED: LEADER OF THE VELVET UNDERGROUND. CONSIDERED ONE OF THE ALL-TIME GREAT ROCK SINGER-SONGWRITERS.

JANIS JOPLIN: ICONIC '60s PSYCHEDELIC SOUL SINGER, DIED AT TWENTY-SEVEN OF AN OVERDOSE.

JONI MITCHELL: CANADIAN SINGER-SONGWRITER WITH ROOTS IN FOLK MUSIC. POPULARIZED OPEN TUNING.

NICO: SINGER FOR THE VELVET UNDERGROUND, MODEL, ACTOR. COHEN HAS GONE ON RECORD AS SAYING HER SINGING STYLE WAS VERY INFLUENTIAL TO HIM.

OSHIK LEVI: ISRAELI SINGER WHO ALSO ACTED IN NUMEROUS FILMS AND TELEVISION SERIES.

PHIL SPECTOR: VOLATILE PRODUCER WHO ROSE TO FAME WORKING WITH THE RONETTES, THE CRYSTALS, AND IKE & TINA TURNER. WORKED WITH THE RAMONES AROUND THE SAME TIME HE WORKED WITH COHEN.

Rogues' Gallery

LEWIS FUREY: CANADIAN COMPOSER, DIRECTOR AND ACTOR. **CAROLE LAURE:** CANADIAN SINGER, ACTOR AND DIRECTOR.

DOMINIQUE ISSERMANN: FRENCH FASHION PHOTOGRAPHER KNOWN FOR WORKING WITH DIOR, TIFFANY, AND CHANEL.

KELLEY LYNCH: COHEN'S LONG-TIME MANAGER. ALLEGEDLY STOLE OVER $7.3 MILLION FROM HIM. FINALLY SENTENCED TO EIGHTEEN MONTHS IN PRISON IN 2012 FOR VIOLATING A "NO CONTACT" ORDER BUT NOT THE EMBEZZLEMENT.

JEFF CHASE: MUSICAL ARRANGER WHO ASSISTED COHEN WITH EARLY DEMOS AND CONVINCED HIM TO CEDE HIS RIGHTS TO THE SONG "SUZANNE."

JOHN CALE: FOUNDING MEMBER OF THE VELVET UNDERGROUND WITH A WELL-REGARDED POST-VELVETS CAREER. INFLUENTIAL PRODUCER FOR THE MODERN LOVERS AND PATTI SMITH.

JEFF BUCKLEY: AMERICAN MUSICIAN, KNOWN FOR HAVING A FOUR-OCTAVE VOCAL RANGE. DROWNED AT THE AGE OF THIRTY. "HALLELUJAH" WAS A POSTHUMOUS HIT FOR HIM.

REBECCA DE MORNAY: AMERICAN ACTRESS WHO ROSE TO FAME OPPOSITE TOM CRUISE IN RISKY BUSINESS.

RUFUS WAINWRIGHT: CANADIAN-AMERICAN SINGER-SONGWRITER. SON OF LOUDON WAINWRIGHT III AND KATE McGARRIGLE; BROTHER OF MARTHA WAINWRIGHT.

KYOZAN JOSHU SASAKI: JAPANESE TEACHER OF ZEN BUDDHISM, FOUNDER OF THE ZEN RETREAT AT MOUNT BALDY IN CALIFORNIA.

Bibliography

Cohen, Leonard. "Bells." Recorded by Buffy Sainte-Marie. *She Used to Wanna Be a Ballerina*, Vanguard Records, 1971.

Cohen, Leonard. *The Flame: Poems and Selections from Notebooks*. McClelland & Stewart, 2018.

www.cohencentric.com

García Lorca, Federico. "Little Viennese Waltz." *Poet in New York*, edited by Christopher Maurer. Translated by Greg Simon and Steven F. White, Farrar, Straus and Giroux, 1988.

Guillot, Claire. "Dominique Issermann: 'Leonard Cohen avait un côté funky.'" *Le Monde*, 12 November 2016, www.lemonde.fr.

Kubernik, Harvey. *Leonard Cohen: Everybody Knows*. BackBeat Books, 2014.

Lemmens, Kateri and Charles Quimper, ed., *Moebius: Pour Leonard Cohen*, no. 133. Triptyque, 2012.

www.leonardcohen.com

www.leonardcohenfiles.com

Marom, Malka. *Joni Mitchell: In Her Own Words*. ECW Press, 2014.

"Ma vie avec Leonard Cohen: "Je l'ai entendu travailler deux ans sur 'Hallelujah.'" *L'Obs*, 11 November 2016, www.nouvelobs.com

Monk, Katherine. *Joni: The Creative Odyssey of Joni Mitchell*. Greystone Books, 2012.

Reynolds, Anthony. *Leonard Cohen: A Remarkable Life*. Omnibus Press, 2010.

Simmons, Sylvie. *I'm Your Man: The Life of Leonard Cohen*. McClelland & Stewart, 2013.

Tordjman, Gilles. *Leonard Cohen*. Le Castor Astral, 2006.

Philippe Girard was born in Québec, Canada, in 1971. He published his first comic in a children's magazine when he was eight years old and has since published more than twenty books. His comics have received the Joe Shuster, the Bédélys, and the Bédéis Causa Awards. This is his first book with Drawn & Quarterly. He lives in Québec City.

Helge Dascher has been a contributor to Drawn & Quarterly since its early days—translating Guy Delisle, Michel Rabagliati, the *Aya* series and many others. Karen Houle is a Governor General Award shortlisted poet. They recently collaborated on the animated film *The Physics of Sorrow*.